SEA AND ISLANDS

Hammond Innes not only writes about the sea; he knows it. His ocean-going yacht, *Mary Deare*, was designed and built to his specifications, and he and his wife Dorothy have covered many thousands of miles exploring the coasts and islands of Europe from Scandinavia to Turkey.

The first part of this book is a record of these journeys; sailing among the coves of Ithaca to pinpoint the site of Odysseus's palace or looking at Troy as the Greeks first saw it – from the sea.

The second part is complementary to *Harvest of Journeys* – a record of his subsequent travels. They range from the Western Isles, which gave him the background for *Atlantic Fury*, to remote Addu Atoll in the Indian Ocean for *The Strode Venturer*.

HAMMOND INNES

Sea and Islands

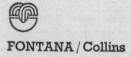

FONTANA / Collins

First published by Wm. Collins 1967
First issued in Fontana Books 1970
Second Impression December 1973

Printed in Great Britain
Collins Clear-Type Press London and Glasgow

The quotations from the *Iliad* and the *Odyssey* are
taken from E. V. Rieu's translation, published by
Penguin Books Ltd

To MARY DEARE and all those who have
crewed in her

Contents

Illustrations

*Most of the photographs in this book were taken by
the author or his wife*

For those interested in the details of the boat in which these voyages were made, *Mary Deare* was designed by Robert Clark to my requirements; these were that she should be able to race without ignominy and at the same time be able to sail anywhere in the world. She has, therefore, certain unusual features for an ocean racer. She is 42 ft overall and her beam is 11 ft, yet her draught is only 6 ft. Her six bunks offer equal comfort, there are 32 lockers and drawers for stowage and she has four large ventilators by way of the mast. She carries 150 gallons of fresh water and 45 gallons of fuel, giving her a range of 500 miles under engine. She has a masthead rig with Bermudan mainsail and a trysail for storm conditions. Her wardrobe of foresails includes: racing and cruising spinnakers, genoa (No. 1 jib) and ghoster (light weather genoa), yankee (No. 2), working jib (No. 3) and storm jib (No. 4). Her auxiliary engine is a Coventry Victor flat twin diesel. Her steel hull was built at Scheepswerf, Zaandam, in Holland, and motored across the North Sea by Robert Clark and myself for completion at Whisstock's Boatyard, Woodbridge, Suffolk. She was launched by my wife on July 17, 1959.

In the race and the five voyages recorded here I have referred to the friends who crewed in *Mary Deare* by their Christian names, as is customary on board. Their full names are given below the title of the voyages on which they sailed.

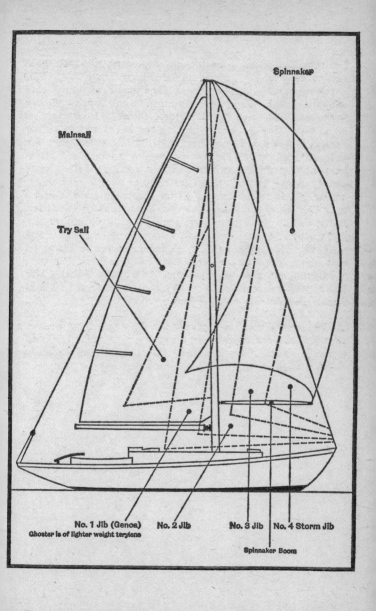

Spinnaker

Mainsail

Try Sail

No. 1 Jib (Genoa)
Ghoster is of lighter weight terylene

No. 2 Jib

No. 3 Jib

No. 4 Storm Jib

Spinnaker Boom

'I came upon it from a tussle with the sea—and
I was young—and I saw it looking at me. . . .
A flick of sunshine upon a strange shore. . . .

Joseph Conrad

PART ONE

The Sea

INTRODUCTION

This first part of *Sea and Islands* is a record of the voyages I have made in my boat *Mary Deare* during the past six years. In an introduction to my earlier travel book, *Harvest of Journeys*, I said that the sea seemed to infiltrate into my novels of its own accord. This is largely because, for a long time now, I have spent at least two months of each year cruising in foreign waters. My wife, who loves the excitement of sea travel, but not the sea itself, has come with me on every voyage; together we have sailed many thousands of miles, exploring the coasts and islands of Europe from Scandinavia to Turkey. Accounts of these voyages were originally written from *Mary Deare*'s day-to-day logbook and published in the Journal of the Royal Cruising Club. In revising them for general publication, I have tried to convey an impression of sailing as a way of travel, as well as give an account of the places to which our boat has taken us. Even today, the sea remains a very effective barrier, and those who sail in boats large enough to have their own accommodation are made free of a world of small anchorages and isolated communities often inaccessible by other means.

It is no easy task to express in words all that the sea has meant to me, but I hope that the cumulative effect of these 'logs' will convey something of its fascination. There is, however, one disadvantage to travelling in your own boat. As owner, skipper and navigator, your inland travel is to some extent limited by responsibility for the safety of the boat. It is for this reason that I have divided the book into two parts, the second being devoted to travel in which the journeys inland dominate the sea environment.

I

DISMASTED

Crew for North Sea Race—1961
Major C. R. 'Bob' Stirling
Michael Hopkinson
Cavendish Morton
David Pierson

'Of passionate men in battle with the sea. . . .'

John Masefield

An ocean race—what place has this in a book of travel? Nobody can see it except the participants. It is difficult even for others to follow it or understand it. Nevertheless, ocean racing is an exciting, fast-growing sport, increasingly in the news, and to sailing boats it is what motor racing is to cars—the test bed of new methods, new ideas, new materials. And since this whole book is about sea travelling, much of it under sail, it seemed that a description of this violent and testing form of sailing would be a reasonable introduction to the subsequent voyages to little-known islands and anchorages. That I have chosen to describe the only race that proved disastrous for me is because it is the one most indelibly imprinted on my memory.

The North Sea Race has always been one of the most popular of the Royal Ocean Racing Club's events, attracting a big foreign entry. It is run early in the season, at Whitsun, and is usually reckoned to be tough. The number of boats entered has risen steadily and on this occasion eighty-two crossed the starting line. The course is Harwich to the West Hinder light vessel off the Belgian coast, thence north to the Smith's Knoll light vessel off Norfolk and so to the finishing line at the Hook of Holland—a big Z covering the southern part of the North Sea. Because of its finishing point this event is generally known as the Hook Race.

When we arrived in Harwich in the late afternoon of Thursday, May 18, 1961, the Dutch contingent, twenty strong, was already massed under Harwich Town and some of the British boats that had come up a fortnight before on the Southsea-Harwich race were lying to the buoys provided by HMS *Ganges*, the training establishment for ratings at Shotley on the other side of the estuary. We anchored just outside them. The wind was from the north, about 15 knots and very cold, suggesting a cold, wet beat most of the way.

We were racing this year with a complement of six, which is on the light side for a 16-ton ocean racer. Bob and Michael had already joined ship to help bring her round from the Deben estuary so that now there were four of us on board, including my wife, Dorothy, and myself. We had tea, changed into our shore-going rig and took a launch to the Naval pier. The sun was shining and it was warm ashore as we walked up to the *Ganges* Mess for the pre-race cocktail party. The big room was packed, a sprinkling of wives among the men, and crews pouring in by car from boats lying miles away up the East Coast estuaries. The talk was of boats and prospects, everybody relaxed, for the race starts near the top of high water and this was not until three-thirty the following afternoon. So confident was I that *Mary Deare* could cope with anything in the way of bad weather that my only concern was that we shouldn't miss the new herring. Whitsun was early that year. But at dinner a Dutchman at the next table assured me that the first of this delicacy had already been landed. 'Ja, ja. Is already kom. Is good, ja?' This with a wealth of demonstration as to the way it is eaten—head thrown back and the raw sliver held aloft by the tail.

Next morning we were up at six forty-five for the weather forecast: Wind northerly backing north-westerly, force 3–4. The burgees of the neighbouring yachts showed that it had already gone into the north-west, confirming once again that forecasts are more often an indication of what is actually happening than what is to come.

There was much to do that morning. Spinnaker, genoa and No. 2 jib to be stopped—that is, rolled along the line of

the hoist and tied with rotten cotton so that the sail can
be set in position and broken out at the moment required.
The main standing rigging had to be tightened. I had been
out two weeks before with full sail in a strong breeze; the
forestay wires had been stretched and checking the line of
the mast by looking up the track of the mainsail slides I had
noted that the top of the mast above the upper spreaders was
bending very slightly to leeward under the weight of the
genoa when heeled in a strong breeze. Somebody had to be
hoisted up the mast to tape the outermost edge of the upper
and lower spreaders, a thing the yard had forgotten to do.
There are screws here and if they are not covered by tape
they rapidly produce chafe on the Terylene mainsail when
running before the wind.

By ten-thirty the other two members of the crew—Cav and
David—had joined ship. By eleven-thirty all work had been
completed. Both forestays had been tightened two turns on
the rigging screws and the upper shrouds that run from the
chain plates amidships to the top of the mast had been
tightened one turn. We retired below for a drink and a discussion of tactics.

The start at Harwich is easterly across the line to the
Guard Buoy not much more than quarter of a mile away,
thence southerly to the Beach End Buoy about two miles,
easterly again for four miles to the Cork Sand Buoy and
then south easterly to the West Hinder just over fifty miles.
It looked like genoa across the line, hoist spinnaker at the
Guard Buoy on starboard tack and a spinnaker gybe at the
Beach End Buoy for the run down to the West Hinder on
port tack. All of which really requires a practised crew that
have worked together regularly, for the spinnaker is big, a
nylon sail bellying out in front of the boat and carrying a great
weight when full of wind. It is boomed out on one side
(opposite side to the mainsail boom) and to gybe it the
boom had to be detached from the spinnaker and transferred
to the other side, all at the exact moment course was altered
and the mainsail brought across. Our crew had never sailed
together before as a team.

Further, we should be rounding the West Hinder light
vessel at night. This would mean hoisting genoa and hauling

down the spinnaker at the moment of rounding for the beat north, a tricky operation to be carried out in the dark. We had another drink and hoped it would all work out. A large lunch then of soup and cold chicken and salad. By the time we had finished, the small Class III boats were getting under way. Owing to the large entry, this class was being sent off in two waves at two-fifteen and two-thirty. Our own start—Class II—was timed for two forty-five.

We got the weather forecast at one-forty. It was the same except that it suggested that the wind would strengthen to force 5. We hauled up the anchor, stowed it below with the chain, turned into the wind under engine and hoisted the mainsail. I cut the engine then and the genoa was hoisted, but it had been wrongly stopped and had to be lowered. The wind was very light under the shelter of the land and I had drifted down-tide among the Class I boats, so I re-started the engine and motored towards the line as the starting gun for the first wave of Class III went. In a matter of moments, it seemed, they were round the Guard Buoy and going away under spinnaker, a brave, multi-coloured sight.

I switched the engine off and we jogged around under mainsail whilst the second wave of Class III went away. Our own class was manoeuvring towards the line now as we waited for the ten minute gun. Time hung heavy, then the five minute gun. Dorothy started the stop watch and began the count-down. Four minutes, three minutes, two . . . I had the genoa broken out. We were drifting up close to the line—too close, I thought, and gybed. In a 220 mile race I preferred to start a few seconds late rather than risk having to put about in the midst of nearly thirty boats because I had crossed the line ahead of the gun.

I was planning to manoeuvre myself towards the starter's position close under Harwich pier, but I was blocked by another boat. By the time we were clear of it all the twenty-eight boats were moving down on the line. The gun went. Too far out across the estuary we had little wind and it took longer than I had expected for *Mary Deare* to gather speed. We crossed the line with the tail-end group, tension un-relieved, for the Guard Buoy was coming up and we were being pressed by a Belgian closing us on port side. It was a

near thing. We rounded the buoy very close and broke out
the blue and white spinnaker, the Belgian's bows a few yards
from our stern. For a moment we had only half a spinnaker
set, the rotten cotton of the stops holding in the light air.
A couple of hard tugs and it bellied out and we were away
down the estuary, closing with *Thalassa*, veteran of many
Hook Races and, on handicap[1], rated second boat in our class.
We were rated twenty-third. A gust and a slight shift of wind
enabled us to cut under her stern and move away on the
windward side of her, constantly adjusting the sheet ropes
to stop the spinnaker collapsing. Behind us the big Class I
boats, which had started quarter of an hour behind us, were
coming up fast. *Swerver*, a Dutch boat and the final winner
of this class, rounded the Cork Sand Buoy just ahead of us.

Once round this buoy the alteration of course for the West
Hinder light vessel made spinnaker work easier. After playing
with the sheets for a time we got it properly set and then we
were pulling into the smaller Class III boats that had started
ahead of us. It was a wonderful sight in the bright sunlight.
We were in the centre of a great fleet of yachts all with their
spinnakers set, all going well. They looked bright as flowers
in the sunlight, every sort of colour, and the sea sparkling.
But when I finally relinquished the helm to the watch on
duty and got down to my navigating, I found that the glass
had dropped from 1020 to 1012 millibars. It was a biggish
drop and boded no good. The shipping forecast confirmed it.
The wind was already strengthening out of the nor'nor'west.

We dined in comfort—Dorothy serving a Boeuf-en-Daube
(prepared at home in advance) followed by cheeses and fruit,
the boat rolling slightly and a powerful surge of water at the
bows as she ploughed along at around 7 knots. We had passed
through a large number of the smaller boats and for a time
sailed level with *Sposa II*, rated top boat in our class. As
evening closed down we pulled away from her. Some of the
Class I boats were still behind us and away to the north we
could see *Thalassa*'s green spinnaker. In a lull, *Jabula*, one
of the fastest and best-sailed of the smaller boats, began to

[1] All boats entered for RORC races are measured and, after making
various allowances, are given a time factor, which is their handicap,
or rating.

close up on us. But then the wind strengthened again and we pulled steadily away from her.

Darkness came. We switched on port and starboard navigation lights, stern light and masthead light, and those not on watch went to their bunks for the four hour run to the West Hinder. About eleven I got up to check navigation. The beam of the Noord Hinder light vessel loomed to the north. For a time the actual light was visible. At half-hour intervals I was getting the radio beacon of the West Hinder loud and clear on my radio direction finder. Position right where it should be—over the bows.

Midnight, and I was up on deck, searching for the West Hinder light. Not a sign of it. But all around us the firefly glow of the fleet, masthead lights and stern lights. Somebody up front had a great, white beacon in the cockpit powerful enough to be the beam of a lightship . . . all very confusing. It was like being in the centre of a huge fishing fleet—lights everywhere.

I went up for'ard and leaned my back against the mast, bracing myself to the surge and roll of the boat. Above me hung the great canopy of the spinnaker, full and taut with the weight of the wind. No sound up there, but from the bows a great noise of water as we creamed along with the surf of a breaking wave-top; and then suddenly the sound would drop away as we slid into a trough, only to start up again as the stern lifted and *Mary Deare* plunged forward. It was wonderfully exhilarating just to stand there and feel the boat so alive and driving furiously towards the Belgian coast.

But all I cared about at that moment was the West Hinder light. The boats ahead were spread out in a fan and we looked centrally placed. But with the loom of the Noord Hinder falling away to the port quarter, the West Hinder should have been visible. Stern lights of the leading boats, dipping in the waves, gave flashes that were hard to distinguish from those of a light vessel. Four every 30 seconds I was searching for. I am blessed with remarkably long sight, which has so far survived the close work of writing. I can usually see a rock or a buoy, the vague blur of land on the horizon, before any of my friends. But now the blink of the West Hinder eluded me.

Going back to the cockpit I looked astern and saw the white-capped tops of waves, saw the way the man at the tiller seemed to be lifted right up and then thrown back again. There was quite a sea running and I remembered with a tautening of nerves that a crew who had not sailed together before would have to drop that wind-filled spinnaker as we rounded the lightship, hoist the genoa, and at the same time we should have to haul in the mainsail. I didn't like the thought of it in the dark. So many things could go wrong, and the wind was force 5 now—17–21 knots.

Bob was at the helm and we stood talking about it for a while, our eyes searching the horizon beyond the plunging compass light. David had gone for'ard with the glasses. His sweatered figure appeared in the red of the port navigation light. 'I think I can see it now. Away to starboard. You have a look.'

I crawled for'ard again and he pointed to a gap between the stern lights of two boats. I, too, thought I saw it. It meant we were too far north. But the tide was flooding southwards. A quick mental calculation of the probable distance off and I realised we were as well placed as we could have expected.

It was time we began to get organised for the 300° change of course. David took the helm and I told him to head for where we thought we'd seen the loom of the light. Bob and I clambered for'ard to grapple with the spinnaker net. This is a cat's cradle of strings hoisted for'ard of the mast to prevent that most frightening of all spinnaker misdemeanours, the wrapping of the sail around the forestays. Once a spinnaker spills its wind and begins to wrap, it goes on winding round and round, sewing you up in such a tangle that the only answer may be to hoist a man to the top of the mast. It was something that didn't bear thinking about, in the dark and with a sea running.

Back in the cockpit I found David sailing with the wind dead aft and still not quite headed for the loom of the West Hinder. I watched for a moment, and then we both saw. not the loom, but the light itself. It was nearer than I had expected. Two miles, perhaps three—and still on the starboard bow. There were three courses open to me; to hold on and when we were just north of the lightship drop the spinnaker and run down on to it under the genoa, to gybe the spinnaker right away, or to continue as we were, but sail the boat 'by the lee'—in other words, with the wind on the wrong side. This last meant taking a risk, for if the wind got behind the mainsail the whole boat would become unmanageable.

No question which was the right thing to do, but it was dangerous and obviously I was the person who should take the risk with my own boat. I relieved David at the helm and began half an hour's very concentrated steering, my eyes fixed on the leech (the rear edge) of the mainsail, watching for the slightest back-lift, my whole mind concentrated on that and the feel of the wind at the back of my right ear as I stood four-square to the stern, sensing every slight shift of wind direction.

I heard David and Bob discussing how best to handle the spinnaker on the turn—heard them only vaguely, for every now and then the leech of the mainsail lifted on a surge and all my nerves were bent on bringing the boat safely down on the tide to arrive just south of that slow-flashing glimmer of light. The lead boats were rounding it now, the big Class I boys. I could see them pulling away, coming up towards us to cross our bows. Our closer rivals were moving in from left and right, closing us fast. I could see more than the lightship's lantern now. I could see her riding light, could see the whole ship.

'Is it all right with you if we hoist the genoa first?' This from David.

'Yes, of course.' It would act like the net, stopping any chance of the spinnaker wrapping.

'We'd like to take the boom off first. All right if we leave the spinnaker loose-footed? It'll only be for a moment.'

'Yes.' What else could I say? The light vessel was coming up very fast now and we were still to the north of it. This was no time to argue with the foredeck about the best way to handle that monstrous wind-bellied pile of nylon. I was sailing more and more by the lee, edging south with every tiniest shift of wind, willing myself and the wind and the seas to get *Mary Deare* the right side of that anchored iron hulk that was now sweeping the sails with a brilliant white light.

The watch below were coming up on deck, bringing with

them the heavy orange bulk of the genoa sail bag. They dragged it for'ard along the plunging deck, passing out of my line of vision. I was aware of activity up in the bows, but I had no eyes for anything but the lightship and the mainsail. Twice the wind caught the back of the sail and only the boom guy—the thin wire brace running from the end of the boom to a block and tackle in the bows—prevented the boom from slamming across in an unintentional gybe. Each time I just caught the boat before she became unmanageable.

The light vessel was looming over the bows now, her beam beginning to sweep above our sails. Out of the tail of my eye I saw a big boat closing me on the port side, saw her butcher's-striped spinnaker belly further and further out ahead . . . something wrong there; the halyard must have slipped. She seemed to be coming down on us. A quick glance and I saw they were in real trouble. The spinnaker was falling away towards the bows, the stripes billowing out and smothering the for'ard part of the boat; it was all picked out in the swinging beam of the light, in photographic flashes.

'Speed it up, if you can, Bob,' I called. 'There isn't much time.' The light vessel was right over our bows, the tide sweeping us across it, and the boat with its spinnaker trailing was coming in on us, forcing me to turn away from her. The wind hit the back of the mainsail. I swung *Mary Deare* back and for a moment we were headed for the other boat. But we were just clear of the light vessel and the genoa was up, the spinnaker boom on the deck. 'Have you let go the boom guy?' I called. I thought the answer was Yes, but it was lost in the spill of a wave and the surge of the boat. The spinnaker was free on the port side. They were hauling it in under the lee of the main. As it came down I told Cav to haul in on the main. The big boat was rounding-to right alongside the light vessel, her decks alive with figures heaving the trailing spinnaker back on board.

We were clear and I rounded-to myself, neck-and-neck with another boat, squeezed in by it as it closed from starboard. 'Haul that mainsheet in,' I yelled. Cav gave a great heave, all his weight on it. There was a snap and the trailing end of a wire came curling into the cockpit. The boom guy had not been let go. But we were round, with the genoa and main hardened in, the spinnaker down and the boat driving. Close alongside a white hull wallowed—*Kiff* rated only four above us. But we were pulling away, and clear of the lee of the light vessel, we gathered speed, conscious of the boat heavily heeled, conscious, too, of the weight of the wind and the size of the sea.

Gradually things were sorted out, the spinnaker gear all stowed, the decks tidied by the safety-harnessed figures that crawled and clutched their way in the rearing ghostly gleam of the navigation light.

'About fifteenth boat, I think.' David, who when he wasn't underwriting was doing parachute drops or Marine Commando work in small canoes or frogman's suit, was fiercely competitive. 'I counted them. About fifteenth round the Hinder, wouldn't you say, Bob?' His voice sounded excited as well it might, for we were rated 42nd in the fleet.

'About that.' As always Bob's voice was quiet, non-committal.

I handed over the helm to Cav and Michael. Cav, who is a painter, still had the picture of our rounding the light vessel clear and vivid in his mind. It was fixed in his memory, as it was fixed in mine—a mental picture so sharp that it would stay with us until it could be reproduced on canvas and in words. 'Fantastic,' he said. 'Absolutely fantastic. It was like Piccadilly Circus—all those boats converging and the swinging beam of that light and the spinnaker coming down in a tangle over that poor devil's bows. Fantastic.' He was still burbling excitedly about it when I went below and got down to my charting.

The course was north, but the best we could do was about 20°. That would take us up past the Noord Hinder and away on a long leg that would never meet Smith's Knoll. Some time in the morning we should have to go about. But for a few hours we could stay on this tack and get some sleep. I pushed open the hatch. 'Don't pinch her,' I said. 'Keep her sailing all the time even if you do see boats up to windward of you.' Michael was a very good dinghy helmsman who had sailed with us to Spain the previous year. I knew he could be relied upon to keep the boat going really hard. I undressed to my underwear and slipped into my sleeping bag in the quarter berth, which is just below the main hatch.

Sleep was impossible, but I dozed, pressed into the side of the bunk by the angle of heel, hearing the water thundering past the steel hull close beside my left ear, my body riding with the plunges, feeling the slams as she dived into the troughs. The slams got worse and I thought: 'We must be running straight up the Hinder bank—these are the overfalls.' I thought of the rigging, hoping I'd tuned it right, remembering the two turns I'd taken on the forestay, the turn on the main upper shrouds. But she was a tough boat, built as a cruiser to go round the world, down round the Horn if I wanted to—the designer's words, not mine.

I suppose I slept. I remember seeing Cav in his oilskins. He seemed to be clambering along the upper side of the dog-house above the galley. He was peering out of the port dog-house window and his face, with the tousled iron-grey hair, was lit intermittently by light. A storm? Lightning? Or was it the sun coming up? The first grey light of dawn was showing. No, of course—it must be the swinging beam of the Noord Hinder. 'Is that the North Hinder, Cav?'

He turned to me and nodded. 'Abeam now and quite clear.'

'Enter it in the log book, will you—time and mileage run by the log.' I closed my eyes. The movement was very trying. Ninety miles from the West Hinder to Smith's Knoll. Beating like this would add another—how many?—thirty, forty miles? It wasn't going to be pleasant. I could feel the cold through two layers of blanket and a down sleeping bag. We'd be feeling very battered and tired by the time we rounded the next mark and started the downhill run to the Hook. But it would be daylight all the way and we had a good crew. It's the crews that crack usually, not the boats. Certainly not *Mary Deare*.

The watch changed. Cav and Michael came below. 'We've pulled up on several more.' Michael was struggling out of his oilskins.

'How many can you see now?'

'One or two,' Cav said. 'Up to windward of us. Another astern and down wind. *Mary Deare*'s going very well—just her weather.' He had started his sailing life way back on the big 'J' Class boats. The time was just after four. 'Dawn beginning to break,' he added. 'Nasty-looking sea.'

I lay and listened to the slight change in the boat that follows a new hand on the helm. How long ought we to continue on this tack? Should we make a long leg of it and then one across to the Outer Gabbard lightship and one up to Smith's Knoll? Or should we take short tacks, back and forth up the direct line between the West Hinder and Smith's Knoll? I thought three long tacks. It would be easier on navigation. I was beginning to worry about that. It's hard to concentrate on figures when the world is standing on its head, and I'm not fond of figures. Some of these liner boys would be horrified if they had to navigate the way we have to—wet and cold on a chart that's never still.

And then I was listening to the slams as she hit the seas. For a time they had been much less, as though the wind had lessened. But I knew the easing of the motion had been due to the fact that we had cleared the Hinder bank and the seas had become more regular. But now the tide had turned. It was running north. Wind against tide—the seas were getting steeper, breaking more often. I clambered out of my bunk, pushed open the hatch doors. Bob was at the helm. I can see him now—a tall, military-looking figure in yellow oilskins, his glasses misted with spray, his head bare and his neck muffled in a towel. 'Is she getting heavy on the helm?'

'Carrying a bit of weather helm, but nothing excessive. She's going very well.'

'You don't think she'd sail better if we changed to Number Two jib?'

'No, she's all right at the moment. Might be worth considering later if the wind gets up any more. But not to worry now.'

I went back to my bunk, lying there and feeling with every nerve the movement of the boat, trying to make up my mind whether to order the change. I wasn't thinking of the boat being too heavily pressed by the weight of canvas or that she was in danger. That never occurred to me. And the way we were going I was quite prepared to blow out the genoa if it would win us the race. No, all I was thinking about was whether she would go faster under the Number Two. It is a fact that in heavyish weather boats often lose time by hanging on to big canvas too long. *Mary Deare* I knew from experience slowed up as soon as the lee rail was under and the deck awash. I had proved this time and again, and the signal was invariably a heaviness on the helm.

About a quarter of an hour later my nerves came suddenly alert to the heavy slam of a wave and what I thought was an ugly additional sound. Did I imagine this, or was it premonition? I don't know. All I can remember is that I was wide awake and every nerve tense to the movement of the boat. I began to want very much to order the change down. I tried to balance my knowledge of the feel of the boat below against Bob's experience. He was at the helm and I was well aware that what sounds like heavy weather down below is often an exhilarating sail for those in the cockpit. And so I hung between sleeping and waking again, listening, waiting—discouraged as much as anything by the effort it was going to cost to struggle into my oilskins and go for'ard into the wet and the wind to change the sail. I was only just recovering from a bout of 'flu.

Slam! And another sound. A sound like a sharp crack, merged with the slam. And then a sudden quietness. No rushing of water, no surging roar of speed, and the boat rolling.

The hatch banged open. 'That's your mast gone.' It was David's voice—quiet, but very clear and pitched a shade high.

'Are you serious?' But after that first stupid question I didn't say anything. There wasn't anything to say. The mast had gone, and that was that. I knew it had gone by the feel of the boat. I dived out of my bunk to rush on deck. Cav was there, too. Michael followed. I'd no oilskins on, no shoes. I hesitated and then got my oilskins. The mast gone, there was no desperate hurry. We couldn't put it back on again. It wasn't something you could deal with in a hurry. I remember lacing up my shoes, knowing I would need a firm foothold on that rolling deck. I told the others to get their things on. And all the time I was thinking—'This must be my fault; I got the forestays or the shrouds too tight.' And yet I didn't see how that could have dismasted us.

Up on the deck the grey light of day showed steep, ugly seas—all grey. It was five o'clock in the morning and the

Noord Hinder was way astern. Bob was already up for'ard, heaving in the genoa, which had fallen over the side. The mast had gone at the upper cross-trees. The topmast section was suspended from the splintered remains by a wire halyard and was banging to and fro against the starboard shrouds. As far as the lower cross-trees the mast was splintered, the mainsail track torn away; below that the mast was intact, the lower shrouds still standing. At least we had something on which to rig a jury sail.

I was thinking about this problem as I went for'ard. The genoa was inboard by then. We got the main boom sheeted hard in, pulled the trailing mainsail in over the guardrails. Dorothy started to come on deck. 'Tie-ers, please,' Michael called. She never did get on deck, poor girl, but was forced to remain below in that rolling madhouse whilst the hatch kept banging open in her face as one or other of the crew demanded this or that—a pair of pliers, the genoa bag, a rope to use as lashing. And then things began to be bundled below for her to sort out.

I remember, after the mainsail was partly lashed, somebody called out, 'Have you got heavy duty wire clippers on board?' These are recommended equipment for ocean racing and I had toyed with the idea of getting a pair that year, for the lifeboat had had to go out to two boats during the Southsea-Harwich race, one having been dismasted. But to be of any use they have to be really massive things and anyway I had thought that though others might be dismasted, it wouldn't happen to *Mary Deare* with her stalwart and relatively short spar.

Now I doubt whether I shall ever carry such a tool. Had I had a pair on board we should undoubtedly have sheared through the wire halyard from which the topmast was suspended, probably some of the standing rigging, too. We might well have lost the topmast section then and with that gone the evidence of what had caused the dismasting would have been lost. It might even have been put down to the rigging having parted.

'No,' I said. 'We'll just lash it.'

It took time to lash that banging lump of mast with all its trailing wires. By then boats were piling past us, all the yachts we'd left behind us, the hard sailing wasted. It was a bitter moment. An oilskin-clad figure in the cockpit of one boat added insult to injury by taking a photograph of us. And a little later Mike called out that there was another boat in trouble. But she was only reefing and changing to a smaller headsail. She went on her way and about this time I saw a batten lying on the deck. It started me salvaging what I could, thinking ahead to the time when I'd have to cope with setting all this to rights. It was then, I think, that I made up my mind to head for home, not down-wind for a Belgian port.

We saved all the battens—those plastic stiffeners that hold out the back edge of the mainsail. I even rescued the burgee flag and its staff. The signal halyards were undamaged. We cut the slides from the mainsail to free it from the topmast section and bundled it down below to Dorothy, who somehow managed all alone to stow the huge pile of wet sail up for'ard out of the way.

In forty-five minutes exactly everything was lashed and stowed, the decks cleared and I had started the engine. We headed east with the seas on the starboard bow.

That I should head eastward under engine for the English coast may seem the most natural thing in the world to anyone who does not understand about ocean racers. In fact, *Mary Deare* was one of the very few boats in the fleet that could have undertaken this sixty-mile voyage against wind and sea. Most ocean racers are equipped with auxiliary engines. Those without are penalized on handicap, for the original idea was that the races should be between cruising boats. Now, however, engines tend to be small in relation to the size of the boat, designed to do little more than get the ship in and out of port. Moreover, when racing, most of them carry the minimum of fuel to reduce weight. This means a small range under power and the engine itself often incapable of pushing the boat satisfactorily against the wind, certainly not against a biggish sea as well. Doubtless for this reason the other English boat to be dismasted turned down-wind and put into Zeebrugge in Belgium.

Mary Deare, however, was designed very much as a cruiser, which is why she rates below much smaller boats. In the original design discussion I had stipulated a Coventry Victor horizontal twin-cylinder diesel because this engine had the best thrust-weight ratio and I was determined that the engine should be powerful enough to earn the space it took up. To some extent the boat was designed round it and the tank, which was fashioned in one piece with the steel well of the cockpit, had a capacity of some 45 gallons of fuel. The manufacturers claimed a consumption of only half a gallon per hour, which should give us a range of 500 miles under power.

I remember before the race I had discussed with the boat-yard the possibility of removing most of the fuel to reduce the weight aft. They always fill the tank at the end of each season to preserve it during the winter lay-up. But once filled it is extremely difficult to drain and I was very glad now that the boatyard had said it was impossible. I had run the engine for perhaps four hours so far during the season. If the yard had really filled it up at the end of the previous season then I had a virtually full tank. I just crossed my fingers and hoped, and nothing would induce me to dip to find out. To run for the Belgian coast meant shipping a new mast out with risk of damage and it would then have to be rigged by a strange and perhaps unsatisfactory yard. We were due to leave three weeks later for Sweden and I was determined to get the boat across to England.

Only one of the crew suggested that it might be better to turn down-wind and run for it, and I was relieved to hear Bob's quiet voice say, 'Skipper's right. I'd rather be out in open water if the engine's going to pack up and the wind goes on rising. Better that than a lee shore.' And so we plugged on, the engine note not varying. But progress was slow. We thought perhaps 2½ knots. The seas were unpleasant in the squalls and it was bitterly cold. The boat rolled violently, the shattered remains of the mast swaying wildly. Sixty-odd miles at 2½ knots. 'It's going to be a slow business,' Bob said, sitting at the helm with his towel round his neck, his hair streaming water. We should go a bit faster when we get into shallower water and came under the lee of the English coast—about 20 hours altogether we reckoned.

Sickness caught up with some of the crew in the wild unbalanced movement and I sat at the helm hour after hour, praying that the tank really was full, that the engine really would only consume half a gallon an hour, that the fuel lines wouldn't choke or the injector nozzles carbon up, things that require a good engineer to put right. It was like that time two years before when Robert Clark, the designer, and myself, with a Dutch journalist, had motored the empty hull across from the builder's yard in Holland for completion in England. We had gone out into a gale first time with a qualified engineer on board and had had to put back to the Hook of Holland. The engineer was sick and had to be sent home and when I told Robert I'd always sworn I wouldn't do the trip without an engineer on board, he had replied, 'You don't refuse to go out under sail unless you have a spar-maker on board for fear your mast may break—why insist on an engineer in case your engine fails?'

I thought of that remark now. We'd broken the mast and there was nothing that a spar-maker could have done that we hadn't done. Now it was up to the engine and I didn't think an engineer could have done much if it broke down, rolling as we were. The rolling, which was very violent, affected us all, and when we weren't on deck steering, we clung to our bunks as the only safe place. God knows how my wife had managed to produce hot drinks immediately after we'd cleaned up the mess and salvaged all the gear.

Some time during the morning we sighted a yacht headed north under sail. She was a long way away, but watching her, I envied her her tall mast and her sails. Around midday a ship ploughed across the horizon to the south. She looked like the Harwich train ferry, but I couldn't be sure. It is very difficult to be sure of the course of a ship passing you at the limits of visibility, but I thought she was headed a little south of our own course. If so, we were to the north of the Galloper light vessel, which I wished to sight before we closed the East Coast banks.

Twice Cav and I saw what looked like a light vessel to the south of us. But each time it turned out to be a fishing boat with a steadying sail. And then suddenly there it was—definitely a lightship. It couldn't have been anything else but the Galloper; nevertheless, I turned south and closed it until we could see the name painted white in huge letters across her red hull.

The time was then just after three in the afternoon. We had thirty miles still to go. We did this in 5½ hours, and in the grey light of evening entered Harwich estuary. We dropped anchor in the Orwell River, close under HMS *Ganges*. I switched the engine off and all was suddenly peace with the curlews piping on the mud banks and a bitter cold wind driving up the estuary. The time was 8.30 p.m.

Below in the warmth of the saloon, already neat and tidy again, with a cloth on the table and the bottles and glasses out, we drank a toast to the sturdy little engine that had brought us so uncomplainingly through a dirty sea more than sixty miles from the scene of our disaster in just over fourteen hours. We were thinking of the rest of the fleet then, some of them still beating up to Smith's Knoll. 'They'll be tired and cold,' we said. 'Wet, too. They'll have a bitter night of it.' So we tried to console ourselves.

Fortified by a few drinks I surreptitiously got the dipstick and went up into the cockpit. But David had seen me go. 'I wonder how much fuel we *have* got left?'

I gave him the dipstick and unscrewed the top of the dip tube. The steel rod was inserted and when he drew it out he stared at it in amazement. 'It's hard to believe,' he said. 'But you've still got three-quarters of a tank left.'

Down below the post-mortem had already begun. Why had the mast broken? Only Cav with a painter's eye for detail came near to the truth—a constructional weakness. This we established a few days later at Whisstock's yard when, with the designer, the spar-builder, Claude Whisstock, Bob and myself all present, we took a saw to the salvaged topmast section. This revealed that there was also a bad crack on the starboard side—the side that would have been free of pressure during the race. In other words, the process of disintegration had started either earlier that season or the previous year. Robert Clark is not only one of the most brilliant yacht designers, but also one of the most experimental, and in *Mary Deare*, one of the first ocean racers whose crew were relieved of the chore of setting up backstay runners every time she was put about, he had compensated for their absence by giving her a mast that was not normal, almost round section, but very elongated fore and aft; as somebody said when it was building, it looked like a 'plank on edge'. This type of mast is commonplace now, but at the time it posed a problem for the builder. Most designers specify solid sections by way of the cross-trees to strengthen a hollow spar at this vital point, but to achieve lightness Robert Clark's masts were usually hollow throughout. In the absence of specific instructions to the contrary, *Mary Deare*'s had been constructed this way. The effect of this was that the thrust of the cross-trees—the rigging spreaders—had not been trans-mitted to the mast as a whole, which would have been the case in the then conventional round mast, but was concentrated solely on the flat side—concentrated, therefore, on $1\frac{1}{4}$ inch thickness of planking. The result had been almost inevitable. As the spar-builder said, it was like pressing on the centre of an empty match box. But knowing the cause of it was little consolation. We had finished fifth in our class the previous year; this time, rated 42nd in the whole fleet and lying per-haps better than 15th, our chances on corrected time had looked as good as they would ever be for a heavy boat like *Mary Deare*. Nor was it any consolation to know that 36 other boats—almost half the fleet—had been forced to give up for one reason or another. And now there was all the work of getting a new mast built and stepped in time to meet our deadline for Sweden.

II

ROCK-HOPPING IN
SCANDINAVIA

Crew for Sweden and Norway—1961
Michael Hopkinson
David Hare
George Dunkerley
Major C. R. Stirling

We arrived at West Mersea late in the afternoon of Friday,
June 16, just as *Mary Deare* was being towed out to the
Quarters, her new mast gleaming yellow in the sunlight. The
last time I had seen that spar the great planks of sitka spruce
had just been glued and clamped and the two spar-makers
were only beginning the work of planing it into shape. That
had been barely a week ago, the big loft full of the smell of
glue and raw wood. It looked very different now as we
climbed on board from the club launch, the wood no longer
raw, but varnished to a high gloss, the winch farings beautifully moulded, the whole great stick a work of art of which
the craftsmen could be proud. They were working on the rigging and after getting our stores on board and giving the yard
hands a drink we went back to the club. The sun set. Our
crew arrived and out beyond the mud banks exposed by the
tide we could still see the dark figures of the two men working on the shrouds.

We slept on board that night and in the morning motored
round to Brightlingsea to take on bonded stores—gin and
whisky and cigarettes. And then in the afternoon we sailed,
hoisted full main and genoa. David had not been on the Hook
Race with us, but for Michael, I think, and certainly for
Dorothy and myself, the sight of that new spar carrying full
sail again, driving the boat through the water, was wonderfully satisfying; and this time there were solid sections by

34

way of the cross-trees. The forecast had not been particularly good and I decided, therefore, to take the longer route by the Dutch coast.

The last of England dropped astern as night fell with the distant gleam of the Shipwash light and we broke out the duty-free. Dawn came cold and grey with gale warnings, but by midday the front had passed across and *Mary Deare* was sailing herself. It was hot and the sky was clear, but we never saw the Texel light off the Dutch coast. In the early hours of Monday morning, with the BBC giving us more warnings of gales we closed the ST2 buoy. This is one of a line of buoys marking the steamer lane to the Elbe. Heavily reefed we identified the P2 buoy at noon. Wind force 6 now and as Tuesday dawned we were broad reaching in a lumpy sea and the ER light vessel off the Danish port of Esbjerg was straight ahead of us. The log, which had been streamed as usual at the Sunk light vessel off Harwich, read 304 miles—a difference of only half a mile from the reading two years before when we had sailed this same course on our maiden voyage to the Baltic by way of the Limfjord.

We took the Skagerrak at night, keeping close to the Danish coast. To the north the sky was pale, a cold Norwegian summer light. And then it was blotted out by heavy rain squalls. For those coming through the Skagerrak and entering the Baltic ante-chamber of the Kattegat for the first time, the Paternoster light off the Swedish coast is a comforting guide mark. Its reddish colour and the iron stilts of its framework make it impossible to confuse with any other mark, and if it is day and the visibility good, then the huge bulk of Karestan Castle, visible almost from the Skagen light off the Danish coast, pinpoints Marstrand. It looks at first like a stranded hulk and reminded me of Churchill's monstrous grain elevator seen from twenty miles out in Hudson's Bay.

The entrance to Marstrand, after almost four days at sea, seemed unpleasantly constricted by rock. A week later it would have seemed luxuriously wide, so quickly does one condition oneself to rock-hopping in the inner leads. The shelter in Marstrand itself was absolute, but there were few boats there and it was bitterly cold, the place sunless and grey, with only a few oilskin-clad figures on the waterfront. We began to wonder what had induced us to sail 584 miles, mostly under heavily-reefed main and No. 3 jib, to finish up in this grim little hole in the rocks. England, according to our radio, was sweltering in a heat-wave.

We stayed in Marstrand two days, pretending that we were waiting for Midsummer Night, which they were celebrating on June 23; in fact, we had no alternative. The weather was vile. A gleam of sun on the Friday afternoon encouraged us to venture across the water in the little tram-like ferry and trek inland to gather greenery with which to decorate our mast. This is the custom on Midsummer Night, a relic of pagan days perhaps, but certainly appropriate on a coast where the skerries and most of the out-islands are ice-worn to the bare rock without the slightest vestige of anything growing—not a blade of grass, nor a tuft of heather, not even the most stunted tree.

It is always a mistake to announce in advance that you intend to leave the following day, particularly in a foreign port, for having done so, you have no choice but to go. I had hoped for a quiet-weather introduction to the narrow rock channels and the Swedish system of markers. Instead, it was still blowing a gale on the Saturday morning as we slipped back on to the stern mooring buoy, put five rolls in the main and hoisted No. 3. We were the only boat going out and up to the final moment of slipping our new-found Swedish friends were still arguing as to whether we should make directly north, which meant a short open sea passage, or whether it would be better for us to take the inside route through the narrows and into Hakefjord.

I decided on Hakefjord, but only at the last minute. The markers leading to the narrows looked confusing and there were rocks awash with the waves breaking white; only the fact that a small steamer had come through the previous day convinced me that there really was a way through. Because of this decision my introduction to Swedish channel markers was made in a flurry of spray with *Mary Deare* careering along at almost her maximum. In fact, the channels through the rocks in Sweden are superbly marked, and once you have had the benefit of a trial run, you never lack confidence again, however narrow and difficult it looks.

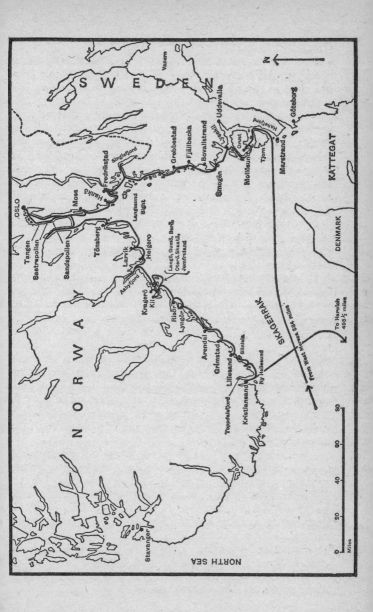

After that first wild dash, the shelter of the narrows was so complete that at times we barely had steerage way and even thought of shaking out a few rolls. But out in the open in Hakefjord it was a very different matter, with the wind funnelling up this fifteen mile inlet to Uddevalla and the gale blowing spray so thick that it was difficult to identify the various islands for they presented an uninterrupted land front, the gaps between opening up only at the last moment.

We were just over a week in Sweden. Gales and calm, the bald rock of the skerries, the green lushness of the *sunds* (narrows) and canals; it was a week of contrasts. The light glimmered with that cold, bright, northern look; and when the sun shone it had a brittle quality. Dawn broke in the east as daylight faded in the west.

The inner leads through the skerries are well marked, the brooms and beacons supplemented by target-like splashes of black and white on the islands. Moreover, the passages through the rocks are drawn in for you on the charts so that instead of searching desperately through a magnifying glass for a way through, you can see it at a glance. Nevertheless, a magnifying glass is as essential at the chart table as binoculars are in the cockpit—and the Norwegian charts are much, much worse; far more rocks to the square inch.

Memories of that week are still very vivid; Mollösund in the dark of a storm, all fishermen's huts with their stilted feet paddled in the waters of the Sund and a howling wind rattling a million haddock drying on the rocks; superb shrimps eaten in the sheltered quiet of Hamburgsund with wooden coasters toc-a-toc-ing by, deep-laden and smelling of strange cargoes; the kind hospitality of the Runos, father and son, hailed as workmen on a quay that proved to be their own; Hunnebostrand, seen in the blazing glory of a cloudless evening, bright contrast to the doll's house quaintness of Gullholmen in the wet.

Best of all, perhaps, the thrill of sailing out of Mollösund, a gale still blowing, the sun shining, six rolls down and No. 3, the speed indicator showing eight and a half knots and all the sea ahead a foaming lather of white as the waves poured over submerged and awash reefs; *Mary Deare* heeled well over and the next markers, two miles away, barely visible through the driving spray—and just seaward of us, outside the rocks, a steamer making heavy weather of it, a blurred shape in the salt haze of wind-whipped spray.

What a frightful coast this would be, so bald and bleak, so full of rock, if to these navigational hazards were added the tides of Brittany! As it is, a rise in the water level is no more than a surface movement of the sea—a sure sign of foul weather from the west; a fall, of course, presages fair weather. Navigationally, the most dangerous stretch we encountered was the shallows north of Skåpesund, immediately after the rather low bridge; the Runos insisted on providing a motorboat escort. I didn't go up to Uddevalla, but I was advised that if I did, and sailed north-about the island of Orust, I should beware the Malö strömmar where the current runs up to ten knots and there is danger of losing control. They call this 'the place of the boiling waters.' One other navigational hazard that, like Odysseus, I endeavoured to keep from my crew, is the little fishing port of Smögen where I was told you find the prettiest girls on the coast. No explanation is given—and since I did not stop, I have no proof that these holiday migrants are all as beautiful as Swedish sailors say.

The end of June found us sailing up Singlefjord. This is the boundary between Sweden and Norway. Bare, grey rock to starboard, the dark green of dense tree-growth to port. It is as marked as that, a natural geological boundary; and as always the people changed with the scenery—a gentler, softer, kinder people.

We tucked ourselves away for the night in a tree-ed inlet on the north side of Kirkö Island and drank our gin in the placid quiet of still waters—the call of a bird, the creak of oars from a boat trolling; no other sound and the mirror-surface of the inlet a dark reflected green. Two cottages, half-hidden among the trees. a rough stone landing place, cows grazing—it was called Urdal. And at six in the morning the sun woke us, hot for a change and heady with the resin-smell of Norway spruce. We put the dinghy over the side for the first time since leaving England, bathed from large flat rocks, lay basking, and refreshed, climbed the wooded slopes to look down on *Mary Deare* riding to her reflection. Two weeks of

wind and cold; and now in Norway this perfect peace, this
gentle greenness, above all the smell:

> Incense of heat, haze-wrapped, green;
> The trees marching to their still reflections. . . .

A cockpit breakfast, and then away to Frederikstad, sailing
the buoyed channel till it narrowed to the width of a Broads
river. And after lunch, through the lifting bridge, through
the shopping centre with its white-wood buildings lining the
stream, past towering ships standing so big in the yards they
almost blocked our path. And in the afternoon, gliding in
sunshine through a maze of rocks with 90° turns in the
channel, we made Hankö.

Months before, my Norwegian publisher, Per Mortensen,
had written—*You must make Hankö for the Regatta.* It was
Friday, June 30, the penultimate day. Garnholmen (*holmen*
means island), black with people massed on the rocky point by
the lighthouse, was the starting point, and all seaward of it
the horizon was filled with the many-coloured sails of yachts
racing. With a good breeze, full main and No. 2, our ensign
streaming against the white of our wake, we crossed the line
close under Garnholmen and lay-to till the first two classes
finished. Then up through the narrows in a litter of boats
that included King Olaf's, dipping our ensign to the *Norge*
and fetching up in Hankö roads, using a 12-metre's vacant
mooring next to the King's.

Salmon for dinner that night at the Hankö Hotel, with King
Olaf, supported by his admiral, presenting the day's prizes on
the lawn below our table; and in the morning Carl Mortensen,
Per's brother, came aboard for a drink. Afterwards we slipped
and followed his *Carmensita* out for a grandstand view of the
day's racing, coming back in a tight pack of boats of all classes
with the ocean racers straggling in from a twenty-four-hour
race.

Hankö must be one of the world's most beautiful regatta
centres—completely sheltered with big houses set in trees
and plenty of room for the boats. A gin or two aboard *Carmensita* and in the quiet of the evening we hoisted sail and
stole away, drifting quietly north round Hankö Island and up
through Rauöfjorden with the sun setting and the sea greying

to steel. In the fading light we dropped our hook in the little sheltered hole of Evjesund where nets hung drying on gaunt poles under a full moon.

Next day we made our first crew change, dropping David off at Moss to endure the stink of that smelly place until his train came in. Once through the bridge and clear of Mosse Sundet, we hoisted spinnaker—an ironical touch this, for in the fortnight he had been with us David, one of Britain's top dinghy sailors, had never seen the spinnaker set.

We were headed up Oslofjord now and had allowed ourselves three days to cover the thirty miles so that we could explore it thoroughly. Sandspollen, Saetrepollen, a sheltered anchorage under Tangen, close in by the boatyard, and another at the head of the Hvalstrand inlet; and then into the island channels just west of Fornebu Landet, oil-slicked, but still a charming little playground to have on your doorstep if you work in Oslo.

The evening of July 4 saw us hitched on to *Carmensita*'s mooring in the Dronningen. We had been the only English yacht at Hankö. Now we were almost the only yacht at all— acres of moorings, all empty, hardly a soul at the club. Next morning Per Mortensen flew in from Paris to greet us. Lunch at Blom's, famous for its smörgasbord—dim, Edwardian atmosphere, all wood panelling and plush, the walls flaunting the heraldic designs of the 'exclusive' Blue Nose drinking club. In the afternoon we had a tour of the Mortensens' new publishing house—in addition to publishing books, they have a corner in Norway's magazines, all deriving from the nationwide correspondence school founded by their father. At six we gave a party on board *Mary Deare* for the press. At eight we were sitting down to dinner with more journalists in Najeden, the restaurant next to Nansen's *Fram*.

The food here is some of the best in Norway. Certainly the *gravlaks* is out of this world. *Gravlaks* is raw salmon, buried—hence the prefix *grav*, grave. The salmon, which has to be a fat one, is salted, peppered, and then compressed for three days—a hundredweight flat stone does admirably. With the coffee Per said: 'You must sail tonight . . . No, I am serious. If you wish to be out of Oslofjord tomorrow, then you have to leave now.' And he explained that every day during the summer months the wind comes in from the south about eleven o'clock.

At midnight they saw us into our dinghy at the club steps. 'You really go, at this hour?' This from 'Veronica', the *Aftenposten*'s columnist. 'Of course,' I said, and after that we had no choice. We hoisted the dinghy straight on board, slipped and motored out into the quiet of that milky Nordic night. Somewhere beyond the wooden silhouette of the club house a car's horn blared us farewell. We kept to the east side of the fjord this time, sailing under main alone, the wind from the north. One by one we ticked off the lights, one by one the storage tanks of well-known oil companies slipped astern, silver under bright lights; at three-thirty in the morning I was hauling in the breakfast mackerel. At four-thirty Filtvet Fyr was abeam; we were out of the narrow section of Oslofjord. By ten we were breakfasting in an inlet south of Bjerkö Island below the whaling port of Tönsberg, surprised to find we had dropped our hook a cable's length from *Carmensita*. Fifty miles, all downhill, and Oslofjord virtually behind us. As we turned in to catch up on our sleep the wind swung 180° to prove Per's point.

Before us now lay some of the most beautiful coastal scenery in the world, all fjord sailing, steep and wooded with towering crags, sheer cliffs, narrow twisting channels and little ports with white wood houses gleaming in the sun. Forestry is the main industry and rafted logs an additional hazard. The land-locked water was relatively warm, its clarity inviting—but everywhere there were jelly-fish; not the transparent, gelatinous type found on English coasts, but, like untidy poached eggs, coloured from cream through yellow and ochre to a dark orange red. They are stingers, and unpleasant, if you do not carry the necessary antidote. There were others, too, long-streamered, spongy creatures that looked like shaggy dahlias. We had a collection of the Sherlock Holmes stories on board, and re-reading *The Lion's Mane*, wondered whether this wasn't the same filthy species of jelly-fish that had sparked Conan Doyle's imagination. It was a cold summer and only very occasionally was the water warm enough to drive

the things into the deeper, colder layers and so enable us to
bathe.

West from Oslofjord to Kristiansand there are a host of
inlets, fjords, channels, rock cruising grounds and harbours. A
whole month spent in this one area would not be too much.
No tides to worry about. And though the Norwegian charts
only mark the way through the trickiest rock litters, leaving
you to figure out your courses for yourself, they do mark the
anchorages—a fluked anchor for big ships, a four-pronged
anchor for small boats. Wherever an anchorage is marked you
can be certain of good holding, usually in heavy grey boulder
clay; this even in small enclosed holes surrounded by sheer
cliff or rimmed with loose stone. The anchorage marks show
up well on the charts, but it is not so easy to differentiate between the red and black spar buoys.

Though there is no tide, there is a west-going set along the
coast, and in the bigger fjords an outward flow after heavy
rains. The set can be quite fast and in the neighbourhood of
reef areas like the Rakkeboerne just south of Larvik care needs
to be taken in thick weather. Going inside it is necessary to
search the chart very carefully for the faint lines of luftspans.
These are the overhead wires carrying electricity from island
to island, and in brackets the chart gives their height. Exact
knowledge of the height of your mast plus burgee above the
waterline is advisable! I had not made a note of this before
leaving England with the result that, where it was a matter of
inches clearance, I was never quite sure.

With time to spare and my chart marked up by the Mortensens, who had lived and sailed on this coast for years, we
were able to go into dozens of little places that hardly ever see
an ocean-going yacht. Anchorages like Kil and Kjölebrönn
(Kilsfjord), Skudodden and Blesviken (Deledfjord) and Skin-
ner (Toppdalsfjord) eat up time for they are way up long,
often windless fjords—a drifting, peaceful, leisurely sail with
the surprise of something unexpected at the end of it; Kilsfjord and Deledfjord, in particular—the one with its jutting
cliffs and forest running up to mountains in the distance, the
other full of sombre holes and quarries, and a freighter lost
among the woods at the end with the current glissading

through the narrows, and in the mist-shrouded gap behind, great log pens ready for rafting. But the most beautiful fjord of all is surely Aabyfjord.

Dorothy and I were on our own then, Michael having left us at Larvik. Within an hour of his pier-head jump at this exposed port it began to blow. We were then in Viksfjord, feeling our way through shallow waters. We should have had a miserable week-end of it, for it blew a gale, but the Pausts, flying the Maltese cross of their shipping line from the flag-staff on their island of Rodholmen, made us free of their home and put us on their own mooring. And when we had dragged that, we moored stern-on to their lantern-lit pier with twenty fathoms of chain out—a lot of chain to bring in on a Monday morning, alone and with the hydraulic winch choosing that moment to go on strike. With many warnings about the current setting on to the Rakkeboerne, we sailed in cold sunlight round into the Langesund Bight, anchored the night at Helgeroa, and in the morning watered at the fuelling point in Langesund narrows. That was how we heard about Aabyfjord. Even the Mortensens had never been there.

It looks on the chart much like any other short fjord or inlet on the coast. And yet, inside . . . it's difficult to explain, the charm so elusive, but it seemed to us to have a fairy-tale quality. The sun was shining. Everything was warm and bright, the colours strong in the rocks, and the narrows through the islands not grim iron-clad gaps, but pleasant openings welcoming us in. Summer houses perched on rocks, a cove with fishing shacks, and at the very head of the fjord, with the echo-sounder showing the comfortingly shallow depth of six fathoms, the rattle of the chain shattering the stillness sounded like 20,000 tons at least coming to rest. Peace in the fading light and small boys paddling canoes, a solitary fisher-man. In the morning, stealing quietly out under sail, people left their breakfasts to photograph and wave, and a boy, on a verandah perched high above the water serenaded us on his accordion.

Wild was the contrast the following night as we slipped through the grim grey gut of the Langaarsund—two miles of sheer rock canyon with the overcast clamping down on us, the rain beginning to fall and the light going out of the sky as though some fiend had drawn a blackout curtain across it. We anchored for our sins inshore of a moored 12-metre, on a bank I hoped was sand. The wind was south-westerly and we were right under the lee of a towering wall of rock, the shore less than twenty yards away. The heavens yawned, pouring out rain like a waterfall. That night Kristiansand recorded its highest ever rainfall in twenty-four hours—five inches, I was told. The trees lashed furiously and at two in the morning the wind swung through 180° and we began to drag. By the grace of God I was standing by the chart table, smoking a cigarette, wishing I'd accepted the paid hand's invitation to moor alongside the 12-metre. Too worried to sleep I was right there, watching the shore, when it began to slide towards me. The anchor had dragged off the bank and the chain was straight up and down in God knows how many fathoms of water. I motored out with nearly twenty fathoms of chain hung from the bows and the anchor never touched once, and we came to rest in the hollow-toothed inlet to the south of Gumö Island just as the first glimmer of daylight began to show.

Langö, Gumö, Berö, Skaatö, Oterö—these, with the out-island of Jomfruland, form the land hulks in a sea of rocks six miles by six that is one of the best cruising areas on the coast; a maze of channels, excellent shelter, innumerable inlets and anchorages. I was unfortunate in my too-brief visit—plenty of chain and the stern hauled tight into the rocks and you could ride out anything here, safe and in the most beautiful rock scenery.

We went up Kilsfjord, spent a wet night in the land-locked peace of Kil's wooded valley, and the following afternoon hit the only rock we touched the whole trip—bang in the middle of Kragerö harbour whilst motoring slowly, waiting our turn at the watering point. One of the many advantages of a steel boat is the knowledge that there is 3/8ths of an inch of steel plate wrapped round the lead keel, but it was an odd sensation as the boat porpoised, plunging the bows in almost to the decks as though she were a submarine submerging.

George, first of our crew for the voyage home, arrived from England, exasperated by an endless train journey down the coast from Oslo. His spirits soon revived for the town was en fête and it was my birthday. The Kragerö Days, as they call it, was building up to its climax, all the countryside packed into the town, jamming streets and quays, youths glassy-eyed with drink and the girls with that entranced stare that shows the mating instinct in the ascendant. There was a fair on the jetties and dancing in the streets, bands playing and boats with singing loads of youngsters milling around the harbour. We had a disturbed night, and in the morning found ourselves at sea, actually out in the open sea—a strange experience for us after weeks in which we had barely poked our bows beyond the last rock. A night at the top of Deledfjord and then in bright sunlight we sailed to breakfast in Risör.

Of all the ports along this coast Risör is the most beautiful—though Lillesand runs it a close second. A rectangular harbour surrounded on three sides by white-painted wooden houses not unlike the old colonial homes of North America. Trees and grass and flowering shrubs, seats along the quays —it had a relaxed old-world atmosphere of great charm. We shopped by dinghy, buying salmon at 7s. a lb. at the excellent fish handlers, and sailed for Lyngör in a hurry to beat the wind. West-going along this coast the mornings are always a rush, for the wind follows the sun and shortly after midday comes in strong from the sou'west.

Lyngör is another of those sheltered narrows lined with holiday houses that remind one of the English Broads. It was full of boats and the wind whistled at the watery cross-roads where a luftspan blocked the only unspoiled stretch. That night we lay at Dybvaag, just east of Tvedestrand. The church there is five hundred years old—black and white timbering, walls three feet thick and a beautiful graveyard laid out on the slope of a hill among the pines. The church was closed that night. 'There is indaid some person,' the sexton told us, and later we saw him digging the grave and surreptitiously putting aside old bones, brown with age. A converted 12-metre came in—two paid hands and an old man alone. Despite high taxation a great number of Norwegian yachts have paid hands, for they use their yachts like cars, leaving work shortly after three and going straight out for an evening's sail.

Arendal, Grimstad, Lillesand; and then we were at the gateway to the Blindleia. All the way down the coast we had heard about the Blindleia, and Carl Mortensen, met again in Arendal, said, 'You must go. It is very good cruising—very beautiful, and you must visit Brekkestö. The entrance is west of Lillesand, very narrow, and there is a bridge.' He glanced up at our mast. 'I think you will make it. If you clear the luftspan, then you are all right. The bridge is a little bit higher.'

We saw the bridge almost as soon as we left the white gleam of Lillesand's painted houses, a concrete arch bridging the rock canyon, its supporting pillars uncomfortably close together. A luftspan sagged across the entrance. We sailed through with ten feet to spare and I was puzzled by the story of a 12-metre hitting the wires with its mast and cutting the electric current to the island of Justö. The bridge looked not higher, but much lower. Two white beacons (*varde* in Norwegian) lined us up; once beyond the beacons there was no turning back—it was too narrow. I was motoring now, the wind fortunately ahead so that I could hold almost stationary. I had no desire to get dismasted twice in a season. Much practice had shown us that you cannot judge the height of your mast in relation to bridges from the cockpit or from for'ard. The best position is at the shrouds. 'I think you're just all right,' Dorothy said. And then from the bows, where he was ready to fend off, George shouted, 'The luftspan—right above you now.' I saw it then, the luftspan Carl had meant, a string of wires only a foot or two from the bridge itself. Our burgee almost scraped them. The bridge was about a foot higher.

We were through and after that we entered an enchanted area of rock and water and trees—a little wilder than Aaby-fjord but with something of the same beauty. Once this was a lost world inhabited only by seafaring people. They even had their own navigational school. Now it is a holiday resort. Anchored in Kjöbmandsvig for the night, where the old sailing barges used to be laid up, we were the only boat. In the morning we sailed out through a narrow gut into a choppy, unpleasant sea so littered with rocks and *varde* that I lost my way and was glad to scrape into Brekkestö for breakfast without doing myself any damage. Brekkestö, all white wood amongst the rocks, was bright and gay. We sailed back into the Blindleia through narrow fjords with speedboats like fast cars going in to shop. Heading back to Lillesand for water, we took the narrows with the mainsail set and a following wind. We were no longer worried about the bridge and there was much talk of setting spinnaker and doing it in style! But it was almost 2 p.m. and the wind, punctual as ever, was coming in again out of the sou'west. By the time we saw the bridge *Mary Deare* was making a good six knots; I swung her round in the little expansion chamber just before the canyon and by the time we'd stowed the mainsail the wind, funnelling up the narrows, was blowing a good force 7.

A night spent way up Topdalsfjord, where like mountain goats we scrambled up the towering pine-clad rocks, and then we were at Kristiansand to pick up Bob and so complete our crew for the beat back to England. The weather he brought was foul—a big depression coming in from Iceland. We had promised him one night in a painter's paradise before we took to the Skagerrak; a wild beat westward. well reefed, and in the afternoon we dropped the hook in the sheer rock expansion chamber of Ny Hellesund.

This is a superb little hole, Celtic-looking—Brittany or Cornwall perhaps; but wilder, a place for trolls. It must look pretty in the sunshine. But we never saw the sun. The wind whistled through the gut where the village perched precariously on slopes of rock. *Mary Deare* cavorted wildly to the blasts. The barometer was 1008 and falling fast. We weighed and let go a little closer to the shore, paying out chain and heaving her stern-on to a sheer rock wall equipped with iron mooring rings. We strapped her in tight with two stout wraps and it blew all next day with scud reaching down to the tops of the cliffs above us, the rain driving almost horizontal, the barometer down to 994 and the forecast putting the whole big depression right on top of us the following morning.

Time was running out. It was already Wednesday; Bob had to be back for the Fastnet Race and George at his desk in London on the Monday. Thursday dawned wild and wet, and we were still moored there 500 miles from home with the whole North Sea ahead of us. It blew all that day, and

Friday we woke to the alarm at 0630, hoping against hope.
The forecast gave sea area Fisher as west force 8, veering
north-west 4–5. At ten the barometer was down to 988, but
the direction of the cloud wrack flying overhead had shifted.
North-west now. We weighed, put three rolls in the main
and hoisted No. 3.

Out beyond Songvaar Fyr the wind was definitely north-
west, the sea moderate—we were still under Norway's lee.
By twelve-thirty it was blowing much harder, the glass was
down to 984 and we were going very fast, the lee rail awash,
the cockpit half full, over 8 on the speed indicator and the
seas getting steep. Time to do something about it; we
dropped the jib, reefed down to six rolls and plunged on
under main alone. Two hours later it was blowing force 8—
I think 9 in the gusts—and a most unpleasant sea, very
steep and breaking. Two small coasters passed us, rolling
crazily and lifting on the combers to show half their keels. As
the day wore on we went into watches, one man alone at the
helm, secured to the guard rail by the clip of his safety harness,
the others below, strapped into their bunks by the canvas lee-
boards and fully clothed, trying to get some sleep, at least
some rest. Even so, it seemed a long time. With the hatch
doors shut it was very lonely up there in that grey waste of
tumbling water, wind and spray beating at one's eyeballs, the
boat heaving up the steep face of a wave to fall crashing into
the trough beyond. And it was wet. In one watch Bob was
up to his neck in water twice, for we were still going to windward fast. No question of heaving-to in the confined waters
of the Skagerrak. Below, it was quieter. But the hull magnified
the sound of the bows slamming into the seas and when one
broke aboard it was a sledgehammer sound. The movement
was very trying. We clung to our bunks, feeling the down-
slam of the bows, waiting for the crash of the next wave
breaking, and when we went on watch the effort of struggling
into our oilskins against the unpredictable plunging of the
boat, the final battle with the webbed braces of our safety
harness, was utterly exhausting. As night fell Dorothy
achieved a stew, balanced astride her wooden galley pen,
the gimballed stove swinging wildly. She served it at the
change of the watch, and whilst we spooned it out of mugs,

gratefully absorbing the energy-giving warmth of it, she made soup for the night watches and then went to her bunk.

We saw no ships that night, no stars—nothing but the dark shapes of waves looming, the glimmer of their crests. The compass light's pinpoint glow was the focal point for the helmsman's eyes, the only comforting thing in that waste of darkness as he sat solitary in the cockpit trying to ease the boat over mountains of tumbling water. And in the cold grey dawn Denmark's shallow coastline showed as a series of dune-humps far too close. The wind had eased a little; we set the jib and had fast, uncomfortable sailing all that second day—120 miles of it. Saturday we shook out the reefs. By Sunday we were motoring in a flat calm. We reached Harwich Monday evening only one day late—495½ miles in 4 days 7 hours.

Looking back on that voyage now, it is not the gale at the end that lingers in my mind, but the long days that preceded it, when we were sailing in bright sunshine through narrow rock passages into fjords so land-locked that, once entered, they seemed like burnished lakes, and always the scent of resin from the spruce. Throughout those days we were in Norway, dusk and dawn merged into a strange, unearthly twilight, turning the sea to a milky film, the rocks and headlands, even the boat, to ghostly shadows. In those short nights the whole world seemed bewitched, and the days were endless —vistas of rock and sea, with every white-painted wooden doll's house flying the country's flag from its own pole, and beyond the beacon and the rock, above the glissading green of spruce, the glimpse of jagged heights.

III

THREE THOUSAND MILES
TO MALTA

Crew for Malta—1963
    Major C. R. Stirling
    Captain Ian Peradon
    David Hare
    The Earl and Countess of Huntingdon
    Richard Marson

It was Dorothy who insisted that we take *Mary Deare* down into the Mediterranean. She wanted to explore the Isles of Greece. This decision, made shortly after laying the boat up at Whisstock's yard in Woolbridge following our Scandinavian cruise, was one of the most rewarding we have ever made. But it was a big step that required a lot of advance planning. Where to leave *Mary Deare* when we got there? And the voyage down?—clearly there was no point in adding over 400 miles to the distance by taking our own East Coast estuary as the point of departure. It was agreed, therefore, that we have one final season in the Bay of Biscay, lay up in the West Country and start from there the following season. So in the summer of 1962 we sailed to La Rochelle and up the yellow waters of the Gironde to visit the *caves* of Bordeaux and taste the clarets that would later come to Britain at much higher cost. We continued south as far as the Basque coast of Spain, to San Sebastian and Santander, and then back by way of Ile d'Yeu and other out-islands of the Bay of Biscay that we had not visited before, laying *Mary Deare* up for the winter at Brixham in Devon. We were all set, except that we still had no idea where to base the boat in the Mediterranean.

That bitter cold winter of 1962-63 I flew out to Addu Atoll, a coral group in the middle of the Indian Ocean, almost on the equator, to get the background for a novel I later called *The Strode Venturer*. I had already spent much time poring over charts of the Mediterranean and, with my eye on the Aegean, Malta stood out as the most sensible base. I had never been to Malta, but Homer's description—'the navel of the world'—still seemed apt. And then, returning from Addu Atoll in February, providence in form of blizzards in England diverted my plane to the Malta air base of Luqa. A few hours in the island confirmed my choice of winter quarters, but when we sailed three months later I still did not know just how or with whom I was going to lay the boat up. I left it in the lap of the gods, relying on my friends in the island.

The plan was to make Gibraltar direct so that we would have half of May and the whole of June in which to sail the Western Mediterranean. Apart from crew changes, I was already committed to a definite date in St. Tropez, my French publishers having organised a big press party there in connection with their publication of *Furie atlantique*. There were five of us on board when we sailed on May 4, 1963— Dorothy and myself, Bob, of course, and David, also Ian, who would be with us all the way to Malta. He was just out of the Army, ex-skipper of the LCT in which I had first tried to reach St. Kilda. He had advised me on all the technical details of these craft when I was writing *Atlantic Fury*.

In the event, we did not make Gibraltar direct. After beating 400 miles with the wind consistently westerly, and in such cold conditions that at night we were wearing as many as four sweaters under our oilskins, we ran into trouble. At 2300 hours on May 7 I noticed the foresail shivering; the wind was not all that strong, but feeling uneasy I handed the genoa. We then found the fore and aft rigging very slack. Not knowing what the trouble was we lowered the main. This was done with great difficulty as the halyard was sticking. After an hour's work tightening up all the rigging in the dark we tried to hoist the main again, but the halyard was now completely jammed. We hoisted No. 3 jib and waited for dawn. I was reluctant to send a man up the mast in that confused sea; we tried it with a tail line to the bos'n's chair, but the motion prevented David, the most agile member of the crew, from getting further than the first cross-trees.

We were then 240 miles south-west of Ushant, having in four days of hard beating at last made our westing. The choice was to proceed to Corunna or turn east to La Rochelle. The latter I knew. It is the premier sailing port in France with a fleet of more than 50 ocean racers and a famous yard— Hervé's. Reluctantly we turned for the French Biscay coast, knowing we should then be well and truly embay-ed, all our hard-won westing lost. On the evening of the 9th David managed to get to the masthead. He reported part of the stainless steel welding sheared and the mast cap fastenings for the twin forestays dangerously weakened. The main halyard still being jammed I had him rig a strop at the upper cross-trees to carry a block and we were then able to hoist our trysail.

We reached La Rochelle in rain and very bad visibility early on May 10—a race against tide, sailing blind into the Pertuis Breton with only one glimpse of the Baleines tower at the north-west tip of Île de Ré. By midday Philippe Hervé had been up the mast and discovered that, following the welding failure, the main through-bolt that carries the spinnaker block on the for'ard side and the topping lift on the after had been drawn down through the glueing of the mast and was jammed tight on to the sheave of the main halyard. Unbelievably the mast, after opening to allow it to pass through, had closed up behind it.

That afternoon we went into the trawler basin, unrigged the ship and had the mast lifted out by one of the big dockside cranes. It was the week-end of the Vouvray Cup Race, but despite urgent demands on their time from their own people Hervé's got to work on the mast first thing Monday morning, stripping down and completely refashioning the mast cap. At 0700 hours on the Tuesday morning we were back in the trawler basin and in one hour flat we had stepped and rigged the mast. We tuned the rigging in the tidal basin and an hour and a half later, breakfasted and with everything stowed, we slipped out of La Rochelle, taking the last of the outgoing tide as it ran fast over the bar.

That night we were hove-to in a gale forty miles off the mouth of the Gironde. This is a bad place to be, right on the edge of the continental shelf. The seas were not only very big and breaking, but strangely phosphorescent. At some time during the night I remember seeing Bob at the helm, just after we had taken a big sea over the bows—the whole front of his oilskins was spattered with bright globules of spray so that he seemed to glow with light. The seas themselves came out of the night with such brilliance that they looked like the loom of small, brightly-lit towns.

Bad luck dogged us. Attempting to start sailing again in the dawn—we had been hove-to for more than six hours—the main slammed across so violently that the boom-end fitment carrying the main sheet blocks sheared. Fortunately the engine started at a touch and by heading into the wind we were able to recover the boom without damage and lash it to the rail. We hoisted the trysail then and Ian started to make strops to carry the blocks. These were so good that they served the remaining 850 miles to Gibraltar.

I still have in my log the Atlantic weather map for noon May 12 with Low 'O' shown as a mass of concentric rings like an enormous bull's eye centred over the North Atlantic. There were gales all round the British Isles and by the time we reached Cabo di Villano the gales had reached south to us. Nevertheless, we could not complain; we had recovered all our lost westing in three days and now, down the coast of Spain and Portugal, we roller-coastered for over 200 miles, first with trysail and storm jib, and later, when the waves were over 15 ft, under the storm jib alone. Against my entry in the log of 'a day of perfect sailing and not pooped once', Bob wrote: 'Lucky you! I was waist deep twice between 0015 and 0020 hours.'

At 1305 on May 21, seven days out from La Rochelle, we rounded Cape St. Vincent in glorious sunshine, the boat driving at near her maximum with full main and No. 3, wind force 6, the seas bright, the sun warm. 'Nobly, nobly . . .'— the long, sharp-etched cape ran away into the sunset and next day we were in the Straits, our luck changed, no Levanter and sailing east amongst the tanker traffic with the spinnaker white and blue against clear skies and a sun-lit sea. We handed it as the wind veered and with the genoa set took to the African shore, going about when the Rock showed up. Everything was very bright and clear, Tarifa on one side and Tangier on the other, white against the purpling hills; and the Pillars of Hercules, those twin rock bastions, standing huge and magnificent, just as they had stood for the Phoenicians, for all the sailors of olden times since that cataclysmic readjustment of the earth's surface first blasted a passage into the Atlantic for these land-locked waters. And there, bang over the bows as we stood across the straits close-hauled, the huge peaked Rock of Gibraltar glowed magnificent in the sunset.

Closing Gibraltar Bay we had our first taste of the fickleness of the Mediterranean, the water ahead suddenly white and the wind gusting force 7 off the Spanish mountains. And so into one of the most uncomfortable ports I have ever visited. No doubt because it is so near the old smuggling port of Tangier yachts are not made very welcome in Gibraltar. We were berthed in the destroyer pens where the walls are high and you need to be an Alpine goat to get ashore. In fact, *Mary Deare* suffered more damage to her topsides and fenders in one night there than she had suffered before in the ports of eight foreign countries.

David, already several days overdue at his desk, disappeared abruptly in a taxi commandeered for him by the dock police and just made the night plane for London. Bob took off two days later after taking us on a tour of the Rock —the apes, the subterranean gun emplacements, the almost sheer concrete slopes of the water catchment, all the unique facets of this extraordinary place where he had served during the war. The views from the underground emplacements showed acres of empty dock, but though the Navy is largely gone, the apes, in two separate bands, are on the increase, gathering each day for the benefit of visitors and demonstrating their agility by leaping from car to car. We were at the airport again the following day to welcome Jack and Margaret, and that night Gibraltar staged a storm of such appalling ferocity that even in the shelter of the pens the whole boat trembled. Throughout the night lightning stabbed at the Rock, thunder crashed and the rain fell in torrents. In the morning I rang the forecasting office. Light easterly winds, no chance of a westerly, and constant references to the swell. In fact, we motored out into a calm; but it was the swell I remember. It was like no other swell I had ever seen—akin to the turbulence of a tidal race; no overfalls, but big seas flopping about uncontrollably.

The boat did likewise, though we were motoring at 5 knots. So violent was the motion that it took me over half an hour, working alone on the foredeck, to get No. 3 hoisted in the hopes of steadying her. For Jack and Margaret, straight from the stability and comfort of a hotel room, it was sheer hell.

Dawn next day showed the coast of Spain crystal clear with the snows of the Sierra Nevada sixty miles away looking white and close against a cold grey sky. Contrary to the forecast a breeze came up from astern. By midday we were under spinnaker, the swell almost gone and small whales lolloping around. A turtle was also sighted and the first of the Balearic shearwaters cutting the waves with inclir d wings. The nights were warm now, the days hot. The deck became a place for eating, sleeping, sun-bathing. We forgot about oilskins and in the dark hours of the dawn watch on the last day of May I picked up the shape of Formentera Island. Day broke and Ibiza emerged from the haze, white houses piling up to the walled mass of the Citadel. It was a most beautiful landfall and we felt suddenly rewarded for the month's voyage of nearly 2,000 miles.

The town is still largely unspoilt, the port very much a working port, the point of entry for all the island's needs. It still has the haphazard easy-going air of a past age. Other sailors in from the sea have described Ibiza, but coming straight from Atlantic waters the first sight of it remains a unique experience touched as it is with the magic of the Mediterranean. The dark interiors of its small shops yield embroidery, gaily-painted pottery, wrought iron, straw-work —there is even a herbalist—and over all hangs that warm southern scent that is compounded of charcoal fires, olive oil and herbs. Late that night we climbed steep cobbled streets to Il Corsario, and from this excellent restaurant, looking out over old tiled rooftops to the harbour and the rock-bound coast beyond, we watched one of those still, slow purpling sunsets whilst eating local prawns and cigales, that peculiarly Balearic crayfish that looks like a submarine armadillo.

But though Port Ibiza still has the charm of a place just

'discovered', the island itself was developing fast. All along the coast, on every beach and cove, villas were going up, and the price of land bordering the sea had risen astronomically. We sailed out in perfect weather to beat through the narrows that separate Formentera from the main island, and out of the midday haze there suddenly emerged the magnificent Dolomitic peak of Islote Vedrá, a bare rock island 1,253 ft. high that marks the western extremity of Ibiza. In quiet conditions, such as we had, the narrow gut between presents no difficulties and by late afternoon we were tucked into Port des Torrents, a small cove on the western arm of San Antonio Bay. Just back of this cove was a ranch-like restaurant and here we had the benefit of our second moon as we dined in a setting of splendid simplicity. There is no such thing as in-doors here—you are out in the maquis under a lacing of bamboo and the talk and the wine flowed whilst the moon set.

I was prepared to sleep late the following morning, but the uneasy movement of the boat woke me shortly after six. A slight northerly swell was snatching at our chain and ruffling the nearby rocks. We sailed, hoisting spinnaker off the north-ernmost point of the island and heading for Palma in Majorca some eighty miles away. A shift of wind—fortunate in the circumstances—caused us to hand the spinnaker. We barely got it into its bag when a black cloud, materialising out of nowhere, was seen coming up astern. One moment it looked perfectly harmless, the next I saw a line of white below it. I had time only to turn up into the wind before the squall hit us. We got the mainsail off and within moments were running at 4–5 knots under bare poles.

I took note of the warning, grateful for this relatively in-nocent demonstration of the speed with which conditions could change. The wind came in strong from the south-west to give us an uncomfortable ride to Palma, where night caught us so that we had to probe the length of the new breakwater in the dark; not an easy entrance until you know it.

Our original plan had been to explore the Balearics, but now time pressed. Cables from my French publishers had been chasing me and I had agreed to be in St. Tropez on June 8. It was already June 3. All next day we were stormbound. Our delayed arrival at Gibraltar meant that Jack and Margaret had to leave us, their time up. We sailed on June 5, just Dorothy and myself and Ian.

Reefed we headed out of Palma Bay to face the down-draughts from Majorca's mountainous north shores and the 250-mile haul across the notorious Gulf of Lions. But the gods were kind. The wind took off as we ploughed north towards the jagged outline of Dragonera, the 1,181 ft. island off the north-west tip of Majorca. It would have been perfectly safe to take the narrows inside the island, despite the eddies and down-draughts against which the Pilot gives such explicit warnings, but I went outside, feeling that the three miles extra were worth it for my peace of mind. The magnificent north face of Dragonera glowed pink in the sunset. We took it very close, barely a cable off, and all the moonlit night, and on through the dawn, we sailed the spectacular northern coast of Majorca, and then we started across the Gulf of Lions.

I had with me the first edition of the Mediterranean Pilot, dated 1916, of particular interest because it was written largely with sail in mind. One should, of course, always read the Pilot after one is safely in port! My entry in the log for 0410 the following morning reads: 'And suddenly five ships in a red dawn with a horizon cloud below the morning star like an elephant trumpeting and the moon a perfect orb low astern.' These clouds—presumably over Corsica—became fantastic as sunrise approached, wind-blown and flaring red until all the east was aflame with a fiery uprush of vapour that at one point looked like the emergence of some new-born island.

I thought the morning sky boded ill, but throughout the day the sea remained calm. We sighted our first big whale, a family travelling east, the venting of the bigger cetaceans showing thick and dark against the blue sky. As night fell the light on Ilede Porquerolles came up. Dawn found us sailing into the Hyères roadstead; we took the narrows between Port Cros and the little island of Bagaud, ghosting in a limpid quiet with Port Cros fast asleep and only the odd fisherman to share with us and the sea birds the morning's still luminosity.

And so we arrived in St. Tropez at noon on the day we

had agreed, and the following morning the French press descended on us and for twelve hours *Mary Deare* kept open house. And when it was all over, and Richard had joined ship, we felt suddenly relaxed; no more firm dates to meet and the pleasures of pure cruising ahead of us. Richard is known as our 'large hand'. Six foot four and fifteen stone, his muscles toughened in the forward pack of the Harlequins, it is always a joy to have him aboard, particularly when there is ground tackle to be recovered. Inevitably in St. Tropez we could offer him plenty of *divertissements* in the way of cables and old hawsers to unravel. We sailed at noon on June 11, exhausted by good food, all the hospitality we had given and received—and of course the fun of shopping at those famous boutiques, Choses and Vachon, where girls are so absorbed in trying on clothes that the scene has the semi-nude quality of a farce.

We beat out into a rising sou'westerly. The French Navy was out in force and with the wind and sea rising fast we found ourselves in the path of three minesweepers. One moment they were steaming to cross our bows, the next they had changed course and were headed directly towards us. I was appalled to see that they all had paravanes streamed. Signal lamps flashed, but there was nothing we could do about it, only hold on and hope for the best, for we were then very pressed. They reduced speed for us and immediately we were across the bows of the leader we hove-to, changed down and reefed.

We had purchased fresh sardines at the fish market that morning and all day the smell of them plagued us in the cockpit as we broad-reached across steep, uncomfortable seas towards Corsica. Strange how often rough-weather greets a new crew. Richard took to his bunk and did not surface till the early hours of the following morning. He claimed an innocent and sober week-end, but the rest of us, suffering from long hours at the helm and the smell of the sardines which I had somehow managed to gut, were not impressed by his assurance.

Our first sight of Corsica was a mass of tumbled rock seen through a haze of mist and spray. Later we caught a wild glimpse of snow peaks high amongst the piled-up clouds. It

is these clouds that are the key to Corsica's great pine forests.
I had seen these forests on an earlier visit when we had
hired a car and travelled up the east coast, turning on to the
forest road at Solenzara. Here great granite pinnacles bar
the way with the glint of snow against blue skies. The pines
close in, red-scaled boles of magnificent trees reaching a
hundred feet to the first branch. The road climbs up by a
series of hairpins till you stand on the Col de Bavella among
centuries-old trees, wind-torn to strange shapes, and look
down into the great bowl through which you have come, scarred by the ravages of a recent fire. A series of passes reaching up to 4,000 feet bring you to the Col de Verde and the
forest of Marmano, where cables slung across the valley bring
logs for export from the most inaccessible crevices of the
mountain tops.

Marmano is virtually father and mother to all the Corsican
pine forests of the world. It grows the tallest, finest trees,
many a hundred and seventy feet high. Its nurseries supply
the other island forests, its seeds exported to every country
where *pinus laricio* is grown. Stopping the night at the
forest town of Ghisoni, we were shown over the Marmano by
the Chef du Forêt. He was a startling figure—tall, power-
fully-built, his desert-darkened face unshaven, his eyes blood-
shot. Wearing the faded green jacket of the Eaux et Forêts, he
had the battle-weary look of a resistance fighter. He had, in
fact, been fighting a fire for three days on the other side of
the mountains and he had had no sleep.

Fire, not exploitation, is the disaster threatening these
great natural forests. We had had a glimpse of this in the
Bavella—all blackened devastation with Italian foresters
felling what was left. The fires are caused by the shepherds,
who persist in the age-old custom of burning the undergrowth
to encourage grass much in the same way as 'swaling' is still
carried out on Dartmoor. It is against the law, but there is
nobody in these remote areas to enforce the law; and so for
the gain of a few francs a solitary man will destroy great areas
of new growth that would otherwise have grown on into big
timber, replacing the existing trees that have taken three
centuries to reach maturity.

And in maturity, how magnificent these trees are! Up over

the Col de Sorbe and half the way to Corte you drive through a towering cathedral quiet. And at Corte, the old capital—another citadel on another crag—you have the Restonica Gorge. We went up it at dusk, the single-track forest road, unwalled and with sheer drops to the torrent below, winding up through ranks of unbelievable crags that looked in the fading light as iron-bound and deadly as the Gates of Hell.

But for the forest there would be no road into this fabulous gorge, or into the Asco and the dozens of other places that most countries would regard as inaccessible. Even so, though Corsica is only a hundred miles long and fifty broad, it takes a lot of nerve-racking driving to make much in the way of real progress. One wonders what it must have been like for Letizia Buonaparte, fleeing feud-torn Corte in 1769 along old mule tracks to give birth that August to France's future Emperor on a little couch in the family mansion that can still be seen in the old quarter of Ajaccio.

West from Corte the road climbs the greatest gorge of all, by the Scala de Santa Regina and its serried granite pinnacles to the high valley of the Niello where the chestnuts and the walnuts grow, where tall church belfries stand outlined against perpetual snows and the war memorials, with their long lists of Italian family names, stand witness to six hundred years of Genoese oppression and the fighting instincts of a mountain people.

There is only one way out of this high mountain valley—by the 5,000-foot pass of the Col de Vergio and down through miles of tall pines to Evisa where the melting snows stream water through the village and the chestnuts stand two thousand years old and of colossal girth. Below Evisa is the Spelunca, a V-shaped gap that gives a glimpse of the sea, best seen at evening when the sun sets in the gap and all the primeval chaos of granite outcrops is turned blood-red. It is a fantastic sight; and fantastic, too, is the Calanche de Piana —another chaos of red rock, dropping in contorted shapes to blue waters.

England's brief ownership of Corsica was due largely to Nelson's insistence; he wanted the giant Corsican pines for the masts of his warships. Having planted some Corsican pines in my Suffolk woods I had been puzzled by the effect

of prolonged summer drought on young seedlings. Now, seeing Corsica again, this time from the sea, I understood; whatever the wind's direction there is almost always a cloud cap
on the Corsican heights. This will hardly surprise anybody
with meteorological knowledge, for the central spine of mountains rises to a 10,000-ft. mass where the snows are perpetual.
The lie of this cloud mass on the slopes is a sure indication of
the future wind direction.

By afternoon we were crossing Ajaccio Bay and the town
that gave birth to Napoleon was just visible in the haze. By
evening we were tucked into the quiet seclusion of Campo
Moro. We anchored there all next day, revelling in the fact
that we now had time to please ourselves, sail or not sail as
we wished. We bathed, climbed in the hot sun to the great
Pisan tower on the headland, watched a religious procession
with people from all the hill villages round come to bless
the waters in which only *Mary Deare* lay anchored, and in
the afternoon Richard set off alone to see the menhirs of the
Rizzanese Valley, fired by descriptions of the Neolithic burial
statues which Dorothy and I had seen at Filitosa.

For those interested in archaeology the south-west corner
of Corsica has the fascination of the newly discovered, particularly Filitosa which is unique—quite different from the
Nuraghi Bronze Age culture of Sardinia, from the remnants
of early man to be found in Malta and the Balearics, though
all have the same period in common, dating from around
3500 B.C. Filitosa was known as a place of archaeological
interest as early as 1810, but it was not until 1937 that the
first of the menhir-statues, 'Le Paladin', was discovered, and
it is only in the last ten years that the full glory of the burial
statues has been uncovered. The grave mound itself makes
use of the fantastically eroded stone of this part of Corsica,
but it is the statues that are unique—great hunks of pale-
coloured granite up to 7 or 8 feet high, some left unembel-
lished except for the face so that they look like petrified
mummies, others with head and shoulders carved, even the
tonsure clearly visible, still others with the body decorated
with sword or dagger. A few of the smaller statues found
close around the subterranean grave have the rib-cage carved,
even an arm. The place itself, heavily overgrown with myrtle

or ilex, has an almost Grecian atmosphere, the country round very beautiful.

Had we had the time to revisit Filitosa, it would have been very easy, for Porto Pollo, just across the bay from Campo Moro, offers reasonable shelter, and from Porto Pollo it is only 4 kms. to Filitosa. My interest, however, is now centred on something I was told by a villager in Guinchetto above Sartene. He had worked for an archaeologist, who was uncovering a cave-dwelling in the mountains, and he assured us that there he could show us rock paintings perfectly preserved. This cound be the link between this proto-Corse culture and the remains of earlier settlements found in Spain and the Dordogne area of France.

The maquis, which makes this part of Corsica a difficult one for archaeologists to work in, also makes it hard going for the adventurous seafarer. A map is essential. But walking this wild country has the fascination that here, for the amateur as well as the professional, is an ancient world only just being brought to light—a lucky chance and you could be the first to discover something priceless.

Further south, at Bonifacio, we touched for the first time the classical Greek period. A fjord is something almost unknown in the Mediterranean, yet this is what Bonifacio is—a narrow fjord cut deep in limestone cliffs and appearing even narrower because of its sheer sides. The wind was rising in the Straits between Corsica and Sardinia as we rounded-to off the lighthouse of Madonetta. I would like to have sailed in as Odysseus did, but the sea was slopping in the caverns and I didn't know what conditions would be like in that lime-walled passage with the great Citadel crowding the top of the cliffs above. The passage bends to the right and half-way down it you leave the turmoil of the sea and come into the glass-smooth peace of the most enclosed harbour in the western Mediterranean. Here, if you agree with Ernle Bradford's deductions in *Ulysses Found*, was the unfriendly land of the Laestrygonians where that 'talkative bald-headed seaman' lost all the rest of his little fleet. Bonifacio is more friendly now. It was Sunday, the sun shone warm and we breakfasted on the waterfront, bought fruit and vegetables and sailed at noon with 3 rolls down. The wind had risen further as we plunged out of that limestone fjord into the Straits of Bonifacio, and with those fabulous undercut cliffs that so insecurely support the huge Citadel dwindling astern, we had a magnificent run across the Straits to anchor for a meal in Porto Liscia on the Sardinian side. And so in the fading light, with rainstorms sweeping the islands, to the friendliness of La Madalena.

A day here is well spent, for permission of the Navy is no longer required to visit Caprera Island and the house of Garibaldi. The Risorgimento still means much to the Italians and I was interested to find a naval rating on guard at the tomb. This visit was of particular interest to Dorothy, whose grandfather had sold his Australian estate (a large slice of the Riverino now worth millions) for a ridiculously small sum to follow the sword of the Italian hero.

We sailed at 0400 the following morning into what is surely the best cruising ground in the Western Mediterranean, a world of rock and islands, reminiscent of Norway's inner leads. We had a lazy, dreamy sail with the rising sun gradually dispelling the early morning mists. By seven-thirty we had opened the narrow entrance of Porto Cervo, which is little more than a cable wide. There are many anchorages amongst the islands of this unspoilt coast, but Porto Cervo, being almost land-locked with good holding on patches of sand, is the most perfect. Unfortunately the Aga Khan also thought so. This is now his Costa Smeralda and a short twelve months after we had seen it quite deserted a friend of mine sailed in to find the little cove packed with a hundred yachts, and ashore there was already a hotel and a night club and several villas. But when we saw it they were only just beginning to blast the road through. It was still unspoilt, and we lay off a small sandy beach, our anchor down in three fathoms, and not a soul there.

We sailed at noon, keeping close inshore and making lazily through the narrow rock channel of the Galere Passage, no boats, no houses, the world to ourselves. It was the utter, deserted peace of this area (now, alas, shattered for ever) that charmed us. And then, suddenly through the heat haze, a towering cliff rising fantastic in its abruptness. This was Cape Figari, and soon beyond it another great heap of rock—

the enormous shape of the island of Tavolera standing magnificent like a petrified monster stranded on the coast. We
went inside this 2,000-foot-high island and spent the night in
Porto Taverna where a few modern villas, built to a pattern
and rectangular as chicken houses, marked the sad shape of
things to come as Germans spearheaded Central Europe's invasion in search of the sun. It was a limpid beautiful evening
and the shape of Tavolera Island loomed in the dark, strange
and remote-seeming, its huge bulk mirrored exactly in the
sea's still surface.

South again the following day, beating sluggishly in a light
southerly that was hot and humid. The shore was hazed over
and we saw little of it until we tacked in towards Capo di
Monte Santo. This is the highest headland on the coast, rising
abruptly to 2,400 feet, its limestone cliffs fluted and holed
along the waterline by numerous grottos. In the evening quiet
we motor-sailed close along the cliff-face. All these cliffs
along Sardinia's east coast are steep-to and in the limpid
conditions we experienced we could have gone in bows-on to
any of them and moored. Again it was reminiscent of Norway,
particularly the Sognefjord, but the rock was different, its
weathered brown not the effect of ice, but of hot sun; and
the sleeping surface of the sea steamed.   •

The only real harbour on the east side of Sardinia is
Arbatax, conveniently placed just over half-way down the
coast. The approach is simple for it is tucked in under Bel-
lavista, a prominent red rock headland which is visible for
miles and has a lighthouse on its conical summit. We motored
in as night fell and had the harbour almost to ourselves. It was
hot and humid and mosquitoes were bad for there are swamps
in the flat land behind, and though this is good for esparto,
we wondered how effective the anti-malarial campaign had
really been. The same thought had been in our minds at
Taverna, for the Gulf of Terranova once had an ill reputation and it is not difficult to comprehend the significance of
Malladormiti which is the name of one of the inshore islands.

We stayed a day at Arbatax, lured by the promise of the
only taxi. First it was in for repairs, then the driver was said
to be in hospital. Finally, three hours late, the owner reluctantly agreed to take us inland to one of the grottos high up

on a limestone ridge. We found the grotto, a monstrous cave
going down 300 feet into the bowels of the earth. But it was
an hour's climb on foot and as a result, and because of the
delayed start, we never got to Buromini, the greatest of the
Nuraghi settlements. But the mountain villages were in themselves worth the expedition—primitive medieval caverns of
shade, every doorway framing a group of black-garbed, gypsy-
skinned inhabitants whose dignity of bearing matches their
high surroundings.

That evening we witnessed a Saint's day procession, very
similar to one we had seen at Campo Moro. Here no effigy
of the saint was carried; a small boy held the cross and
behind, on either side of the road, a single file of children
followed by women, with the men bringing up the rear. They
went down to the waterfront and then, all singing, returned
to the church with the sun setting in a protracted crimson
glow, the great circle of the mountains mirrored in the
waters of the harbour and jewelled with the lights of villages
and towns clustered high on their slopes. Whilst the procession was proceeding to the harbour the juke box was
blaring in the garish café-bar that was part of the new
promenade. What appeared to be an anti-clerical group had
established themselves here, letting off fireworks in an appar-
ent attempt to drown the singing. Twice they fired rockets
directly at the procession—once when it reached the waterfront and again when it entered the church. It seemed symbolic of the old and the new, the struggle in Italy between
Church and Communism.

South from Arbatax the only shelter is in small river estuaries. As elsewhere in Sardinia, and Corsica too, the anchorages are marked by old defence towers. I think it is probably
true that if one were to find oneself off these shores with no
large-scale chart one could safely regard any of these towers
as indicating some shelter with reasonable holding.

Cagliari was our next stop. We fumbled our way into this
recently-extended harbour in the dark, managing better than
we deserved, having no up-to-date large-scale chart. The
most exciting item in this citadelled capital of Sardinia is the
small bronze votive statues of the Nuraghi to be seen in the
Archaeological Museum. This is at the very top of the Citadel

and we were driven there by a kindly telecommunications operator whom we had met in a trattoria. The people of Cagliari are like that—enthusiastic in their welcome, anxious to help the stranger. Perhaps it is because they have always lived by trade. The outside world is not something to be shunned but to be welcomed with open arms.

Cagliari did us proud the day we left—the Navy dressed overall, the Sardinian flag, with its strange device of four black blind-folded heads, everywhere in evidence and the scream of escort sirens. Antonio Segne, President of Italy, was paying a state visit to the island of his birth. Richard had left that morning. We were just the three of us again and in the sultry heat of the afternoon, off the island of Cavoli, a school of whales came to play with us. They were strangely pale, some almost totally white, about 10–14 feet long with blunt heads and beautifully tapered bodies. They were so close that we could see the valve of their air vent opening and closing. Two mainland ferries drummed through the heat haze and Cavoli, the south-east corner of Sardinia, faded away.

That night the mainsail streamed with condensed humidity. At dawn an American naval ship passed us flying signals indicating underwater operations. After that nothing, a dead, brassy sea, its flat surface empty except for a lone dolphin and a solitary turtle playing with an old box, and the sky heavy with moisture. Rainstorms came and the flat calm surface of the sea was poppled, as though it felt the urge to leap up to join the clouds. It was ugly sirocco weather and later the sea became still more unpleasant, jumping about uncontrollably as though we were in some tidal race. It made me think of Terrible Rock and the shoal called Graham's Bank that had arisen in old submarine upheavals and I wondered what it must be like here in a gale, the sort of gale that had caught the oared galleys going to the relief of the Knights of St. John besieged in Malta by the Sultan Suleiman's army in 1565. The heat haze that surrounded us should have cut down visibility, yet we sighted the high craggy shape of the island of Marittimo about 30 miles away.

Once again we were off course, this time to the northward. More than once we had had cause to doubt the compass. But

there was, in fact, nothing wrong with it; in each case it was
due to the unpredictable currents.

I wish now we had gone inside Marittimo and put into
Favignana, but it was night and I was doubtful of the currents, doubtful about what the sultry heat might portend. The
morning found us off Marsala in an area where the sea is
capable of surging violently when a change of wind causes
currents to meet and clash. We motored through great numbers of Sicilian fishing boats, dirty-looking but friendly, and
then caught up with a large school of dolphin. We followed
them for a time to watch them flocking round our bows,
twenty or thirty of them in layers, and in the clear water we
were able to get good photographs. Then a breeze came up
and Sicily faded in the heat. That night we could see the
lights of Agrigento astern of us as we made across to Malta
with the third moon of our voyage hanging in the night above
us, and at five-thirty in the morning Dorothy, alone at the
helm, raised the steep north-west face of Gozo. Through two
months—more, through all the winter's correspondence about
laying up—we had been aiming at this. It was an exciting
moment. But it was the end of the voyage.

We gave thanks to Poseidon as was his due, pouring the
libation down our thirsty throats, and the wind stayed light
and steady so that we coasted gently south-eastward past
Gozo with its great churches standing against the blue sky,
past the little island of Comino, to enter Grand Harbour at
1700 hours and tie up at the Customs quay. We were brown,
browner than the Maltese. So many days sitting in the unshaded cockpit roasting in the sun, days when the deck had
been too hot to walk on in our bare feet and we had cooled it
down with buckets of sea water; cooled ourselves, too, standing under the curved white wing of the genoa and sluicing it
over our heads. Now, in place of the sea's wide circle of
visibility we were hemmed in by great battlements and walls
of honey-coloured stone, and in place of the solitude of small
anchorages we had the sprawling mass of Valletta. When we
went round to our berth in Sliema Creek the contrast was even
greater. It was the feast of St. Peter and St. Paul, the narrow
streets all draped and lined with painted wooden effigies and

teeming with people, the machine-gun blatter of firecrackers ripping across the water, the sky above the churches pock-marked with little balls of smoke. Independence was in the air, the docks half-empty, our Mediterranean fleet already almost non-existent. At the time the Maltese were worrying about the future. But having sailed there I was convinced they could not lose the battle for economic survival, for their island is still as Homer described it, the navel of the world—the central, focal point of the Mediterranean—unique in its miles of deepwater creeks, in the people themselves, who have a maritime tradition reaching back to the Phoenicians; a racial affinity, in fact, that reveals itself in both their nature and their language.

A week later we laid *Mary Deare* up at the shipyard on Manoel Island and that night, travelling along the Sliema Creek road on our way to the airport, we saw her across the water, tethered to the shore and looking strangely forlorn without her mast. It would be ten months before we saw her again.

IV

THE AEGEAN

Crew for the Aegean—1964
    Major C. R. Stirling
    Michael Calascione
    Freda and Raymond Hughes
    David Hare
    John Faircloth
    Rosheen and Michael Vernon

Malta was to be our springboard to the Greek islands. But on Christmas Eve I received a cable informing me that *Mary Deare* had been damaged in a severe easterly gale. The fact that a lot of other boats had also been damaged was no consolation to me as the file grew due to changes in management at the yard and the tardiness of the insurance company's surveyor. The new yard manager had promised she would be ready on time, but Malta was a thousand miles away and many of the yachts wintering there had their owners on board. Moreover, in the early months of 1964 the situation in Cyprus was beginning to look very ugly. As well as making the Aegean a hazardous sea for British boats, it might also affect the yard's ability to handle civilian work.

It was, therefore, with some misgivings that Dorothy and I flew out on the night of April 23/24 as planned. Friends met us at the airport; a brief sleep and then breakfast of coffee and strawberries on the balcony in bright warm Mediterranean sunshine. Our spirits soared. And on arrival at the yard we found *Mary Deare* riding at her moorings, the mast stepped, paint and brightwork gleaming. We went aboard. Only the closest examination showed the area of bulwark where repairs had been carried out, and below, where in England our last fitting out had proved a disaster, the whole interior gleamed—not only was paint and varnish work well done, but she had been carefully cleaned. We had allowed a week to get her ready for sea and this, with time off to attend the Malta round of parties, proved about right. On laying up we had stripped absolutely everything out of the boat and taken it into store. This was a big Nissen hut with wired-off compartments and because of the wind-blown dust that had penetrated into it we were three days re-cleaning and stowing all gear. However, this type of store has one great advantage —it ensures a sufficient circulation of air to offset the extreme humidity of August and September. Nothing had rusted, nothing had rotted or become mildewed; even the radio direction finder was still working on its old batteries.

We sailed on the afternoon of Sunday, May 3, 1964, bound for Pylos at the south-west corner of the Peloponnese, a distance of 368 miles. With us was our old friend, Bob, and Michael, a Maltese friend relatively new to sailing. I estimated that with luck we might pick up a light on the Greek coast in the early hours of Thursday morning, but it was, in fact, early on Wednesday morning that Bob called down that he could see something that looked very much like land. There was a certain amount of haze and some cloud, but what he had sighted was definitely land, and as the shape of it hardened, it became an island with high ground stretching north behind it. We were less than 5 miles off, yet we were only 68 hours out of Malta, the log reading no more than 283. There was, of course, only one explanation—the westerly which had carried us to Greece must have been blowing long enough in the Western Mediterranean to have built up a strong east-going current, though wind and current charts for the month of May give no indication of this possibility. The island was Proti, just to the north of Pylos, so that we were less than ten miles off the rhumb line.

Gone now were the clear blue skies. Thunderclouds lay black over the mountains as we ran south before a wind that was being deflected and increased in strength by the high land. Coming from the north it is not easy to find the entrance to the great bay of Navarino in which Pylos lies. We probed several false openings, not wishing to be blown past it and have to beat back. It was a vessel steaming out of what appeared to be a solid cliff face that finally established the

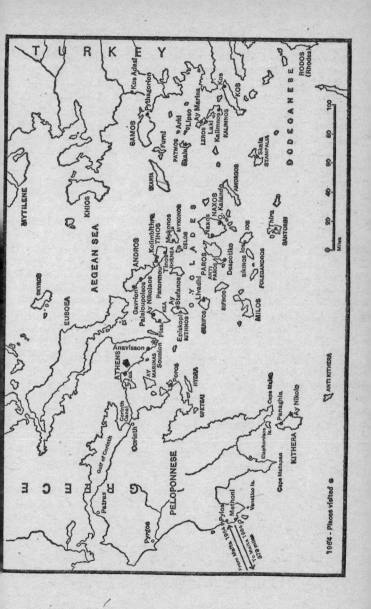

entrance for us. It is a fine, craggy entrance with an island of rock and a natural bridge, and inside one of the finest natural harbours in the world. Here in 1827 Admiral Codrington with 27 allied ships assured Greece her independence by sinking no less than 53 of the 82 Turkish warships anchored there in support of their army. Now Greek shipping lines were maintaining a succession of tankers there to provide cheap bunkering facilities. Looking after these ships was the main business of the port. Pylos had only recently been made a port of entry for yachts and, contrary to what we had been led to expect from some accounts of sailing in Greek waters, formalities were carried out expeditiously and with great courtesy. In fact, during the whole cruise in Greek waters—seven weeks, over 2,000 miles and 38 ports—we were treated with courtesy and hospitality, and only once was Cyprus ever mentioned. The island Greeks seem to regard the sea much as the Bedouin regards the desert, a peril which entitles the stranger in from a journey to respect and a kindly welcome.

Pylos was the home of wise Nestor and Homer always refers to it as sandy Pylos. We saw no sign of sand. What we did see, from the heights above the town, was a blazing sunset. It emphasised the jagged rock entrance to the great bay, and etched black the heights of Palaeokastro and the medieval bulk of the castle built on the site of Demosthenes's stand against the Spartans, and as we walked a rough track up to the point men and women were coming in from the fields with their goats and donkeys that were barely visible under their burden of coarse withered grass. As night closed in, we sat under the trees of a waterside taverna drinking our first resined wine—the retsina of Attica—with a little plate of *meses*, an hors d'œuvres of whatever is readily available locally, in this case anchovy and cheese and cucumber. The bottle finished, we moved to the *estiatorion* in the square, were invited into the kitchen to choose our meal from the pots bubbling on the stove or from the ice-chest full of the day's catch of fish. The trees in the square, where Codrington's statue stands surrounded by old guns, were motionless in the still air and the night was luminous and warm. And so back to the quay, to haul our boat in close and go aboard for a final nightcap and our first night of uninterrupted rest in the quiet friendliness of a Greek port.

Shopping for the boat is always a pleasure in a new country. It not only brings you in contact with the people, but it gives you a kaleidoscopic insight into their lives, the things they eat, the things they need for home and work, the trades of the town, too. We stayed a day in Pylos, enjoying the shops and the food and watching another flamboyant sunset, seen this time from the huge Turkish castle behind the port, night closing in as we came down the path through the pines. Next morning we motored out into the bay, and as we passed through the entrance, the engine faltered, black clouds coming from the exhaust. It was not difficult to find the cause of the trouble, for all the after part of the ship, the paintwork, even the sailbags, were coated in an oily black film. The flexible exhaust, always the weakest point of an engine on rubber mountings, had broken. We had had this trouble the previous year and the repairs made at Gibraltar should have been checked during the winter. However, no good cursing the Maltese engineers; the question was, did we turn back into Pylos, still only a mile and a half away, or go to Athens where we could get the exhaust properly repaired. Athens was over 200 miles away. But a breeze had sprung up. We hoisted sail and headed south. All we needed now was wind, and the wind was fair as we slid quietly past Methoni, with the tower of its Venetian fortress standing in the water, and turned the corner of the Peloponnese inside the islands of Sapienza and Skhiza. By afternoon we were watching the thunderclouds building up over the long, 8,000-ft-high Mani Peninsula that runs out, knife-edged, to Cape Matapan. That west wind carried us to the open anchorage of Panaghia in Kithera, the windy island that lies off the south-east tip of the Peloponnese like a guardship to the Aegean. We went ashore, bought bread and walked in the hot, heady scent of pine and thyme, and in the morning the wind was still there to blow us across to Cape Malea—the sea blue, not a cloud in the sky and that chuntering sound of the bows trampling the water underfoot, the boat galloping with the white spread of her canvas fully stretched. And then suddenly, off Malea, the wind left us. For almost 36 hours we lay drifting and wallowing in the swell, in a sea that was slicked and filthy with the congealed oil debris of a winter-wrecked tanker. The sun was hot, no shade from sails hanging limp and slatting to the roll. That night we had just the faintest whisper of an off-shore breeze and I saw Bob up for'ard, a tall silhouette by the forestay, crying plaintively to the moon, to Poseidon, 'More wind! More wind!'

It did not come until late next day, a gentle zephyr. But though it carried us only slowly north, the relief at feeling the boat moving at all, of seeing the sails drawing at last, was intensely felt by all of us; she had suddenly come alive, like a sleeping beauty waking, and the gentle suck and gurgle as she slipped through the water was at that moment more beautiful than music. Another night at sea with its routine of lone vigils at the helm, sleepy with no sense of time, and then at last we came to an anchorage under the island of Aegina. Ayia Marina bay is immediately below the great Doric temple of Artemis Aphaia. The sun was setting as we rowed ashore. Twenty minutes to reach the temple, they said, if we walked fast. The track, which soon deteriorated into a water course, climbed steeply through pine trees each with a cup attached below a slit in the bark to catch the resin, resin that would go into the wine of Attica to make it retsina. We lost our way, and when we found the temple at last it was closed and night was falling. But it didn't matter. We could see the shapes of its columns bulked huge against the first pale stars; more exciting, we could see across the water the lights of Athens, thought we could just make out the Acropolis illuminated. In a mood of complete happiness we stumbled down the pale glimmer of the track, drunk with the resin scent of pines, to eat at a taverna looking out over the bay where the only light was the pin-point gleam of *Mary Deare*'s riding light. And in the morning we sailed to Athens, roaring into Zea heavily reefed with the rain falling and the wind howling. We were fortunate to find a berth at the outer end of the breakwater; fortunate, too, to get hold of Leonidhopoulos immediately. He runs an excellent repair and maintenance service for yachts and I shall long remember his cheerful chief engineer. He was a fat man with a penchant for two words of English— 'no good' and 'out'. When he saw the exhaust he beamed:

'No good! Pi-ipe ouhut! Ouhut! Everything ouhut!' Thirty-six hours later a new exhaust line had been installed, the cylinder valves reseated and the engine was running perfectly.

Bob left us at Athens, treating us to a farewell party at the Royal Hellenic. Few yacht clubs can have such a perfect position, perched right above the Tourkolimano basin with a panoramic view of the city, its sprawl of lights covering all the hills beyond Phaleron Bay. For that and for the Acropolis I can almost forgive Athens its very ordinary appearance, the sense of a city living off past glories. The Acropolis is overwhelming in its impact, one of the true wonders of human creation—simplicity combined with a stage setting of extraordinary dramatic effect. I think Bob, who had not seen it before, found the right words; he described it as one of the great experiences of his life. This is what draws the world to Athens, every race on earth treading the foot-worn stones, an endless procession paying tribute to the theatrical beauty of its conception—and perhaps to something less obvious, for here is tangible expression in stone of the ideas on which the social structure of so many nations is based.

The engineers gone, we set to work with detergents and hot water on the oil-filmed paintwork aft. Raymond and Freda arrived, so that, with Michael, we were five on board, and that evening, the boat and ourselves both clean at last, we all dined together at Tourkolimano where fish restaurants line the waterfront. We sailed in the morning, a slow beat along the north shore of the Gulf of Athens aimed at Cape Sounion and the Temple of Poseidon. The wind died and we put into Anavisson.

We were astir at five, the sails hoisted and the anchor up whilst the kettle boiled. In the pale light we slid into the channel between the mainland and Nisos Gaidhouro (Nisos means island) and over a shoulder of rock, suddenly, there was the temple standing sharp and clearly defined upon its jutting headland. We breakfasted in Limin (Port) Sounion, the temple bright above us, shining crystal white in the sunlight as though pickled by the sea's salt spray. Later we stood by the great marble columns and stared seaward as all those old Greek mariners must have done centuries ago coming to that cliff-top temple in hopes of placating Poseidon with their offerings. Like ourselves they would have been embarking on a voyage to the islands, perhaps as far as the Turkish shore, or maybe they were traders and voyaging south, to Crete or west round Matapan to distant colonies. Like ourselves, they would be wondering what lay in store for them out there in that 'wine-dark' sea as Homer so often describes the Aegean.

Standing on the marble slab where Byron, one of the first of thousands, carved his name, I could just see *Mary Deare* riding at anchor. So, I am sure, had those old Greek mariners turned from the sea to look down upon their boats, much frailer, both in construction and gear, much less able to face the elements, and in the calms only the muscles of the rowers instead of a diesel. Let us then bow our heads and pour a libation to this ancient god, for we, like those before us, go out upon this myth-haunted sea, and though it is summer and our boat is steel, we are strangers to it and remember that he is not only god of the sea, but Poseidon the Earthshaker.

From Sounion's temple it should have been possible, one felt, to see all the islands of the Aegean. But even Kea, first of the Cyclades and not twenty miles away, was invisible in the haze. We lunched ashore—squid and octopus with the first bottle, then dentici, a fish of the bream family, with fresh lemons and the inevitable salad of cucumber, tomato and cheese that we were to find in every port. The wine was good, dry and only slightly resined, and as always with retsina it made us neither sleepy nor thirsty. We sailed shortly after three, no port in mind, our plans still fluid. In Malta the Commander-in-Chief had invited us to rendezvous with his ship at Skiathos, one of the islands north of Euboea. He would be there on May 25 on his way back from Turkey and could offer us gin and baths. This would mean abandoning Dorothy's idea of being at Delos, birthplace of Apollo, for the sun god's birthday on May 22.

As we cleared Cape Sounion the wind came in from the north. No question of taking the inner passage between Euboea and the mainland. We headed east, and as we cleared the southern tip of Makronisos, the wind came ahead, veering east-north-east as it swung round the bottom of Euboea and still too light to get us into Limin Ayios (St.) Nikolaos on Kea before dark. We switched the motor on, driving for the vague outline of the island standing nearly 2,000 ft up out of the sea. The setting sun glinted on its rugged outline revealing a deep cleft. This was a little fine weather bolt-hole for caiques called Ormos (bay) Pisa or Poises. We took a chance on it, feeling our way into the first of many island bolt-holes that the Pilot describes as 'affording shelter to small vessels with local knowledge.' The result was an uneasy night with the sound of water slapping rock too close and the wind blattering almost vertically down from the heights above.

Apart from the Mediterranean Pilot Vol. IV our Bible throughout was Henry Denham's *The Aegean*. This sea guide to the coasts and islands of Greece was most conveniently published the previous year, and knowing that I was bound for his own happy hunting ground, the author had kindly sent me a copy. It is the perfect introduction to island landfalls, for it not only gives the port information necessary before sailing in, but also geographical and historical details in conveniently concise form. Only on one point did Denham mislead me. He indicates in his introduction that the Meltemi, the prevailing north wind of summer, may be expected to begin in early July. From this I leapt to the quite erroneous conclusion that there was no Meltemi during May and June, expecting to have to motor a great deal of the way. In fact, the Meltemi blew intermittently all the time we were in the Aegean, so much so that we came almost to rely on it. We had our first experience of it sailing out of Ormos Pisa on May 18; wind north-east 2–3 and fitful under the lee. We sailed south, beat east through the straits between Kea and the next island of Kithnos, and then south again, running in steep breaking seas for the shelter of Loutrain, sometimes known as Port Irene, where old thermal baths are still in use. The soft curves of Kea's outline had looked beautiful and very feminine in the bright morning sunlight, but there was nothing either soft or feminine about the hard rock outline of Kithnos, and the surface of Ormos Loutrain was all white water right up to the line of houses that fringed the shore. We handed the jib and jogged in close under main. It looked so sparklingly pretty in the sunlight, but it was no good, the whole bay was wide open to the nor'easter that was now blowing a good force 5

and still increasing. Regretfully we turned south and ran close
along a steep-to jagged coast, strangely folded and stratified,
to turn into the shelter of a long north-running crevice of a
bay called Ormos Ayios Stefanos. Here we lay two nights anchored by the Meltemi, the days all sunlight and blue skies,
the sea sparkling with white-caps.

This enforced stay proved in retrospect one of the high-
lights of the voyage. Kithnos is one of the less visited islands
and is consequently quite unspoilt. For us, who had come a
long way always with the Cyclades in mind, this first real contact with the islands made a deep impression. Three hours'
climb, a thousand feet up a rough mule track, brought us to
the island capital or *chora*, Kithnos; oleanders and figs in the
valley and on the slopes long bars of gold where the barley
stood ripe in hard-won terraces. Dry-stone walls patterned
with up-ended slabs scored strong lines across all the hills.
They were harvesting in the fields, the men in straw hats, the
women in bonnets bleached by the sun, and they waved to us
as we passed. High on a hill-top stood a little church that
looked like a mosque with its rounded cupolas and, on a
ridge, the first of those ingenious windmills that are so much
a part of the island scene. Down into Kithnos, blazing with
whitewash in the sun, even the paving of the alleys daubed
with it, a tracery of intricate patterns. At the local taverna,
for a total of 53 drachmas, the five of us drank fresh lemon,
beer and retsina, ate bread and sheep's cheese, octopus, olives
and little squares of mutton, and finished with Turkish coffee
and loukoumi. It worked out at about 2s. 6d. a head, which
shows how cheap living can be in Greece, provided you are
content with the local produce and do not demand the things
that have to be imported.

Kithnos had something of a Moorish quality, its maze of
narrow twisting alleys constantly bewildering, constantly de-
lighting. There was a truck road up from the caique port on
the other side of the island, but it did not impinge upon the
main body of the village. Like most villages in the Cyclades,
you either rode an ass or a mule or you walked on your own
two feet. Though tiring physically, with the warmth of the
sun trapped in the alleys, we all found it mentally very restful.

Not so restful was our anchorage in Stefanos. All night

Mary Deare was snubbing at her chain, trembling to the wind blasts, and in the morning it was gusting a good force 7 through the cleft in the hills to the north. Two black pigs bathed at the sea's edge, cows lay on the sand; it was a hard row to the shore, but once there the wind was gone and all was peace and sunlit warmth. We visited the little whitewashed church on the left side of the beach. It was more shrine than church, about 14 ft by 10 ft, with simple paintings and a few offerings. Throughout the Cyclades every port, every anchorage, almost every deserted little hole in the rocks where a caique has paused or a fisherman kept his boat, has a similar shrine or church, and in almost every case it is positioned on the left as you enter.

Another two hours' hard climbing took us to Dhriopis where a line of windmills thrust their bare arms against the blue sky. It was cold on the top, the wind blowing hard, but in Dhriopis itself the air was still and warm. In the church two priests were measuring and making a drawing of the bishop's chair. Like most Greek Orthodox churches, there was a great deal of panelling and such seats as there were had been placed along the walls. It was full of painted and silver icons, sconces for candles and chandeliers of Venetian glass. The power of the Greek Orthodox Church in the islands is considerable and rests, I would say, very largely on the character and training of its priests. These men, with their beards and their long hair pinned at the back of the head, represent a power bigger than the island life that is all most of their flock know. In their flowing black robes and strange headgear they move among them with assurance and a great air of authority. The people of these high villages are broad-faced, almost Asiatic-looking, the men stocky like highlanders, the girls rather big, not pretty, but with fine eyes and a good complexion.

The young people are leaving Kithnos—Kea, too, and all the poorer islands. It is a hard life. You can see that in the lined faces of the old. But it is a good life all the same, and you can see that, too—in their sense of repose, of absolute tranquillity. What, in fact, we were seeing in the two days we tramped the mule tracks of Kithnos was a way of life that had hardly changed since the Achaian hordes sailed past to the siege of Troy more than thirty centuries ago.

That evening the wind dropped and in the morning we sailed, clear skies and good visibility at last. We passed south of the penal settlement of Nisos Yiaros and when we came into the lee of Tinos we motored close inshore to get the benefit of the down-draughts. A short fast sail and then the genoa had to be handed in a hurry. It was only my second attempt at deliberate down-draught sailing and I had under-estimated the force of it. Snug in Tinos harbour, stern to the main street, we were suddenly not strangers in from the sea to be welcomed, but foreign visitors to be importuned and exploited, for Tinos is a kind of Greek Lourdes and religion an industry. We made the pilgrimage up the hill to the great church, saw the healing icon that had been rushed to King Paul on his death bed, did the vaults with the strange baptismal fonts, the art gallery, the museum. None of it was what we had come to the Cyclades to see, but since the water is supposed to be the purest in Greece, we transferred twelve cans of it from the tap on the quay to our own tanks. The Meltemi blew strong all night, the lights on the quay swinging and *Mary Deare* straining at her stern warps.

Ashore in the morning for stores a woman with gold teeth who was married to a sailor sold us boxes of Tinos loukoumi and prophesied three days' respite from the Meltemi. In case a flat calm resulted we each purchased a string of amber-coloured beads. These beads—called I believe *tespihler*—were introduced into Greece by the Turks during the long centuries of occupation. There are twelve beads running loose on the string and a single bead secured at the end with a tassel. Old men sit handling their *tespih* by the hour in the sun, letting them drop two by two along the string. Young men twirl them as they sit over endless cups of thick sweet coffee. Others play with them as they walk the streets. I never saw a woman with one—only the men. A panacea for restlessness? 'It is the climate—it makes us impatient, quick-tempered,' a Greek shopkeeper told me. 'It means nothing. It's in the blood. It's the sun that does it.' The beads are on my desk now as I write. They are smooth, almost silken to the touch—they slide on the string, click gently as they fall—it is something to do as I search for a word or a phrase, something to occupy my hands where before I would have reached automatically for a cigarette.

It was now Thursday, May 21, the eve of Apollo's birthday and time to go to Delos. All enthusiasm, we had set the alarm for 0500, but it was gusting so hard nobody stirred. We sailed just before midday. The gold-toothed lady of the loukoumi stall was right. There was now no wind at all. We motored for a while, and then it came in from the north again, giving us a nice gentle ride to Delos. By three we were in the narrow straits between Delos and Rhenea with ruins littering the foreshore and sprawling up Mount Cynthus and groups of tourists being shepherded by guides. There was a cruise liner north of Remati Island which lies in the middle of the strait and another lurking to the south of it. I slipped under its stern, and turned for the shore. With the wind in the north the place to go was Fourni Bay. Denham gives an excellent diagram and I had his book open in front of me as I felt my way in amongst the rocks of that strange kidney-shaped cove. The surface of the water here was glass, magnifying the movements of fish and so crystal clear we could see our anchor lying like a forgotten toy on the white sand bottom. This little cove, so hidden away, so small, so shallow, was completely deserted. We bathed, had tea, and then, the cruise liners gone, the whole island to ourselves, we went ashore in the dinghy to climb through fields of vegetables and barley towards the tumbled rock slopes of Mount Cynthus. It was a magically beautiful evening and as we climbed the view over the sea and islands spread wider and wider. Beyond the last stone wall imprisoning patches of agriculture the grass was blue with the bloom of sea lavender, that same blue that the Greeks chose for their flag.

What is there so special about Delos? It is not just the ruins of the port and the ancient city. There are ruins scattered all over the Eastern Mediterranean's shores, many far finer than Delos. Is it the myth then or the beauty of the place or the sense that this is where our civilisation started? The myth is an attractive one. Hera's hatred of her husband's mistresses had doomed Leto to wander the earth seeking a place in which to deliver the child she was carrying. Poseidon took pity on her and struck wandering Delos with his trident, causing the island, which before had been sometimes above and sometimes under the sea, to be still and fixed. Here Leto was delivered first of Artemis, the moon goddess, described in the myth as arriving just in time to assist at the birth of her brother. Apollo was born on the top of Mount Cynthus. Zeus himself came down for the birth and at the moment of birth great columns of granite rose up from the bed of the sea to fasten Delos in its place for ever and all the surface of the island was suddenly transformed into a carpet of flowers.

The moon was three-quarters full the night we climbed Mount Cynthus, the earth a carpet of blue. It was not difficult then to believe in this beautiful story of the birth of summer. And as for Delos being fixed in place by Poseidon, this is a volcanic world. And what voyager in the Aegean has not seen island upon island apparently riding in the sky, the milk calm of the sea or the white of the haze disembodying each towering mass of land from the surface of the water, and sometimes the dark ruler-straight line of a current touched by a breeze heightening the effect with a false horizon.

The sun set as we stood on the top of Mount Cynthus, on the mosaic flooring of the old temple with tumbled slabs of marble all about us. The wind had died away. The sky was clear, the air like crystal. At our feet sea and islands stretched in every direction to the limit of our vision. The first stars pricked the eastern sky and the brightening moon rode high above us. The world stood still and all was peace and full of an unforgettable beauty. We walked down the great staircase or the Sacred Way where in olden times thousands had come to make offerings and sacrifice to the sun god, and then we were amongst the ruins of Ancient Delos, capital of the Cycladian Federation. The Cycladian culture is as old as the Minoan, as old as western man's knowledge of how to make and sail a boat. Delos is the hub round which the islands of the Cyclades (Kiklades: *Kukloi*—rings) form a natural cycle, and as boats improved, its importance grew, for it stands halfway along the island trading route from Europe to Asia and is the last natural harbour before the open sea passage to the islands of the Turkish coast.

It must have been a big city, for it has been despoiled by

the shipload and yet there is a great deal still standing. The
work of reconstruction has left a maze of narrow alleys between dry-stone walls with a scattering of cisterns, well-
heads, a marble couch or the drum of an old column to give
one a glimpse of what the houses were like at their last
occupation. Dorothy and I, exploring this maze whilst the
others took another route, almost lost ourselves in the gathering dark for so many of the alleys proved to be cul-de-sacs.
From the shrine of Dionysus to the sanctuary of Apollo is not
far, but daylight was no more than a last faint glow over
Rhenea by the time we joined the others to stand and marvel
at those marble lionesses glimmering white in the half-light,
all damaged and worn by time, yet still proudly standing,
unique in line and a monument to the creative ability of the
man who had sculpted them.

As we walked back through the Sanctuary the frogs were
croaking in the cisterns and a woman with two cats was drawing water from a carved marble well-head for the vegetable
garden she was cultivating between the stone foundations of
some public building of twenty centuries past. There is no
village or settlement on the island; she was there to cater for
the tourists. The few small farms are summer farms. Down by
the reed-grown shore of the ancient port we came upon the
family we had seen earlier threshing and winnowing their
corn with a mixed team of horses, mules and donkeys. They
had just finished a meal of fresh caught fish cooked over a
charcoal brazier, dark gypsy faces above the glow of the fire.
Some were already wrapped in their coloured blankets, for
they were sleeping out, their boat drawn up at the water's
edge, their beasts grazing nearby. 'Kalaspera . . . Kalasperas'
('Good evening'—and the reply: 'Good evening to you.') We
went back by the shore route, Greek remains giving place to
Roman, thick-walled villas with many rooms. It was moonlight now, an unearthly brightness that touched the stones with
the magic of its luminosity, and the sea was like milk patterned
with the circles of fish rising. Below a farm where we had
seen the team of donkeys and mules treading corn in the winnowing circle a man was using a modern pump to spray a crop
of gourds, and as we launched the dinghy on the white sand
crescent of Fourni Bay three black goats stood watching in-

tently from a rock above our heads. That night we were most reluctant to go to our bunks. The moon shadow of *Mary Deare*'s hull was sharp and clear on the white sand bottom of the bay. Our own shadows moved three fathoms down; we waved to them and they waved back. Everything was still, not a sound except the cicadas. The whole place seemed possessed of a magic of its own.

At two in the morning I woke to the movement of the anchor chain. A wind had sprung up and it was from west of south, the only direction that would make Fourni Bay untenable. A swell began to come in. By morning we were rolling heavily and so we motored hurriedly out to anchor again in the old port, a cable south of the jetty. Two more cruise ships had arrived. The traffic to the quay was continuous, augmented by caiques and launches from Mykonos. We rowed ghillie for Michael, who like most Maltese is a fine swimmer and an underwater fisherman. He speared one grouper and came aboard after half an hour blue with cold. Over to Remati then to bathe and lie on the rocks in the hot sun and watch three yachts come in. The anchorage was beginning to look crowded and the wind was increasing with the midday heat. It was tricky rowing back and the moment we got on board *Mary Deare* began to drag. We got under way only just in time for the jetty was then very close. We tried anchoring in 6 fathoms north of Remati Island, but it was no good and in the end we were forced to go under the lee of Rhenea on the west side of the strait. There is a shallow bay here with a sandy beach, and though *Mary Deare* was snatching at her chain all through our much delayed lunch, the holding seemed good enough in 20 ft of sand and weed. But it was no place to spend the night. There was no purpose anyway with the wind too strong to allow us to land on Delos. We left at 1630, sailing for the fun of it through the shallow channel between Mikros (Little) Remati and Delos, just north of the old port, following as best we could the course a Greek yacht had taken earlier in the day. It gave us a good view of Delos, but not having 'local knowledge' and the Pilot simply saying that the passage between the islets and Delos is blocked with debris, we found it a bit of a scrape and were glad when we were through.

The south wind carried us swiftly the few miles north to Mykonos. Here the blue and yellow striped section of quay reserved for visiting yachts is at the root of the northern jetty. The bows of the island steamer virtually hang over this berth and there is not much room. Mykonos is the only island to have a newly built hotel. This is the Leto, but after looking at the dining-room and the menu we hastily abandoned it in favour of the native freshness of the tavernas. It was at Mykonos that Michael left us, catching the night boat to Piraeus, first leg in a difficult journey back to Malta by way of southern Italy and Sicily. The meeting of the boats is one of the great events of the islands. The steamer has barely swung to her anchor before the gangway is down, the first laden launch alongside. We sat at a café table drinking wine and by the end of the first bottle Michael and the Piraeus steamer had gone, he into a new world sharing a cabin with three Greeks, we to feel for a little while the sense of loss, as though a member of our family had suddenly been spirited away.

After dinner we abandoned the tourist belt of shops and tavernas on the waterfront to roam the narrow alleys of the town itself. Mykonos, behind its tourist façade, is full of enchantment, glimpse upon glimpse of moonlit magic—little balconies and staircases, vines trailing, alleys rioting with flowers, the Square of the Three Wells, the Square of the Churches, a cupola gleaming white, the tower of a windmill hanging above steep steps, and away from the harbour the waters of the bay lapping a line of old houses, crumbling balconies of wood, the white of plastered stone, the slop of water and little alleys looking out to sea. Not a soul! Not a soul about anywhere—only in a little dive of a café a boy and a girl twisting sleepily to the tinkle of a guitar.

The joy of cruising in the Cyclades is that no island is like another and each port of call has its own quite individual personality. From Mykonos we sailed to Naxos and moved abruptly into another world, that of a working port. A big cargo steamer occupied one side of the main quay. The yacht mooring was on the north side by a caique loading potatoes. The men crowding the quay to watch us moor looked a ruffianly unfriendly bunch, so much so that we wondered whether this was going to prove the exception, the one place in Greek waters where we dared not leave the boat to feed ashore. 'Kalaspera.' My greeting was answered by one or two. And then a voice said ponderously and carefully in English —'You—are—well-come in Naxos.' By the time the port authorities had returned our 'log', that useful and sensible paper issued at the port of entry and giving all particulars of the boat, the ruffians had become individuals and we were friends.

Naxos is not the sort of place where you would expect a good meal. After careful consideration we picked the sleaziest of the three tavernas on the quay. What attracted us was the gentle smile of the old man grilling fish over a charcoal brazier and the fact that he was serving them with almonds. The chairs were rickety, the table worn, the men eating there the roughest of the crews and stevedores from the caiques. But as soon as we were seated the old man brought a paper table cloth, cutlery wrapped in a serviette (this is common to most tavernas; only hotel waiters handle cutlery with their hands!), glasses freshly washed. The retsina was strong but palatable. The fish was mackerel, fresh caught and beautifully cooked. The usual salad of cucumber and tomato because they were in season. It was one of those little unexpected meals that I shall always remember. Also another two days later at Limin Livadhi on the island of Serifos; again it was cooked by an old man—crayfish purchased live from a trap and served with the usual sauce of lemon juice and olive oil, into which he had worked the coral and brain. It was a dish of which our friend Alexandre Dumaine would have approved, for even when he became premier chef of France he still regarded simplicity as an integral part of great cooking.

We left at dawn, motoring out into the beauty of a white still morning with the mountainous Naxos peaks banked in serried ranks against the sun, the town piled in shadow and Nisos Vakkhos etched black and sharp above a calm sea only lightly touched by cats-paws of wind. A man in a boat held up a squid to us whilst another, much older man—his father probably—had his face glued to an old oil drum thrust like a telescope into the sea. We took the passage inside the Frouros rocks and sailed south through the straits, hugging the Naxos shore. Paros, only a few miles away to starboard, was a blurred shape in the sun's hot haze. By ten-twenty we had our hook down in Kalando Bay, an attractive little inlet at the southern end of Naxos. The usual little shrine to the left of the beach as you enter, but no sign of life—until we sailed after a bathe and lunch when a woman appeared calling a flock of about fifty goats after her. Some of the goats paused to drink from the sea, and behind them the pink oleanders came down to the water's edge.

We had intended spending the night in some bolt-hole among the islands of the south. Most of them were steep-to and rocky, affording no shelter, but Ekhinousa looked promising and the Pilot mentioned an anchorage on Koufonisia. Outside Kalando Bay, however, the wind was south-east so we turned for Paros, thinking optimistically that we might try the Fourteen Foot Passage between Paros and Anti-Paros. I had still to learn the full extent of a mountainous island's deflection of the wind. Not only will it down-draught on the lee side at a force of approximately plus 2 of its real strength, but it will curve round each end of the island, building up boisterously at the extreme headlands and then following the direction of the lee shore sometimes for as much as two-thirds of the island's length. Now, as we approached the southern end of the straits between Naxos and Paros, we could see the darker line of the wind-whipped water and the white of waves breaking. The Meltemi was back, funnelling down through the straits. We handed the genoa, set No. 3 jib in a hurry, and after that we had a fast exhilarating sail with the wind veering easterly, following the curve of the coast as we came under the lee of Paros. The Fourteen Foot Passage was out of the question; at its shallowest point it faced due north and the Meltemi would be piling straight into it.

It was getting late now, the shadows lengthening, the sun low in the sky and the water white all round us. These were not the conditions in which to undertake a night sail—too many rocks and islands, the speed of the boat too boisterous. The only possible anchorage was Despotiko, a rocky inlet to the south-west of Anti-Paros leading to an open water anchorage protected from the west by an island and some shallows. It had once been a pirate's nest and it looked satanic enough for any filthy deed as we rounded its protecting headland of knife-edged rocks in the dusk, finding to our amazement that we were still able to lay it though we were now sailing almost due north. A bald black skull of a rock 500 ft high loomed close to starboard, dark hungry cave mouths gaped aslop with water, and then we were in the anchorage, closing the northern shore to within little more than half a cable. Here we let go the big anchor in 25 ft opposite the outlet of a small stream. I think we should have anchored a little further west. However, the boat lay steady to the chain and the anchor held though the wind was down-draughting hard all night.

Next day it was 3 rolls down and No. 2 as we beat through the narrows inside the island of Strongyli. The wind fell light and it took us seven hours to sail the 31 miles to Serifos. Misted in a heat haze, the white villages lying along its crest looking like drifts of snow. We moored stern-on to the little quay with the *chora* piled white on its 1,000 ft crag, the high hills shutting us in and ravens circling. But after Despotiko the place had an almost tropical lushness—palm trees, flat-topped houses, donkeys heaped with fresh-cut grass; a general air of lassitude in the afternoon heat.

In the cool of the evening we took the local taxi up to Serifos—the *chora* always takes the name of the island. A winding, crazy road, it stops abruptly in a little square by a line of broken windmills, and after that we climbed through narrow alleys to the *kastro* and a fantastic view of the rich valley below. That night there were nightingales singing as well as the inevitable cicadas and frogs.

It was now time to think about changing crews again and we headed back to Athens by way of Episkopi, a cove on Kithnos, and Poros, now a commuter's paradise for Athenians. The mainland shore, so close across the narrow glassy channel, was once the Troezen kingdom where Theseus was born. Again we had to reef approaching Athens after a hot lazy sail in the shallows by Aegina, and again the quay at Zea was crowded with huge motor craft. Though *Mary Deare* is rated Class II for ocean racing, she was still by far the smallest yacht encountered in Greek waters and at Zea she looked positively tiny.

It is a long drag back from the islands and particularly up

the Gulf of Athens, which is 40 miles, the wind seemingly
always contrary. I had not realised how good the steamer
service to the islands was or I would have arranged the second
crew change at some place like Mykonos. However, Zea is
always interesting with a scattering of British, American and
Continental boats in from ports as distant as Seattle and
Hong Kong. Jack and Margaret were due to join us again
here, but cables had caught up with us at Mykonos to say that
a loosened retina necessitated an operation to Jack's eye.
David, an old *Mary Deare* hand, was also joining us, and
thinking we should be short-handed, he brought out with him
another keen dinghy man. David and his friend John stole
aboard in the early hours of May 30 bringing our mail and
news of home, the latest Gallup polls, the results of the Hook
Race—all strangely unreal to us, another world that we seemed
to have shed entirely.

Back again to the islands then by way of Poros and the
two-fathom channel opposite Galata with a distant sight of
Poseidon's temple on Sounion. Kea, Andros, Tinos—a slow
progress searching for cats-paws of wind in near flat calms,
motoring only when our patience was entirely exhausted. All
this time the islands seemed to float in the sky, so still and
flat was the sea's surface. Four days we loitered in little off-
beat ports and coves of the Cyclades though the real objective was now the Dodecanese and the Turkish coast.

Two of these anchorages I particularly remember. The first
was Ormos Palaioupoleos, on the island of Andros, at the
head of which, the Pilot says, 'are the ruins of the ancient city
of Andhros and the remains of its harbour. . . .' It was a perfect day for sailing in close under the slopes of the 3,000-ft
mountain of Petalon and we anchored in 18 ft just over a
cable off the south-eastern corner of the bay, with the lion-
shaped rock to the south-west showing just clear of a natural
rock breakwater. The old harbour is marked on Chart 1820,
but not its entrance, which we found still quite visible when
we explored in the dinghy. With the exception of the key
rock to seaward all the old harbour walls are a few inches to
a foot below the surface of the sea. What chiefly surprised us
was the smallness of this ancient port; a modern caique would
almost have filled it. This gave us a clear indication of the

size of boat used by this ancient settlement and suggested that the boats were normally kept hauled out on the beach.

South-east of the harbour the short beach is littered with sea-worn marble. It would seem that Palaioupoleos is sheltered from the worst of winter's gales and that the remains of the settlement have not been swept out to sea, but simply pounded and worn down on the spot. Column drums of striated marble have been reduced to all sizes, some no bigger than a shin bone, yet all along that foreshore a kind of cement platform inset with marble chippings that must have been the floor of buildings or the sea wall promenade is so perfectly intact that it might have been laid this century. Apart from this, the settlement seems to have dissolved into a tracery of stone walls and terraces on two little hills standing below the magnificent green sweep of a mountainside dotted with cypresses and villas, every valley bright with the ubiquitous oleander.

The other anchorage that particularly interested me was Kolimbithra on the north east of Tinos. This is a curious coast. We noticed it first when beating through Stenon Dhisvaton, the narrow passage between Tinos and Andros, the rocks strangely coloured and the hills behind marked with mineworkings. There is much marble along this coast, giving a brittle jagged look to the cliffs, and the colouring of the other rocks is sometimes livid, sometimes sombre. Mineral out-crops spill everywhere. The whole coastline is wide open to the Meltemi and we were fortunate to be there during a period of calm.

Kolimbithra is an empty little bay with a deserted monastery in place of the usual shrine. A single caique lay anchored close in, the crew all ashore digging with spades in the sand, half-naked and looking like a bunch of pirates. The treasure they sought was the sand itself, which they were shipping to an English company quarrying black and green marble near Panormou; it is particularly gritty sand which is used for polishing the marble before it is exported all over the world. But what made Kolimbithra most interesting was the irrigated land behind, quite different from anything we had seen before in the islands. It was more like a North African oasis, hot, steamy patches of intensive cultivation sur-

rounded by bamboo windbreaks. Lemons, cucumbers, toma-
toes, various gourds, and beyond reach of the irrigated
channels and the power pumps, lush patches of grass with
the first horses we had seen and cows, as well as Barbary
sheep and goats, and in the dusty tracks boxes piled ready
for packing. A French-speaking Greek pressed lemons and
cucumbers into our hands—always a gift of welcome to the
stranger, a flower or a fruit. We left them there to pick up
on our return and he said he would put them in a bag, and
we went on through the soft sunset till we could see the
villages with their pencil-thin steepled churches that looked
like minarets, and all up the valley to the monastery perched
on a distant crag and the inevitable telecommunications
towers on another hilltop. Returning in the fading light we
met the workers from the fields going home by horse and
mule and donkey, and where we had left our Greek friend's
gift, there was now a bag so full of lemons and cucumbers
that it was an effort to carry it back to the boat. Frogs
croaked their chorus in the still water of the valley stream
trapped behind the sands and there were terrapins, little
fresh-water tortoises with their necks thrust out from the
surface of the water like old and rotten sticks.

We sailed at 0440 catching the ghost of an off-shore breeze
that gradually patterned the oil-calm surface of the sea ahead
of us. The voyage that now faced us was the one that had
always worried the ancient Greeks, the fifty-mile gap between
the Cyclades and the Dodecanese. With two keen dinghy
sailors on board we ignored the engine and throughout that
blazing calm day went searching for cats-paws north of
Mykonos, heading east for the Turkish coast and putting our
trust in Poseidon. We had the ghoster up most of the time,
and when we weren't bathing or fishing or drinking wine, we
read the *Odyssey* and the *Iliad*.

By midday the ship had become somnolent in the torpid
heat, until at last we sighted Ikaria, named after Icarus, for
it was from this island's heights that man's first attempt at
winged flight was made. It was into this sea we were sailing
that he plunged when the sun melted the wax gluing of his
wings. Ikaria is the first of the Dodecanese, the islands that
lie close off the Turkish coast, and here the breeze strength-

ened sufficiently for us to exchange the ghoster for the working genoa. A few miles off Akra Papas, the westernmost point,
we heard the rumble of engines. It was a noise I hadn't heard
since the war—the purposeful, solid roar of ships on a set
course. There were fourteen of them coming down on us
from the north and for a few ghastly moments we thought
the balloon had gone up in Cyprus, for north lay the Dardanelles and this was the route the Russians would take.

But soon to our relief we picked up the blare of radios
playing dance music. I guessed correctly then—a pelagic
expedition sailing for Suez and two years' fishing in the Indian
Ocean. A Christmas tree of red lights appeared on the mother
ship which was towing another vessel, probably a refrigerator
ship. We were well clear of her as we crossed her bows, but
were then faced with the ten trawlers in line astern. The wind
had strengthened further under the influence of Ikaria's lofty
mountains and we were sailing fast now, converging on them
at an angle, the sun setting, the sky behind us a volcanic blaze
of red. Would they give way to sail or not? 'They're flashing
you,' David called, and Dorothy came up with me from the
galley where she was preparing curry for dinner—she stayed
to watch and the rice was spoilt, for it was an extraordinary
spectacle. The first three trawlers had already passed ahead
of us, lowering their hammer and sickle ensigns exactly as
the sun's red orb dropped below the horizon. We were now
on collision course with two of these squat, powerful little
vessels. Starboard cross-tree lights flashed, and then together,
as though they were escort vessels carrying out a manœuvre,
they turned out of line, passing close under our stern, black
silhouettes against the sunset. The entire crew seemed to be
on deck, the open bridge crowded—even the cook was there,
immaculate in white. A dozen cameras were aimed at us,
hands waved. 'I think I know the word for Thank you,' David
said. He had done a course of Russian whilst in the Navy.
'Sposebo!' he yelled. More waves—we were all waving—
and a man in the bows raised his pork-pie hat, another lifted
both hands in a Khruschev salute.

We wondered, as those Russian ships went thundering
south, what they had made of us flying the Greek courtesy
flag, but no ensign, and a single shouted word of Russian. A

yacht under sail is rare in Greek waters. Did they guess our nationality? The name on the stern would have been clearly legible in the sunset's glow. Were we the subject of a message back to base via the impressive radio aerials on the mother ship? It was a strange feeling to be alone and under sail in the midst of that powerful little fleet. Then night closed in and Poseidon came between us and speculation, the wind gusting 6 and a steep little sea as we passed close under Akra Papas, the beam of the lighthouse flashing on great slabs of adamantine rock, a glimpse in the night of Milton's *Paradise Lost* as we gybed and gybed again. It was a filthy place, but once clear the wind fell away.

We were under the lee of the island then, motor-sailing through the night and not realising that the Meltemi was once more upon us. It caught us at dawn, funnelling through the gap between Ikaria and Samos, and we drove for the rock labyrinth of the Furni Islands in a flurry of spray. This group is yet another of those old pirate haunts, quite as wild and grim as Despotiko. We tried the anchorage of Ormos Mamaro, recommended by the Pilot but it was such an ugly-looking place that in the end we motored to the northern extremity of this rocky gut on the east side of Furni. Here are two or three cottages in an uncharted cove called Klad-haridha, and some old windmills on a ridge. A friendly fisherman came down from his cottage and out in his boat specially to show us the exact position to drop our anchor—about ¾ of a cable from the sand beach to the north-east in 30 ft mud and sand, and just, but only just, room to swing without touching the rock outcrops on either side. The wind down-draughted furiously but ineffectively whilst we rested and fed, and at 1350 we sailed, going south about Furni with 3 rolls down and No. 3, taking the 10 fathom passage inside Mak-ronisi. A bumpy ride, but good, fast sailing with the wind freeing all the time as it followed the Samos coast round.

With Tigani (now called Pythagorion after the mathematician who was born there) in sight, we made the mistake of shaking out our reefs under the lee of Karavata. Off Hera's city of Heraion we were motoring. And then suddenly white water and the first of the down-draughts. We thought the wind had died with the setting of the sun, but not so, and this area, notorious for its down-draughts, gave us a rousing welcome. The jib came off and then the mainsail, just in time, for a few minutes later we hit the real vortex of the down-draughts, the whole boat trembling and heeling under the vicious onslaughts though we'd not a rag of sail up and were under motor.

Those down-draughts remained with us right into the harbour entrance. The place reserved for yachts was much too exposed and broadside to the gusts, and the place Denham advised was occupied by steamers. The rating from the harbourmaster's office—as usual in white sailor's uniform and as usual extremely helpful—beckoned us to a position in the north of the harbour, free of down-draughts and now having a depth of 9 ft alongside. The harbour is the same harbour that Polycrates built for his marauding warships 2500 years ago. The bollards on the quay are ancient columns taken from the Hellenic city of Heraion; the old stone and the columns have the white gleam of marble and fishermen's nets give a splash of colour as they hang drying in the wind amongst the green of the trees that shade the old stone-paved waterfront.

One huge magnificent column still stands erect amongst the wild flowers and the grasses that clothed the ruins of Heraion. This ancient city, named after Hera, the sister and wife of Zeus, lies a few miles to the west of Pythagorion, one of the few temple cities to be built on the foreshore. We took a taxi there, and then drove on into the interior of Samos, through the green of its wooded hills to heights from which we looked down the length of a deep gorge to the distant vista of a rich fruit-growing country. The day was hot and pine-scented and our self-appointed guide talked incessantly in basic Italian, gold teeth flashing in a dark, square Turkish-looking face. The village taverna, where we stopped to quench our thirst, was full of farmers sitting relaxed in the midday heat drinking coffee. An old woman picked a bunch of flowers from the taverna's garden, presented them to Dorothy and patted her bare arms to ask whether she was not cold. A woman pedlar on a bicycle, with rugs woven in the mountain villages, stopped to trade with us and in the evening, on a hillside behind the port, we explored the water tunnel built by Polycrates, light-

Mary Deare

Reflections in a Scandinavian fjord

Mary Deare stormbound in Ny Hellesund

Dolphins – our most constant and delightful companions – taken from the bows of the *Mary Deare* off Sicily

Coffee with a Turkish innkeeper after visiting Aphrodisias

THE CREW:

David off watch

Ian getting a position as we approach Crete

Dorothy goes below to prepare a meal

Bob searching for a breeze

The siesta watch – Martin and Göran

Phrikes – one of Odysseus's four ports in the north of Ithaca

Dorothy searching the site of 'Penelope's House'

Mooring stern-on to a tree in the narrows between Corfu and Albania – one of the many bolt holes only seen by those who travel in their own boats

I try to get a forecast – this picture shows the comfortable size
of *Mary Deare's* chart table

ing wax tapers as we passed out of the sun's light into darkness through a narrow entrance rock-hewn to the shape of a man's body. This was the first tunnel ever constructed by driving from opposite sides of a hill. It was like a catacomb, a strange and dangerous place, for we were in the pilot tunnel; the main water conduit had been dug out below it and every few yards a vertical connecting shaft reduced our taper-lit passageway to a narrow slippery ledge above a 50 ft drop.

The Dodecanese are much wilder, much grander islands than the Cyclades, and the Anatolian coast of Turkey thrusts great promontories of hard volcanic mountains between them. The whole of this coast with its sheer rock islands has a savage quality that I have not personally seen other than on the Batina coast of Arabia. It has the look of rock just born from the earth's volcanic womb. Air currents and down-draughts make the sailing itself extremely interesting; a wary eye should always be kept on the surface of the sea and an instinct for the effect of rock masses on wind should be acquired as quickly as possible. We found, for instance, that the down-blasts in the approaches of Limin Skala on Patmos were particularly bad, and all headlands seemed to trap us when beating, the variations in wind direction close-in and offshore causing our tacks to bend back on themselves.

We were twelve days altogether in the Dodecanese, visiting most of the islands between Samos and Rhodes. At Patmos it was the thick-walled monastery of St. John the Theologian that impressed us. You can see it from miles away, standing like a huge square outcrop of rock above the snowdrift of the *chora*. It is a grey formidable shape with the castellated roof picked out in whitewash, and inside are a wealth of illuminated manuscripts, ecclesiastical jewels from Russia's Catherine the Great and an aura of great peace and devotion. At Leros it was the deep-indented natural harbours and the wild savagery of the bare rock coast that impressed. Sailing down its coasts was one of the most spectacular passages of the whole voyage. We cracked the straits between Leros and Kalimnos towards evening when the wind had lessened, beating through under full sail, a little nervous because of the over-powering cliff scenery, wondering what the ugly gap must be like in a winter gale. And then into Laki through a gateway in a cliff face that leads to a magnificent hideout, the Italian flamboyance of architecture a reminder that this had been a stamping ground for Mussolini's fleet.

After sailing this island it was easier to understand the disaster of the Kos-Leros adventure in 1943. And so to the sponge islands of Kalimnos and a dawn glimpse of a little duck-like cavalcade of lampari returning from a night's fishing —the mother caique towing first a crew boat in which the fishermen were standing eating their breakfast and then a string of five rowing boats each with two great gas lamps hung out over the stern, the whole little fleet painted in 'house' colours of green and yellow. Ashore great encampments of beehives stood in soldierly ranks on the slopes and there was a green softness we hadn't seen since Patmos. From Kalimnos port in the south the sponge-fishing fleet sails each year in May for the African coast. It does not return until autumn. There is still a little local sponge-fishing—boats close-in under the cliffs with men searching through glass-bottomed drums —and there were two Kalimnos-style boats in the harbour with their decks strewn with small sponges drying in the sun.

Kos, which was reconstructed by the Italians after the 1933 earthquake, is, like Tigani, a harbour of great antiquity. It is dominated by the huge castle built as a northern lookout and redoubt by the Knights of St. John during their tenure of Rhodes. Everything of interest is close around the port, including the aged tree, its limbs strangely supported by Doric columns, under which Hippocrates, the father of medicine, is supposed to have taught. Mosques stand witness to long centuries of Turkish rule. They are empty now. A small mosque we visited had all the inside blackened by fire and under the central cupola an aged bandsaw stood on a carpet of sawdust. But it is the massive walls of the castle that dominate, so that it took me back to my Brittany cruises and the Vauban fortress of St. Martin on Ile de Ré.

We were able to sail out of Kos, hoisting our genoa in the narrow entrance under the castle walls. We had managed to sail out of 90 per cent of the ports and anchorages we had visited, but on this occasion David was moved to say, 'I bet they haven't seen that done for a long time.' We only saw one yacht under sail the whole time we were in Greek waters

—plenty of big sailing yachts, schooners mainly under charter, but they keep their sails stowed and prefer to motor. It was sailing out of Kos that morning that we experienced the most exaggerated effects of land on air currents. We began close-hauled on the starboard tack steering 55°. As we moved over to the Turkish coast, which juts a great headland south of Kos, we were able to lay the curve of the channel, still close-hauled on the starboard tack, until finally we were sailing 225°. The true wind direction remained throughout west-north-west. Next morning in the first pale milky cloud light of dawn it was fascinating to watch the vague shapes of the islands emerge—first Symi to the east, then the great bulk of Rhodes to the south, finally there were islands all round us in a great circle.

At Rhodes we made our last crew change, Mike (taking a sabbatical from ocean racing whilst his new boat was building) with his wife, Rosheen, replacing David and John. We sailed on Monday, June 15, a day late due to the vagaries of BEA and a gale force Meltemi that had been blowing since our arrival. With 5 rolls down and No. 3 we passed out through the entrance, where the Colossus had been set up after Demetrius's failure to take the port in the third century BC, very conscious that we had a long way to go—over 700 miles to cover in twelve days and a lot to see on the way. The wind was north-west, a dead-noser, and though it eased during the day, it left a filthy sea. We motored through the dark of the night and the following afternoon, after a most frustrating sail, we reached Port Skala in Stampalia—154 miles sailed to make good 93 miles on our route back. This island, also called Astipalia and shaped like a butterfly on the chart, is one of the most westerly of the Dodecanese; a nice cosy little port with a mule track up to the *chora* and a startling view.

And then another night sail and the outline of Santorin growing in the moonlight. This was the island above all others that I had come to see, for *The Strode Venturer* was then only half written and I wanted to know what an island looked like that had emerged from the sea. Santorin was a sea-girt volcano, split and blasted open to the sea in a shattering eruption long ago, possibly the same upheaval of the earth's crust that destroyed the Minoan palaces in Crete 80 miles to the south. I stole up on it in the dawn watch, the white drift of villages glimmering faintly in the half light on green cultivated slopes. Then the northern entrance to the drowned crater opened up and I sailed in below fantastic cliffs, crumbling into pumice dust and pitted with old cave dwellings. The light was stronger now and the sun, just rising, caught the lip of the crater rim high above, the town of Thira clinging there, rose-white and startling like a long glacier face lipping the edge. And straight ahead of me was the thing I had come to see, a ghastly slag-heap of an island that seemed to float in the flat calm crater-encircled water. Nothing grew there. It was bare and new, the stuff of the earth's bowels congealed and lifeless. They call it Kammene, which means burnt. It is a sinister cinder excrescence, still active, with smoke coming from its volcanic vent. Caiques anchor here, in a little inlet, to have their bottoms cleaned of weed in 24 hours by the sulphur seeping up from submarine fissures.

We moored to a buoy off the only quay with the crater face rising almost vertically above us and Thira just visible, a toothy line of white houses on the rim. The sun was blazing hot as we climed slowly up to the town by a mule stairway that zig-zags 800 long steps up the cliff face, pausing at each turn of the stairway as the view opening up before us became ever more impressive. But Thira itself has an uneasy atmosphere. A Frenchman, who had made his home there for 40 years, told me, 'I am living here through almost one thousand earth tremors.' He had nearly lost his life when his house had tumbled on to him in 1956. 'You are always waiting, expecting something to happen. We are living on top of an active volcano, you see.' Many of the houses are cracked and leaning, scarred by earthquakes, troubled and insecure. And always a thousand feet below them, the dark cinder-shape of that island, there in the flat burnished bowl of the sea, to remind them that, however rich the volcanic soil of their island home, they are there on sufferance. That evening the blaze of sunset was not just startling—it was melodramatic. We were sitting drinking on the terrace of a new hotel, geraniums red in front of us, down there below the sea darkening to steel with the flow of current through the crater gaps marked on its surface, Kammene black like the burnt-out tortured hulk of an island, and beyond it, the blasted western crater wall standing stark in silhouette against the flaring sky. By leaning over the terrace balustrade we could just see our boat, a tiny toy tethered to the quay. It was night when we went back to it, back down the zig-zag stairway, our sense of the strangeness of the place magnified by the dark.

We sailed next morning, north to Ios, where the heat drove us to anchor in a rocky cove for a swim before sailing in to the little harbour. It was late afternoon, the water blue against the warm stone of the quay. A man was beating a squid against a rock to make it tender, and outside the taverna they were fanning a brazier ready for the night's cooking. We picked our lobster and walked up the track to the *chora*, past a little creek full of bright-painted fishing boats, and children handed us mulberries from the tree they were raiding, dark faces smeared red with the juice of the fruit as they smiled at us. Ios itself was hot with trapped sunshine, a white little town where old men, still wearing Turkish trousers, sat somnolent in streets that were no more than narrow alleys. We cut up through the butchers' quarter, a fly-blown gut flanked by the flayed and dripping carcasses of sheep, to an open place where two men were re-sharpening their knives on a stone. Above us on a ridge stood five windmills, white towers with outflung arms. Everywhere we had seen these old mills, on every saddle, every hill, on every place which would catch the winds. Now, for the first time, we found them still working. The miller himself appeared, jangling huge keys. The round stone tower, entered by a narrow door, has a spiral stairway up to the grinding stones. The driving shaft is a great baulk of timber, the cog-wheels, the bearings, everything wood—the wood best suited to its purposes. Mike was president elect of the Miller's Association of Great Britain. We could not explain this, but nevertheless the two seemed *en rapport*, two master-millers, running the grain through their knowing fingers, the one in charge of five mills of unbelievable antiquity, the other master of one of the most automated group of mills in the world.

Going back, we lost our way in the maze of alleys, found a beautiful iconed church, and in the gloaming came down the stony path to the quay, our lobster and a long night's sleep. The dry islands then, Sikinos and Folegandros, past Milos, debris of another eruption, the cliffs coloured by minerals, scarred with mine-workings. Through the night again to Kithera and the little crevice of a harbour called St. Nikolo. The houses here are mostly abandoned in the winter, for southerly gales pile waves in over the shallow rocks to spill around the Turkish fort and invade the village. The bottom in this tiny inlet is clear sand, the rock walls of it almost vertical. The usual English-speaking Greek appeared, a one-time stoker on the old *Leviathan*, and with a wealth of gestures he described how the wind off the coast of Kithera could come from three directions at once; it had hit a caique he was on 'bong, bang, boom—we are like a barrel', and he rolled his head. Of a sandy bay to the west he said, 'You can do anything you want; bathe your body like crystal—it is the iodium.' Did he mean iodine or some other chemical bubbling out of the cleansing sands? We had one of those unexpected Greek meals on a verandah shaded by vines and the water we drank with it was a crystal drink fit for the gods.

Next day in the Elaphonisos Channel we came full circle, back on our outgoing tracks. Cape Matapan, the island of Sapienza rounded at night, and in the dawn our anchor down off the breakwater at Methoni, the walls of the great Venetian fortress that jut out into the sea glowing a warm honey-gold in the sleepy sunrise. And so back to Pylos to hand in our much-travelled 'log' and bid farewell to Greece. Wisely we purchased broad-brimmed straw hats, for though the voyage back began close-hauled under sail, the wind soon died and in the first 52 hours we motored 237½ miles in an oily swell and great heat. It was only after we'd picked up Gozo beacon on the radio direction finder loud and clear that a helpful breeze came in from the east. With it came a thickening of haze, so that it wasn't until we were within nearly 5 miles of Gozo that we caught a faint glimpse of the island's outline. We turned on to the wind then and had an exhilarating sail to enter Grand Harbour as the sun set.

Rhodes to Malta—this seemed a fitting end to our journey,

for the fortified city that had been our furthest point east was
built by the Knights of St. John before the Turks defeated
them, and here in Malta was the end of the story, the battlements of St. Elmo, St. Angelo, Senglea still standing—here
Suleiman's forces had wasted themselves in the great siege
of 1565.

V

ODYSSEUS'S SEA

Crew for the Ionian—1965
  Major C. R. Stirling
  Michael Calascione
  John Faircloth
  Brian Appleton
  Nancy and John Hunter-Gray
  Göran Grauers
  Martin Hare

Another working winter had passed, *The Strode Venturer* finally written. Now, back in Malta once again, Dorothy and I had spent a week getting *Mary Deare* ready for sea—all the winter-stored gear to be brought from Manoel Island to the marina, cleaned, checked for cockroaches and stowed in its right place, the long lists of stores to last us two months to be purchased and packed on board, water and fuel to be organised, and finally the rigging to be checked and tuned. It is incredible the amount of work involved when a boat has been stripped out and left for ten months, and in the evenings, exhausted, we fell into hot baths and emerged to face the pleasant contrast of Malta's social round. All was ready by the time Bob flew out from England and Michael had finally got away from his job as manager of a Malta flour mill.

We were bound this year for the homeland of Odysseus, but we did not take the direct route, the route he took to the land of the Phaeacians. There were things we wanted to see on the way: Syracuse, where I had had my headquarters in a lighthouse during the war, Taormina, Scylla and Charybdis, the islands of Vulcano and Stromboli, the Calabrian coast. We were, in fact, back-tracking an earlier section of the *Odyssey*, the nine-day drift from the whirlpool of Charybdis to the

Isle of Ogygia. Whether Malta, or perhaps its neighbouring island, Gozo, is really the Ogygia of which Homer writes we may never know, but there was certainly no fair Calypso to see us off with a warm and gentle breeze as we sailed *Mary Deare* out of Sliema Creek on May 4, 1965, and headed north for Sicily; the wind was north-west force 4, the sea lumpy after a week of strong winds. We had a fast passage through the night to Syracuse, but could not land there, for by then the wind was westerly and very strong, the quay quite untenable. We lay anchored under the lighthouse I remembered so distinctly and in the morning it was still blowing hard and we gave the trysail an airing on our way up to the naval port of Augusta. Again we could not land and had to anchor off under the old forts in the north-west corner. An Italian frigate accompanied us out in the morning headed for a game of hunt-the-slipper with a submarine. Etna's symmetrical cone stood magnificent on our port hand as we sailed north. The air was cold, for the great snow-capped bulk of the volcano was interposed between us and the wind; in the end we were completely blanketed and forced to motor.

Taormina is visible a long way off, a splash of white on the shoulder of Etna where it spills a great headland of tumbled rock down into the sea. The thrust of this massive piece of Sicily, which, if it weren't so clothed in cypress, would have the appearance of a Moorish fortress on the Barbary Coast, constitutes the first narrowing of the seaway in the approaches to the Straits of Messina. White water all ahead of us now as we closed this towering headland with the wind down-draughting violently. We had intended anchoring in the little horse-shoe bay of Mazzaro, but the entrance faces towards the Straits and when we poked our nose between the rock awash and the sheer cliffs we found the wind funnelling in. We retired defeated to the south side of the headland and felt our way into a smaller, even wilder cove called St. Andrea dominated by the red rock islet of Isola Bella. We felt our way in on the echo-sounder and a kindly fisherman, in a boat as gaily painted as the carts that litter the island's highways, gave us the exact position in which to let go our anchor.

As a tourist resort Taormina doubtless has its attractions, but the charm of sailing one's own boat in the Mediterranean

is that one sees the unspoilt places—and surprisingly there are
a great number of them even today. The long street, filled with
souvenir shops and bus-loads of packaged tourists, is a thousand feet above the cove where we had anchored, no glimpse
of the sea and the town's past character entirely spoilt. Perhaps in winter we would appreciate it more, but we were glad
to go, sailing out in the early dawn northwards to crack the
Straits. Reference to the old 1916 Pilot was alarming with its
descriptions of the rafoli and bastardi, the counter-currents of
ebb and flood. We suffered a good deal from down-draughts
from the high land wrapped in cloud between Cape Scarletti
and Messina, the wind force being between 3 and 6. We
had, however, the benefit of the counter-current. Just south
of Messina the sea became violently agitated with much white
water. We motor-sailed through it and were then in the
descendi or ebb. After that it was slow work as we fought our
way up the middle of the Straits to pass under the centre of
the great overhead span of electric cables at midday.

Navigationally the Straits of Messina are more straight-
forward than the sailing directions suggest, but wind and
tide funnel through this natural channel between two seas and
in really bad weather it must be a most unpleasant place. We
had only one bad patch, south of Messina; after that we saw
little sign of the overfalls, where current and counter-current
meet, and no sign at all of the dreaded whirlpool or Charybdis. Indeed, the spada fishing boats—at least a dozen of
them—were working the rafoli close in to the north-west
shore, passing back and forth over the very spot. Charybdis
is marked on older charts as lying well out from the low,
sandy north shore, so that the fig tree to which Odysseus clung
above the whirlpool would seem to be the product of Homer's
imagination. Surprisingly, we found Charybdis not marked on
the latest charts, which made us wonder whether there had
been some change recently in the sea bottom.

The spada boats are most curious craft. They are long
and low with a clipper bow, the single mast, which is really
a steel ladder, immensely high, with cross-trees just below
the head of the top-mast to give a precarious foothold for
two look-outs. From the bow a light alloy catwalk, seemingly
longer than the boat itself, extends out ahead supported by

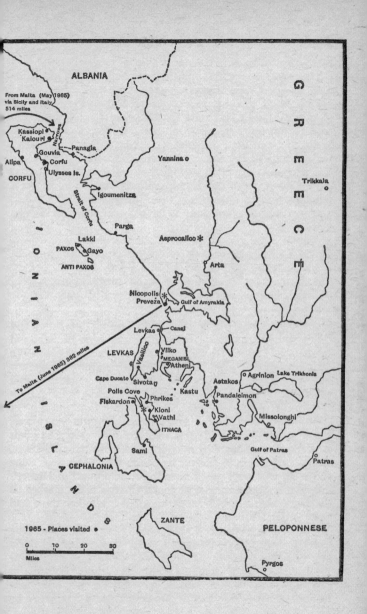

ALBANIA

From Malta (May 1965)
via Sicily and Italy
514 miles

Kassiopi
Kalouri

Gouvia
Corfu
Panagia
Ailpa
Ulysses Is.
CORFU

Yannina

Igoumenitza

Strait of Corfu

Parga

Lakki
PAXOS
Gayo
ANTI PAXOS

Asprocalico ✱

Arta

Nicopolis ✱
Preveza

Gulf of Amyrakia

Levkas
Canal

LEVKAS
Vliko
MEGANISI
Atheni

Cape Ducato
Sivota
Astakos
Agrinion
Lake Trikhonis

Polis Cove
Kastu
Pandeleimon
Fiskardon
Phrikes
Kioni ✱
Vathi
ITHACA
Missolonghi

Sami
Gulf of Patras

CEPHALONIA
Patras

1965 - Places visited

ZANTE
PELOPONNESE

0   10   20   30
Miles

Pyrgos

GREECE

Trikkala

To Malta (June 1965) 382 miles

IONIAN ISLANDS

three stays. The object of all this is to spear the swordfish (It. *pesce spada*) at the point where they are flagging after their long thresh up the Straits against the tide.

On leaving the Straits, Scylla's rocky headland loomed black and sinister on our starboard bow. The sky was overcast, the mistral freshening and the seas steep and breaking. We reefed and headed into it, our objective the Lipari Isles some 30 miles away and dead to windward. The desire to see Vulcano and Stromboli now had to be considered against the reality of weather and time. Michael was due to inspect a semolina mill in Palermo on the 11th and Bob was booked out on a flight from Corfu on the night of the 14th. It was already May 8. Dorothy served a cockpit lunch as we talked it over with the gloomy pile of Scylla receding into the mists astern. The whole coast of Italy was wrapped in low cloud. Reluctantly we went about, shook out our reefs and headed back for Messina; back under the cable span and through the Straits, a fast passage, wind and tide with us now and the spada boats all around us.

Messina, however, was out of the question—it was blowing very hard on-shore. We put into Reggio-Calabria instead and lay stern-to in the north-east corner of the harbour getting our topsides filthy with oil from the wash of the hydrofoil ferry. We had covered 54 miles that day, had sailed back and forth through the Straits, yet we still had time to walk up into the town, replenish our stores and get a meal. The trees of the boulevards threshed in the wind. thunder crashed and the pitch-dark night was rent with flashes of lightning. We were glad to be drinking Calabrian wine instead of beating to windward through the filthy night.

Michael left us in the morning and the three of us got the boat ready for sea. The forecast was wind east-north-east 19 knots. We had a good fast sail in bright sunshine as far as Cape Spartavento, after that the wind died away completely. The forecast had clearly been for the Straits which, like Ushant, manufacture their own weather. By 1425 we were motoring and for the first time since leaving Malta it was warm. We had none of us seen the coast of Calabria before and the thing that struck us most was the dry watercourses winding down each deep-scored valley from great mountains towering inland. These dry river beds, choked with boulders and the debris of winter floods, sweep through the centres of the coastal towns in broad swathes. Night came softly, all stars and moonlight, with the mountains bulking huge; dolphins played around us in water so clear that we could see them well below the keel. The dawn was different, a foul, steep sea. We were into the Gulf of Squillace then and the wind came in from the north-north-west. We reefed 4 rolls and had a rough ride until we were under the lee of Cape Colonne, its Grecian column standing splendid and solitary against the bare laval rock of the headland's platform. Shortly after midday we were moored stern-on to the quay at the north end of Crotone's Porto Vecchio.

We spent 28 hours in Crotone whilst the wind blew hard from the north-east, from the very direction in which we wanted to sail, and the seas piled in against the harbour wall, drifting spray. By 1600 of the second day the wind had backed into the north and eased to force 5. We could now lay the heel of Italy and so we left, reefing 4 rolls and setting No. 3 for comfort. It was well that we did. Fishermen, stormbound in the port after landing their swordfish catch, called to us not to put out. They were, of course, not accustomed to the sea-keeping abilities of sailing yachts, but they knew their Gulf of Taranto. This 70-mile-wide sea encircled by the high lands of southern Italy has apparently a weather pattern quite as unpleasant as the Gulf of Lions. Fortunately the wind backed still further, for by the early hours of the morning it was blowing force 7, the seas steep and breaking. Bob and I parcelled the night watches out between us and we had a fast, exhilarating sail. Just before dawn we caught a glimpse of the light of Santa Maria di Leuca. The sun rose. The sky flared red. By 0830 we were anchored in the centre of Santa Maria bay. There was no question of going ashore. Black clouds were passing over with heavy rain, lightning and squalls of wind. Were these the 'tormentas' referred to in the old Pilot? We had barely finished breakfast when we were dragging under one of these thunder squalls. We re-anchored closer to the shore and turned in for some sleep.

We left at 2200 hours, 4 rolls down again and No. 3 jib. We passed close under the lighthouse and ran slap into a tormenta, or perhaps it was a Tarantata. Whatever it was, it was most unpleasant—sheets of rain and then violent gusts of wind with the lighthouse beam swinging a ghostly arc across taut sails streaming water. I got the jib off, then the main. A batten lost, the mainsail torn, a smell of burning from a short on the lead to the compass light. We put back and when we finally left at 0530 in the morning there were heavy storm clouds over Greece and the visibility was poor. Little more than one hour later the air was so clear we could see Fano Island 35 miles away. Black storms of rain were constantly being funnelled south through the Adriatic narrows. After passing through the edge of one of these we tried full main for a while, but by 1300 we were heavily reefed again and arguing about whether to hold on for Corfu or put in to Fano. Prudence dictated the latter and we anchored close in, glad to be under the lee of this high island as Corfu, Albania, all the land to the east of us disappeared in an ink-black sky.

Later we were told that all the coast was flooded with rain, visibility reduced to a few hundred yards and the temperature so low that people were dressed in the clothes they wore in the depths of winter. We shared the shelter of Fano with a stormbound coaster deck-laden with a cargo of horses. We saw these wretched animals standing motionless in the moonlight as we motored out in the still of the night at 0200 hours. Two hours later the moon was setting, blood red and as full as an orange astern, whilst on the port bow stood high mountains, grey against the reddening sky. An oily swell, as smooth as milk, reflected a kaleidoscope of colours. The day broke clear and bright with Albania's snow-capped Pindus mountains fully revealed, range on range, standing magnificent like a great barrier before us, white at first, then tinged with pink as the sun rose above them. That morning, so crystal clear, so full of the grandeur of high mountains, more than repaid us for all the hours of bad weather sailing. We passed through the narrows between Corfu and Albania to breakfast drifting in the great bay under Pandokrater and enter Corfu harbour at ten o'clock.

Corfu—or to give it its Greek name, Kerkyra—was the administrative centre of what, under British rule, became a union of seven islands. The other six were Paxos, Levkas, Ithaca,

Cephalonia, Zante and Cerigo. Bob, whose grandfather had lowered the British flag when the islands were handed over to Greece in 1863, left us here, an unquiet departure with *Mary Deare* cavorting wildly in a strong north-westerly. John and Brian brought better weather and the sun was hot as the four of us sailed for Paxos, or Paxoi, which is separated from the southern tip of Corfu by a narrow strait, its limestone cliffs as white as the chalk cliffs of Dover. Here the land has the hard, virile look of the Aegean, but the air is different, the light softer, and Paxos is clothed in a ragged mantle of olives. It is quite true that there is something extraordinary about the light in Greece, a quality of brightness, almost brilliance, that I have not found anywhere else. In fact, each time I return from sailing in Greek waters I find my eyes affected by this quality of brightness so that it is some time before I can adapt them for easy reading. This is strange considering that the Mediterranean loses by evaporation two-thirds more water than it receives from the rivers that run into it. But whereas the air of the Aegean sparkles like very light dry champagne, the Ionian, veiled in humidity, has the touch of a heavier, sleepier wine. I never had that feeling of absolute well-being that I had in the Aegean—none of us had.

There are two ports in Paxos, both interesting navigationally. The first is Lakki just across the straits from Corfu, the other Gayo—and Gayo is quite the most attractive port in the Ionian, perhaps in all the islands of Greece. It is still unspoilt, though the Club Mediterranée have discovered it and their caiques full of young holiday-makers regularly put in there, boys and girls of all nationalities roughing it together for the night on deck mattresses after a simple Greek meal served at trestle tables on the quay. The entrance, however, is somewhat alarming. There are, in fact, two entrances, but the southern one, which is between two breakwaters and faces the town, has silted up. All newcomers enter by the northern channel. The approach is behind Madonna Island with its whitewashed convent. Three times I came into this little port. Each time it was early evening with the broom blazing yellow in the slanting sun, the heavy scent of it hanging in the still air of the narrow silent gut that hems one in. This looks so like a rocky cul-de-sac that the surprise of the sharp port-hand turn by the lantern mark, with its sudden glimpse of the sheltered quay, never palls. Here big langoustes crawl beneath your keel tethered to the quay, the waterfront is lit by oil lamps set in red painted lanterns and big white caiques with clipper bows lie against the village square with their nets hung up to dry.

This little white square fronting the quay, with the white church in the middle, is a sun trap, and as you go ashore in the morning to re-stock with food and wine, the blinding light of the place hits you in the eyes. The shops by contrast are cool caverns. They are mostly in the narrow streets that run back to hillsides filled with the gnarled shapes of olive trees so huge and misshapen that you feel they must have been there before even the Venetians came.

The first morning we were there I took the dinghy and leaded out through what was once the main entrance to the port. The bottom was weed at first, but stone and boulder up through the narrow gap between the two arms of the breakwater. The depth was 8 ft all the way with the tower of the church open just north of the top storey of a building on the waterfront. I was then able to make my exit on each occasion by this southern route. But an 8-ft clearance is still running it fine and I must admit that I kept my gaze fixed on my leading marks and never looked over the side each time I made this passage.

Charming by daylight, Gayo takes on an almost magic quality at night. It starts with the lamplighter going his rounds. The oil glow of lanterns about the size of old carriage lamps—a Venetian reflection in the dark water mirror of the harbour—is matched by the flicker of fireflies in the dark of the olive groves along the headland track. The town is white, all white in the moonlight, and in the streets no wider than alleys that run back from the waterfront big water jars, designed apparently to conceal Ali Babas of Falstaffian proportions, stand round and ribbed like Michelin men. The shops gape dark as caves with the faces of Greeks caught like Rembrandt portraits in the soft radiance of single oil lamps.

Paxos is small—about 5 miles by 2½. But its neighbour is much smaller, and very bare in appearance, for whereas Paxos

is partly clothed with olives, Anti-Paxos is given over entirely to the vine. It has no proper port, only a cove on the
eastern side offering doubtful shelter in a bare 8 ft of water
behind a tiny mole. I took *Mary Deare* in twice for the peace
and quiet and the feeling it gave of the Greece of the
ancients. At the head of the cove is a beach of sand with
three or four keel beds scooped out and old wooden capstans
for dragging the boats up out of the water. One boat was still
laid up in its sand berth and over it the owner had built an
arbour of maquis greenery on a framework of barked wood
to protect it from the heat of the sun. A gaily-coloured caique,
painted red, green and white, puts in occasionally with
visitors from Gayo or with stores, but the few people who
live on the island have a hard life. There is little shelter
and their low-built houses, crushed against the hillsides like
the 'black houses' of the Hebrides, testify to the violence of
the west wind, for there is no land between them and the
toe of Italy. In winter they can be cut off, even from Port
Gayo, for weeks at a time.

Southward from Anti-Paxos it is 25 miles to the nearest
point of Levkas. But if you hold to the seaward then it is
nearly 50 miles before you can make port, for the west side
is a bare blank wall of cliffs culminating in Sappho's Leap
and the rocky point of Cape Ducato. Not until you have
rounded this and sailed five miles almost back on your tracks
up the great inlet of Vasilico Bay can you drop your hook.
The first time we visited Levkas we were overtaken by fog
just as we were closing Sesola Rock which lies close off the
cliffs about two-thirds down the Levkas coast. We stood off
for a mile, the sun growing gradually dimmer until it finally
disappeared. Visibility was then about 200 yards, but when
we turned south again we were lucky enough to find a thin
patch and through the grey miasma of the fog we caught a
brief glimpse of the Rock. We could even see the great hole
cut by the waves in its southern flank. Then it was gone
again and we were muffled in thick murk with a cruise ship's
foghorn baying to seaward. We dropped the genoa and fore-
reached gently under main whilst we had a leisurely dinner,
the table fixed, not gimballed, and bright with fruit and
flowers, the candles lit. The odd thing was that as the sun

set we could see the mountainous coast of Levkas high in the
sky, a rose-pink range floating disembodied above a grey void.
The fog thinned as night reduced the temperature, condensing
the humidity until it fell back into the sea from whence it had
come. The sky was clear overhead and, ghostly in the starlight, we saw again the tops of the Levkas cliffs. No sign of
the little light on Sesola Rock, but the beam of Cape
Ducato to the south showed bright. The moon rose blood red
over Ithaca, the dark shapes of mountainous islands crowding
the horizon, and in our nostrils the smell of the land, pungent
and aromatic.

This was the route taken by the rowers of Alcinous, the
kindly king of the Phaeacians, as their ship 'sped lightly on,
cutting her way through the waves and carrying a man wise
as the gods are wise, who in long years of war on land and
wandering across the cruel seas had suffered many agonies of
spirit but now was lapped in peaceful sleep, forgetting all he
had once endured.' They took him to the port that is now
called Vathi and were repaid for their kindness by the wrath
of Poseidon, the Earthshaker, who waited for them on their
homeward voyage and then went up to their ship 'and with
one blow from the flat of his hand turned her into stone and
rooted her to the sea-bottom, where he left her.'

Coming south that first time we passed Sappho's Leap in
the dark. But a fortnight later, in daylight, the white rock was
clearly visible. There was no wind and we were motoring in
an ugly disturbed sea. The straits between Levkas and the
Ithaca-Cephalonia massif are open to the prevailing north-
west wind; they should always be approached with caution,
for not only is the sea disturbed, but even in light airs the
wind funnels through with an inevitable build-up in strength.
It made me think how difficult it must have been at times to
recover the bodies of the novitiates of Apollo's temple. The
white rock is over 200 ft high and the priests who made this
high dive or leap are supposed to have tried to buoy themselves up with feathered wings and even live birds. On this
occasion the disturbance of the water extended two-thirds of
the way into Vasilico Bay, and as we motored up in the
gathering dark to anchor in the little port that same strange
scent filled the air.

Levkas is not properly an island. It is a peninsula joined to the mainland by a broad stretch of marsh and salt flats. Thucydides, writing in the fourth century BC, described it as such even though the first canal separating the 'island' from the mainland had been cut by the Corinthians two centuries earlier. This gradually silted up due to earthquakes and the shift of sand before the prevailing northerly wind. It was re-opened by Caesar Augustus. The present canal, only 32 yards wide at the surface and 16 yards at the base, has a least depth of 18 ft. This narrow waterway, guarded north and south by the great forts of the Citadel and Ayios Giorgios—Venetian in origin, but essentially Turkish in their present massive bulk —is well marked, a strange contrast after days spent in the craggy inlets of mountainous islands.

Southbound from Corfu, the Levkas Canal offers a convenient short cut to a number of safe anchorages, but in no circumstances should it be attempted without previous sight and knowledge of the northern entrance. This entrance is not easy to identify at a distance or in bad visibility, and there are dangerous shallows to the west. Moreover, it is half blocked by a great bank of sand extending at least a hundred yards beyond the light at the end of the breakwater, and the prevailing wind makes all this low coast a lee shore.

I had been through the canal twice, each time from the south, before I dared risk the northern entrance, and even then it proved a fairly nerve-racking experience. The north-west wind had been building up steadily since our departure from Port Gayo at 1030. For three hours we ran under full main and boomed-out genoa, our speed increasing all the time. At 1335 we handed the genoa, pulled down 3 rolls and set No. 3. It was then blowing force 5. As we closed the gap in the mountains that marked the general position of the canal, the wind strengthened steadily as it usually does along this coast in the late afternoon. By the time we could actually see the lighthouse on the end of the mole, a faint white mark against the dark of the Citadel, it was blowing force 6, gusting 7, the seas steep and breaking hard, and nothing but white water ahead of us. We were by then committed to this doubtful route, the water becoming more and more broken as we entered the shallows. It was a wild ride and it got wilder as we drove at the sandy line of the shore, which has to be closed to within a hundred yards in order to turn the sand-bank that lies across the canal entrance. The end came sud-denly, with the boat turned head to wind, sails flapping and sea abruptly calm. The relief of being safe in the shelter of mole and sandbank was considerable.

Levkas port is no more than a quay facing the first bend of the canal. It serves the island's wide irrigated plains and the needs of the caique traffic passing through the canal. The town behind is busy and looks reasonably prosperous. The old church in the square is worth visiting for its icons, but there is little else to see, for Levkas was badly hit in the earth-quake of '48. All to the south now, through Levkas, Ithaca and Cephalonia, the old buildings are tumbled into ruins. Here the dread god Poseidon rules, for this is a centre of seismic disturbance; the most recent, and one of the worst, the 'quake of 1953. Only one person was killed on Ithaca. The people there were lucky in that they had the benefit of a warning tremor. But in Cephalonia there was no such warn-ing and a thousand people died as their homes tumbled about their ears. There has been no major earthquake since, but we were told that in the full heat of summer hardly a day goes by without some tremor, and the drift from the islands has been persistent since 1953. For a people faced with a hard barren struggle for existence, this catastrophe was the last straw. The young gravitate towards the mainland or go north to Corfu to catch the emigrant steamers. We saw one such ship leave the new quay when we were there changing crew; it was packed with young Greeks, women as well as men, bound for Italy, Germany, Britain—anywhere where they had relatives and the chance of work in cities instead of the windy, 'quake-torn beauty of their island heritage.

There are no other ports of consequence in Levkas, and the three anchorages we visited—Vasilico, Sivtoa and Vliko— are much as Odysseus must have known them. Vasilico I came into first at night, feeling my way by the light of a full moon and the echo-sounder, finally anchoring at the head of the bay in 20 ft. There are three protected anchorages here. The outer has a good depth and the protection of a broken mole partly awash. The second is sheltered by a solid quay and is the waterfront of the fishing village. The third is right against the sandy shore, the arms of its breakwaters almost entirely submerged and the space within so constricted that it reminded me of the old port of Palaioupoleos on Andros that we had explored the previous year. Clearly it belonged to the days of ancient Greece when craft were small and invariably dragged up the beach on rollers or slats of wood. As we lay at anchor that night fireflies flickered on the shore like flashes of intermittent rifle fire, and in the dawn the scree on the upper slopes of Mount Stavrota was as white in the sunlight as the snow on the Pindus Mountains. In the heat of the day the waterfront of this little fishing village sleeps under the shade of its plane trees. But earlier it is full of fishermen mending their nets. Donkeys and ponies come in laden with farm produce, and women in the bunched-up brown costume of the country move constantly up from the sunken spring with great round pots of water on their heads. Back from the port is an irrigated plain rich in fruit. A farmer loaded us with oranges as big as melons, huge lemons, and loquats. all fresh from the tree, and also wine—*krasi*—that he had made himself.

Sivota Bay, eight miles to the east, is entirely different— no village here, just three farmsteads at the head of a dog-legged gut in the rocky coast. This is one of the most sheltered anchorages in the Ionian. We came to it first in the dawn. It was a sun trap, already hot, and the gay bright-painted houses stood on their heads in the mirror reflection of the glass-smooth water. In the north-east corner there is a little shrine, the recess of which holds a bottle of oil and a lamp. for like many of these small shrines, it serves the double purpose of a leading mark to light boats in after dark. Here a little stream ran out of the rocks and as we lifted the dinghy ashore a young woman was washing clothes. beating at the pile with a flat piece of wood. Bells tinkled in the hot air and a big herd of black goats came down to drink. The owner was a man of about thirty with blue eyes and reddish hair and a profile right out of an ancient Greek frieze. We walked with him a mile or so up the mountain track that wandered through the grey-green of the olive groves. He kept his goats together by throwing stones ahead of those that strayed, to turn them back, an object lesson in how David became so proficient in the use of the sling.

The atmosphere in Sivota is entirely pastoral. It is as though three nomadic families had settled in a place of supreme beauty that they knew to be suited to their needs. The second time we came there it was even hotter. The cuckoo was calling, ravens circling, and it was washing day. Two women in their bunched dresses were beating at blankets in the shallows, their children playing naked around them, in and out of the water. Donkeys brayed, the air was heady with the sound of goat bells, and as the morning progressed the bushes sprouted the bright colours of blankets drying in the sun and women, children and donkeys sought the shade of the olive trees.

Vliko, half-way up Levkas's east coast, we came to from the mainland after a day's sailing among the smaller islands. The sun was sinking as we passed north of Meganisi with its deep indentations. Meganisi, like all the islands we had sailed through that day, was bleak and bare, but ahead of us now were several very small islands dark with trees. Skropio, the largest of these, but still barely a mile across, had a road bulldozed round it and the sheltered anchorage on the northern side had a big mooring buoy and a landing craft in it, the foreshore littered with the debris of some development project. We thought at first it must be an oil company setting up a drilling rig. Later we discovered that the Greek shipowner, Onassis, had acquired it and was developing the whole island as a gambling centre. Like Porto Cervo, the Aga Khan's development in north-east Sardinia, which we had sailed into two years before when there was nothing there at all, Skropio is in an unspoilt corner of Greece, an area that is quite remote and way off the beaten track. That Onassis should have chosen it for such a project demonstrates the sublime confidence that money and the control of transport gives to a man.

Nevertheless, this is an area that has always attracted the rich. Just past Skropio is the entrance to Vliko and here you sail past old villas big as English country houses tucked away amongst the dark of firs. The water shallows as you turn south. Mud flats to starboard, a small village, and then you are in the narrows, hemmed in by mud and a sea of reeds. At the narrowest point there is a boatyard full of caiques hauled out for repair and above them the dark slopes of mountains hanging high in the sky. Once through the narrows you are in a great basin so sunk among the hills it might be an old crater. Three miles across this shallow sea lies the village of Vliko.

We lay here one night, having let go our anchor close off the Customs House. It is a poor place, but interesting because the German scholar, Dörpfeld, claimed it as the port to which the Phaeacian ship brought Odysseus at the end of his travels. When we anchored there the people were coming in from the fields, ponies, donkeys, women and even men so laden with the coarse verdure they store for fodder that beast and human were almost invisible beneath the great piles. There was a well tap close by the kaffeneion and women passed in endless succession with pots of water balanced on their heads. Most were dressed in the traditional costume, walking with that loose-limbed, belly-thrusting stride that is the graceful legacy of a lifetime of water-carrying.

Dörpfeld lived in a house at the entrance to Vliko and all through the islands you hear about this man who proved to his satisfaction that, in the aftermath of a disastrous earthquake, the names of the neighbouring islands of Levkas and Ithaca became transposed. The theory is about as tenable as the Bacon theory of Shakespeare's plays. Where at Vliko are the two bold headlands at the mouth of the cove? The *Odyssey* is very specific about this. In any case, the Levkas Canal did not exist when Homer described Ithaca as an island. Levkas was then a peninsula, part of the mainland. And there are the words of Telemachus when he refuses Menelaus's gift of three horses: *None of the islands that slope down to the sea are rich in meadows and the kind of place where you can drive a horse. Ithaca least of all.* Even allowing for the fact that it was not an island, this does not fit Levkas where there are several stretches of flat country growing corn or given over to grass and where to this day there are ponies and even horses, as well as the ubiquitous donkey. I suspect that, like so many scholars who claim to be Homeric experts, Dörpfeld was not a sailing man.

On our first voyage south we beat from Sivota Bay across the Straits to Ithaca to make the modern port of Vathi. Whereas Vliko was a trap, its narrows all mud and marsh, Vathi had high land on both sides of the narrows with alternative shelter across the Gulf of Molo for ships that were normally drawn up on the beach. A sailing man would never have confused these two ports. But now that we had arrived in Ithaca, our chief interest was to locate the site of the palace of Odysseus. We were told it was in the north of the island, but we had no precise information as we sailed out of Vathi southbound with the intention of putting into St. Andrea; this little inlet which is supposed to be the place where Telemachus landed to avoid the suitors' ambush on his return from visiting wise Nestor at Pylos. It was a day of little wind until about five in the afternoon when it suddenly blew up fresh from the south-east. The south of Ithaca is very high and bleak and St. Andrea, open to the south-east, looked distinctly inhospitable. We crossed the Straits to Sami on Cephalonia where it blew gale force with very heavy downdraughts so that we did not get away for thirty-six hours. We then motored north in the dawn, up the narrow strait between Ithaca and Cephalonia. Heavy cloud obscured the mountains. The sky was grey, the rippled surface of the sea like steel. We might have been in a Scottish loch. We were soon level with the broken back of Ithaca, that narrow neck of land connecting the north and the south of the island where it is almost cut in two by the Gulf of Molo. A fine position to defend, but hardly the site for a palace. A few miles further north, however, there is a superb little bay, a perfect horseshoe cove called Polis, with a narrow entrance steep-to and high land on either side. At the head of the cove is a sandy beach with the land beyond sloping up to a saddle. A glance at the chart showed that this saddle, right in the centre of the northern half of Ithaca, was almost equidistant from the four main inlets, all natural harbours—Polis Cove in the west, Aphalais Bay to the north, Phrikes to the north-east and Kioni to the east. Seeing it like that in the grey of a cloudy dawn there was suddenly no doubt in my mind; this was the place we had come to see.

It must be remembered that Odysseus was not only king of Ithaca; he was overlord of all the neighbouring islands. And since the nearest, Cephalonia, is more than twice the size of Ithaca, with mountains reaching up to 5,000 ft, to hold its chieftains as vassals he would have to command the straits between the two islands. Polis Cove is the only port in Ithaca from which this could be done. There is no other inlet on the west coast and Andrea in the south is too remote, cut off even from Port Vathi by high rugged country. It had to be the north end of Ithaca, on that saddle. It is the perfect stronghold for a man like Odysseus, looking four ways to four different bolt-holes—shelter for ships whichever way the winter gales blew. It even offers some explanation of the nature of the man. 'What a cunning knave it would take to beat you at your tricks,' is how his own guardian angel, Pallas Athene, puts it. And Homer describes him as 'the wily Odysseus', 'nimble-witted', as well as gallant, stalwart, much-enduring, patient, and like adjectives.

A fortnight later, back at Ithaca again, with five of us on board—John and Nancy seeking warmth, after wintering with their folkboat in Oland Island off the east coast of Sweden, and Göran, the 15-year-old son of a Swedish friend (a fine yachtsman who had trained his son well)—we ignored Vathi and put into Kioni three miles to the north. The tubby, round stone towers of three ruined windmills stand as a guide mark on the southern headland. It is a biggish bay with Kioni tucked into the north-western arm, a steep little place with just room to swing between rock and quay, white villas crowding the hillsides that rise on three sides in a riot of bougainvillaea and roses. The Italianate villas give it the look of a holiday resort, but in fact they are the homes of the people of Kioni, small concrete replacements for the old stone houses destroyed by the earthquake of '53. As in all Greek islands, the Government has connected port and interior by road, but it is so steep and twisting that it is only a small improvement on the old mule track. By the time we had finished lunch, in a bare little shack that did service as an *estiatorion*,

the wind had followed us round and was blowing hard
straight into the harbour. We left in a hurry, our anchor
dragging on the rocky bottom, and sailed round to the shelter
of Phrikes.

Phrikes is a narrow V at the head of a deep bay. Long ago
that V framed the palace and the servants' homes of King
Odysseus. It still looks something of a rover's haven, for on
the slopes above the tiny town two towers stand watch like
ancient keeps. They are, in fact, the remains of windmills,
and in one of them the great wooden shaft and cogged driving
wheel lie with the millstones where the earthquake threw
them. But of Odysseus's palace on the hill behind, nothing
remains, only the dry-stone walls of innumerable corn terraces.

I never want to see Phrikes again. The first night we were
there we spent five hours being chased round the tiny harbour
by a freak storm. We had anchored in the middle with just
room to swing between the cliffs and the stony beach and the
quay. We were warned by fishermen that the wind would increase at sundown—we might drag a little but not dangerously, they said, and it would die down after midnight. The
holding is not good, but when we turned in at about eleven
we were still lying quite comfortably, though the wind was
down-draughting now and then off the hills. The grinding of
the anchor chain kept me awake and shortly after midnight a
particularly heavy gust got me out of my bunk. We were
dragging now and already out beyond the end of the mole.
The wind, roaring down the valley, was incredibly hot, as
though a furnace door had been opened. Engine on, re-
anchor, watch and wait. And then the same thing again,
though we now had more chain out. There is good depth at
the outer end of the quay, but we could not get alongside
for a big Club Méditerranée caique, which had been moored
stern-on and bows to the village, had also dragged. We
watched it hit the quay broadside; thereafter it seemed to
charge all over that part of the harbour, the crew asleep and
entirely oblivious to what was going on. Periodically now the
wind would swing through 180° and then for a while it would
blow quite cold. But each time it switched back to the west

o give us that dry oven heat that I recognised from desert days. This was, in fact, that rare phenomenon, a 'Libbie'— he wind from Libya. At one point the whole surface of the harbour took off in a smoke of spray. We almost grounded on the beach then, but the engine pulled us clear, and in the first gleam of daylight we were able to tie up to the quay, he crew of the caique having at last surfaced and got their ship securely moored.

Soon afterwards the wind died. The day proved hot, and after a late breakfast, we climbed the road to Stavros on the hill above, past gardens heavy with roses, brilliant with the narrow-calyxed pomegranate flower. A meal of fish in the village square, facing an appallingly bad bust of Odysseus, and then we followed a sign-post to 'The School of Homer'. Here were brash new villas blazing with flowers above a valley that dropped in green lushness to a distant glimpse of Polis Cove. At one of these, the Villa Romantzea, which belonged to a Greek confectioner who had been 40 years in Australia, we were directed to the high ground where he said 'Penelope's house' had once stood. More villas, a whole row of them, but now we could catch glimpses of great sea vistas, to the north and to the east. We turned the flank of yet another villa just completed and there was the overgrown rubble of old walls, the ruins of more recent cottages. Had Odysseus trod these stones on his return from the siege of Troy and his ten years' voyaging? Was this where the great hall had stood, the hall where the suitors had banqueted, where the old warrior had bent his great bow and with his son Telemachus by his side had slaughtered the lot? These and other questions we asked ourselves as we scrambled over the ruined piles of rubble, but of one thing we none of us had any doubt—this was the site. It could not be otherwise, for the small eminence on which we stood was the one place that commanded all the seas. East we looked down into Phrikes, north into Aphalais Bay and west to Polis Cove. From this saddle a man could command the weather, the movement of his ships, the safety of his kingdom. It was unique, even in Ithaca, the only place that had such a commanding position. And apart from the rubble, there were the stone-walled terraces on the slopes below. Throughout Greece, wherever there is no natural detritus, the presence of stone walls in great profusion usually indicates an ancient settlement.

There is a little museum close by the site, a bare white-walled room with glass cases full of bits and pieces of pottery. Most of it has come from Polis Cove, including the most interesting exhibits, the finely worked bronze remains of sacrificial supports. It is thought that there may have been a temple at Polis Cove and that the sacrifices were made when the 'black ships' stationed there put to sea. Most of the digging at Polis Cove has been done by an Englishwoman, Miss Sylvia Benton, the museum itself largely inspired by her. It seems strange, considering the world-wide interest in the story of Odysseus, that no attempt has been made to dig on the site of the palace or even to uncover the foundations. Not only have the Greek authorities ignored it archaeologically, but —and this is quite unforgivable—they have been so lacking in interest that modern villas have been allowed to mushroom round it.

That evening in the port of Phrikes a little Greek boy was drowned. The mother, searching along the quay with several men, brought us up from our evening meal and it was John who finally sighted the boy floating out beyond the mole. They had a boat out searching by then and they picked him up and dumped him on the quay close beside us. Maybe they knew how long it would have taken his body to reach that point and realised he must be dead, for they made no attempt to revive him. But in cases of drowning there is always a chance and Göran went to work on him immediately. We were working on him for a full hour—artificial respiration, kiss of life, hot-water bottles, everything. The Greek doctor came, pronounced him dead, but indicated that we should go on trying. The father was away fishing, the mother would not touch him, but stood keening slightly as Dorothy tried to comfort her. In the end one of the family gave a hand, but it was no good. The boy was seven years old and could swim. He had been playing in the fishing boats an hour before he was found. He must have slipped and knocked himself out. In which case he could have been in the water three-quarters of an hour, which is too long. Our blankets, in which we had wrapped him, remained with us, a reminder that the sea is never as kind as it sometimes looks.

Exploration of the ports of Ithaca had been one of our chief objectives and because the neighbouring island of Cephalonia seemed to have a weather pattern of its own, so that we found it a windy place, its high mountains always cloud-covered, our visits there were restricted to the ports of Sami and Fiskardon. Sami is of interest only because, after being laid flat by the last earthquake, it was rebuilt by the British. We knew this before we arrived there, but it was a pleasant surprise to be informed of it by one of the inhabitants in a speech of welcome he made us whilst we were still securing to the quay. The good turns one nation does to another are not always appreciated and this had happened twelve years ago. Though modern, it is a pleasant little port with an underground lake and a grotto full of fantastically shaped stalagmites. But we were glad to leave it, for it is a bad place for down-draughts. Fiskardon, tucked into the extreme north of Cephalonia, clear of the high ground, is much safer as an anchorage. It is also prettier, a half circle of white houses reflected in quiet water, and the remains of a Byzantine castle sprawled over the headland above the lighthouse. Its name, a bastard version of Guiscard, bears witness to the incredible reach of another seagoing race. Robert Guiscard was a Norman, duke of Apulia and Calabria, lord of Sicily. Cattle thief, robber, pirate, he was bold enough and became powerful enough to kidnap the Pope, and he died in this little port at the northern end of Cephalonia in 1085 on his way to attack Constantinople.

If the prevailing north-westerly wind is blowing it is an easy reach across the straits from Fiskardon to the shelter of the Meganisi Channel. This narrow fjord separates the island of that name from the high blank wall of Levkas's south-east coast. A dark wild place with eagles soaring, but by Tiglia Island, in the northern part, the shallows show bright green, the sand white in the blazing sun. Of all the islands of the Ionian, Meganisi was the one we loved the best. Its shape is unusual, for the barren, sun-baked body of the island has a long whiplash tail of maquis-covered rock trailing for three miles in a south-easterly direction. There are four fjords in the deeply-indented northern coast; Port Spiglia, Port Vathy, Abelike Bay and Port Atheni. Of these, Port Atheni provides the best shelter and the best holding; it is also the most attractive. Here it always seemed to be washing day, with the staccato, insistent chatter of women mingled with the braying of donkeys to provide a dawn chorus. They were not only washing clothes and blankets, but also teasing the freshly-clipped wool of their sheep—first boiling it in blackened pots over a furze bush fire, then teasing it out in the inlet's salt water. And at night the solitude of this lonely anchorage was punctured by that haunting bird-note peculiar to these islands, a melodious whistle repeated and repeated as monotonously and persistently as a metronome.

If you land on the southern arm of the anchorage and walk north-east towards the light on Elias Point, you skirt a hill crowned by a ruined windmill and come eventually to a smaller hilltop, a circular eminence with the remains of old stone dwellings and a fabulous view of sea and mountains. The atmosphere of this place is electric with antiquity. It may only have been an old settlement—the old barley ridges below the windmill with their terraced walls certainly indicate a fair-sized village—but the ancient Greeks had a wonderful eye for the positioning of their temples and we all had the feeling that this had once been a place of sacrifice to the ancient gods. We were there at sunset with the hill slopes all about us clothed in flowering myrtle. It was one of the most beautiful places I have ever seen.

If on landing you take the opposite direction, you climb a steep stone track, usually in the company of women carrying water up from the well below, the great pots balanced effortlessly on their heads as they pick their barefoot way over the stones as daintily as that other beast of burden, the donkey. In less than a mile you come to the village of Vathahort. Here you are back in the Middle Ages, the streets rough stony tracks, the houses often so old that they must have survived innumerable earthquakes. It was Sunday evening when we first walked up to Vathahort. The whole village was out of doors, women in their best traditional costumes, mostly green and heavily pleated, with open wicker-stiffened bodice that was undoubtedly a throw-back to the bare-breasted fashion of many centuries ago, though the bosom was now covered by a high-necked blouse held with a gold clasp. The men with their usual courtesy made room for us on the crowded verandah of the kaffeneion. Out of kindness to visitors in from the sea the proprietor cooked us some fish 'borrowed' from a village family whilst his small son, operating a charcoal stove, did a roaring trade in the brochettes that they call solaiki—little skewers of mutton grilled and then sprinkled with rough sea salt mixed with oregon, finally a squeeze of lemon. We never had them quite as good on any other island and the top restaurants of the world would be hard put to it to produce meat more delectable.

Next day we had an exhaust failure when we were barely half-way to the Levkas Canal. We waited for the wind and when it came it was from due north. We beat up to the southern entrance of the canal hoping that a friendly caique would give us a pluck up to Levkas so that we could have the exhaust line repaired. But what traffic there was seemed all southbound. The wind, however, had shifted west of north so that we could just lay the first leg. With my heart in my mouth I drove for the buoys, relying on the heights beyond the salt pans to cause a continuing shift, knowing that if I were wrong there would be no room to anchor, no possible way of avoiding being driven aground. The twin buoys slid by on either side. We were committed then to a channel 32 yards wide that in less than a mile changed direction to nor'nor'west. We came to the bend. The wind was fluky, the sails shivered. We couldn't really lay it, but it was gusting now and each gust enabled us to claw away from trouble and make up a few yards to the west side of the canal. It was only after we were anchored off Levkas port that I realised how tense the passage had been.

We got the exhaust repaired, moved into the quay and spent a wretched night being attacked by mosquitoes. In the morning we found the outside of the boat literally covered with them. North again with a call at the little white mainland resort of Parga and then we started to explore the Corfu anchorages. Gouvia just across the bay from the port of Corfu is by far the easiest. It is also one of the prettiest, for you anchor just beside the rocky island on the north side of the entrance to Gouvia Bay with olive trees and cypresses for company and a magnificent view of the Albanian shore across the Straits. A track leads to a sunny land-locked inlet of the bay where a little church stands with its feet in water, linked by causeway to the shore, and there is an avenue of great cypress trees. Gouvia is little more than a crossroads and some kaffes, but you are then only two miles from the Lucciola Inn, and at the Lucciola Inn there is the best chicken pie, the best moussaka in the island, a whole range bubbling with some of the best cooking in Greece.

Next morning we drifted north under ghoster and full main. Why hurry here? High above you stands Pandokrater, its head bare to the sky, mottled brown and greens and the grey of stone, but wearing a skirt of dense olive and cypress. And across the Straits, Albania—high, remote, mysterious, touched with the white of distant snows. We found the wind lurking in the narrows of the Kerkyra Channel, a line of white water and waves breaking across the Serpa Rock. It was a dead beat. Slowly we closed the little inlet of Kassiopi, handing our No. 3 jib and jogging along under main alone whilst we examined the entrance through the glasses and made up our minds. It looked wide open to the north-west wind, which was then kicking up a steep little sea. However, this proved deceptive. The inlet is deep enough to kill most of the swell and there is a very short breakwater on the west side with sufficient depth off for you to haul stern-to after anchoring in about 10 ft almost due south of the end of it. Above the village there is the remains of a castle that once covered a quite staggering area, and below it, to the north-west, under an eroded cliff of red agglomerate, there is a beach of round white stones like eggs where the bathing is good and great iron pieces of ordnance lie half buried.

It was time to change crews again. We headed back through the Straits. There was little wind and we found ourselves drifting under ghoster towards the forbidden Albanian shore. The plain of Vrana lay green in the dry brown folds of the surrounding hills. We could see the low-roofed houses of a port along the shore. We could also see what looked like a beat-up old trawler heading out towards us, a black shape in

the sun. Cape Stilo marks the border between Albania and
Greece. Beyond it the coast runs east-south-east to the Greek
inlet of Panagia with the Albanian border paralleling it along
a ridge a mile inland. We were just able to lay Cape Stilo
and as we slid close by the off-lying rock islands we could
see the black trawler heading south towards us. It moved
very slowly so maybe it really was trawling; nevertheless, we
had a feeling that we were being shadowed. Inland we could
see what looked like small forts or gun emplacements. They
were dun-coloured and merged into the background so that
they were difficult to see with the naked eye. They were
rectangular in shape and through the glasses we could see that
they were thatched. I think, in fact, they were pens for
wintering cattle.

The wind strengthened as we ran east. A fishing boat with
a white awning was motoring close inshore and on a deserted
beach stood a small, square building flying a blue flag with
a white cross. It was a Greek frontier post and as we closed
the entrance to Panagia, which is lost in a fold of the hills and
difficult to identify, the fishing boat came roaring up astern.
A Greek corporal seized hold of our transom. 'Albunnia!
Albunnia!' he shouted, pointing to the hills above us. 'Boom,
boom, boom.' He made the gesture of firing a rifle. 'Albunnia
non buona.' I agreed that Albania was non buona, but pointed
out that Panagia was Greek territory and showed him the
chart. This fascinated him and a long discussion followed in
basic Italian from which I gathered that the corporal was
very much against our spending the night there and the fishermen were against our entering the inlet at all because we were
under engine and they had their nets slung across the far
end. Finally we abandoned the idea altogether, hoisted sail
again and had a fast beat across the Straits to anchor for the
night just south of Mouse Island, which is called on the chart
Ulysses Island. There is a shallow indent here in Corfu's rocky
coast, sheltered from the north-west wind, and on the cliffs
above, at a restaurant called the Oasis, we dined on terraces
overlooking the sea.

At Corfu John and Nancy left us. David's brother, Martin,
arrived and we headed north again with the intention of cir-

cumnavigating Corfu Island. But in the narrows by the Serpa
Rock we met the north-west wind again. It blew up very
quickly and beyond Serpa Rock the sea was all white water.
We dropped No. 2 jib in a hurry and in the confusion of
breaking waves I thought for a moment that the little Bar-
chetta Rock was a launch heading out to us from the Albanian
coast. That I could have done so was a measure of the way
the towering mass of Albania dominates one's mind in these
narrow waters. We retreated back to the sheltered waters behind Serpa Rock, for the speed with which the wind had risen
suggested a hard blow and I doubted whether the restricted
quarters of Kassiopi would be tenable in a gale. Just south of
the Serpa buoy there is the little port of Stefano, but the holding is said to be poor with a lot of weed. We retreated a little
further to the wider Kouloura Bay. The wind was already
down-draughting off the shoulder of Pandokrater and after
lunch we shifted to the small cove just north of the Venetian
fortress villa now owned by a British Naval Commander.
After dragging twice, we sent our long warp ashore and moored
in the shallows stern-on to a huge eucalyptus tree.

Moored in this way Kouloura is one of the most perfect
anchorages in Corfu. Beneath the shade of the eucalyptus
trees is a peasant's cottage built of stone. Pines and giant
cypress trees climb the hill behind. But the main charm is the
toy harbour below the 'Venetian' villa on the point. It is, in
fact, a natural harbour formed by a small sandbank on which
a protecting wall has been built. It is much too small to enter,
and anyway the warps of the half dozen or so caiques that are
always moored there stretch right across it. These gaily
painted boats are the taxis of the narrows, running a tourist
service through the shallows inshore of Serpa Rock and in
fine weather continuing up to Kassiopi.

We passed Kassiopi next day as the wind came in again
from the north-west. But it was less boisterous this time so
that we had a gentle sail along the white limestone cliffs of
Corfu's northern coast and on down the western shore, which
is all high rock with the black mouths of caves gaping to the
sea's slosh. There is no worthwhile shelter here until you
turn Cape Drasti. There, suddenly, is the little monastery of
Paleocastrizza, standing white on a high sheer headland, and

you turn east into the bay of Alipa, which is surrounded by
grottos and strange rock formations, the shore slashed by
deep, unexpected inlets. The most spectacular of these is
Speridion, named after Corfu's saint whose corpse was
brought from Cyprus, but there is little room here and it is
open to the south-west. It is better to turn into the next inlet,
hugging the sheer cliffs to port with the harbour light above
you on the rock to starboard. The northern arm of Alipa is not
visible until you are completely sheltered. The holding is hard
sand and you can moor stern-on to the refuelling buoy. We
were getting very good at this manoeuvre now; drop the
anchor, launch the dinghy, pay out chain, then motor ahead
and swing stern-on as the dinghy comes back paying out
warp—we could do it all in about ten minutes flat.

A short walk through an olive grove takes you to the shore
of Speridion and Toni Zefiros's restaurant. We booked a
table and climbed the roads to St. Maria di Paleocastrizza.
Woods all the way and a warning in French against cigarettes, which began, 'Aimez les forêts'. Old cannon stand at the
top and the view at sunset is superb. The best view, however, is from the monastery's own garden, which you reach
through a little church full of icons and votive offerings with
many silver lamps, including one with the model of an
aeroplane attached—a thank-offering from the crew of a
plane that crash-landed in the sea off Paleocastrizza without
loss of life. Paleocastrizza means 'old castle'. The monastery,
which when we were there had only six monks, was once a
Venetian stronghold. But as the power of Venice faded the
garrison retreated to the almost impregnable heights of the
peak now called St. Angelo. This castle still stands, but it is a
long climb and after a late night at Toni's, where the waiters
all seemed trained as traditional folk dancers, we were content to do the round of the grottos and get away on the midday breeze, our boatman having warned us, 'piccolo mistrale
oggi—niente vento domani.' We did not put in to the sandy
bay of Ermones where Odysseus is supposed to have landed
after his incredible swim. But we saw it in the distance and
the description fits—the north wind and the iron-bound coast
veiled in spray, and in the end the river mouth. But Nausicaa
is dead and alas we did not see the daughter of a modern

Phaeacian 'tall and beautiful as a goddess'. Nothing called us from the shore, and anyway the wind was fair and we had a date in Asprocalico.

Parga, Igoumenitza, Astakos—these were the three ports of the mainland we had so far visited. On Midsummer's Day, after a night of beauty and peace in our favourite haunt of Port Atheni on Meganisi, we sailed north through the Levkas Canal and, proceeding 10 miles up the sandy coast, turned into the dredged channel that leads to Preveza and the great inland sea of Amyrakia. On the low foreshore at the end of this dredged channel stands an old fortress half concealed by the trees. Its name is Actium and it was off Actium that the fleets of Antony and Cleopatra were routed in 31 BC. It is a strange feeling to come into those shallow waters remembering the great centralisation of Roman power that followed upon that victory. There is a beach café now at about the spot from which I imagine young Octavius watched the battle and Preveza is a modern seaside resort. But a few miles north you can still find evidence of the power of Rome; a theatre on the Greek pattern, a hippodrome, great massive walls half overgrown, the crumbling arches of an aqueduct. These are the ruins of Nicopolis, the city that Octavius, acclaimed Caesar Augustus, built to commemorate his victory.

All the flat marsh area surrounding the gulf of Amyrakia was once a breeding ground for malaria. But despite the warning in the sailing directions there is now little or no danger. The swamp land has largely been reclaimed, and though it was very hot and airless all the time we were in Preveza, we were, in fact, far less bothered by mosquitoes than we had been in Levkas. Agriculture is intensive in the flat lands bordering the inland sea. Small reed- or bamboo-thatched adobes are used for forcing and grass-thatched shelters stand in the fields to protect the sheep from the noonday sun. Cows with big double bells of brass walk the village streets with haughty disregard for lorries, and wherever you go blue haze vistas of distant hills show beyond the quiet waters of that still, empty sea.

We took a car and went north-east towards the old Greek town of Yannina and our date at Asprocalico. The day was broiling hot. Cool glimpses of the empty 'sea', the distant view of mountains purple against a hard blue sky, and in the fields gangs of men and women sweating as they hoed. The flax was green and bamboos rustled with the reeds where the sluggish river water spread to marshlands. We came to the hills and traces of the aqueduct the Romans had built to carry water 45 miles to Nicopolis. Just short of Arta, which was once the Roman town of Ambracia, we turned north and in a few minutes had reached our objective, the Asprocalico gorge. E. S. Higgs, whom I had last seen in Cambridge, was camped with his undergraduate team in an olive grove beside the river. It was cool here under the shade of the trees with the water rushing by, and above us as we talked stood the great arches of Caesar's aqueduct. But Higgs was not interested in Roman remains. Even the older classical Greece meant little to him. A palaeontologist and one of the world's few specialists on ancient bones, it was the prehistory of man that fascinated him, and on this subject he talked endlessly with the concentrated fluency of a man dedicated entirely to his subject.

The previous year he and his team had walked 250 miles from the Macedonian border searching for some trace of early man and finding nothing. And then, right at the end of the season, they had come upon relics of an old chert flake industry. Chert is hard and brittle like flint; it was used for hand axes and arrow heads, the flakes for giving a lacerating edge to the arrow shafts. Finally, in the gorge itself, they had found a cave shelter.

One of the Land-Rovers took us there. The gorge is limestone, much scored by the eroding force of the river. Indeed, at the entrance to the gorge a great hole has been worn through the rock to form a natural bridge high up on the cliff side. This has given the name to the nearby village of Ayios Giorgios, which means St. George. The story goes that when St. George slew the dragon (St. George, incidentally, slew dragons all over Greece and the Eastern Mediterranean!) the beast in the agony of its death throes chewed great lumps out of the side of the gorge. The cave shelter was two or three hundred feet above the road, a shallow, scooped-out recess in the side of the gorge. It faced south, as all old shelter dwellings do, and standing under the over-hanging rock with the river running below us, we commanded the whole sweep and the bend of the gorge. The Asprocalico river—Asprocalico means white stones—is cutting down into the bedrock at the rate of 1/20th of an inch per year. Thirty thousand years ago it would have been at least 120 ft higher than its present level. Black goats foraged on the hill slopes on either side of us and the tinkle of their bells mingled with those of a great flock of sheep moving along the river bank. The bells and the noise of the river were the only sounds.

Higgs's team had only arrived a few days before so that the dig was not yet at an interesting stage. The previous year they had only had time to open up a trial trench. This trench had been dug to a depth of 20 ft and all the way down they had been opening up successive layers of man's occupa-tion of the shelter. At the end of the season they had reached down to the Mousterian level, thirty thousand years back in time. They had then filled the trench in again with rubble and rebuilt the stone fence, for the shelter is still used for wintering goats. Now, at the beginning of a new season, they had just removed the goat fence. What will they find when they have finally obtained all the answers from this dig, which is unique in the Balkan area? Will they bridge the Mous-terian–Cro-Magnon gap? Will they prove that Cro-Magnon man, who developed so remarkably in France and who ousted the Mousterian (a branch of Neanderthal man), came from the east? The rock at the back of the shelter is blackened by fire and at the lower levels the fire marks are covered by a calcareous film. The fire marks are therefore very old, and what Higgs is hoping to find, as his dig opens up the entire shelter floor, is the remains of a hearth or perhaps a series of hearths at various levels. And since these prehistoric people buried their dead beside their hearths, there is just a chance that he may uncover skeletal remains, even a skull.

Leaving the shelter we went back to the Land-Rover and Higgs then took us to see a phenomenon that from the point of view of a sailor was even more interesting. We drove south from the gorge to a point on the road where Caesar's engineers had tunnelled the aqueduct through a hill. The high narrow opening of this tunnel is still there and you can walk into it for about 25 yards before you are stopped by a rock fall. We climbed above the tunnel entrance and at the top of a hill came suddenly upon a strange moonscape of red dunes. This is one of the last vestiges, perhaps even a unique vestige, of a glaciation period 20,000 years or so ago when the level of the Mediterranean was at least 100 ft less than it is today. It was a dry, cold period, and the exposed red earth of the African shore was swept north by high winds. Most of Greece was covered then by a deposit of red dust two or three hundred feet thick. It was easily eroded in later periods of high rain-fall and even this remaining pocket is rapidly disappearing. Recent erosion is marked by the stone ventilation shafts of the Roman aqueduct which now stands proud by anything up to 50 ft. And in the troughs of the red dunes you can see old mountain tops just showing, the breccia of early ice ages lying undisturbed as perfect examples of the effect of extreme cold on rock.

Higgs, talking all the time of a period so remote it was almost inconceivable, walked with his large domed head in-clined to the ground. His shoulders were slightly rounded as though the result of a lifetime peering at the ground for traces of early man. Every now and then he would stop and pick up a piece of chert. This was a Bronze Age chipping— about 7,000 years old; that was 12,000 years; the pale ochre-coloured chippings were older—about 17,000 years. So we went back through time in the oven heat of that dead sound-less world of red, packed dust. And all the time I was remem-bering my charts, the waters we had sailed among the islands of the south, trying to visualise in my mind what the Ionian coast of Greece would have looked like with the sea level lower by 100 ft. All the Levkas marsh would have been dry land, Meganisi barely an island, the great inland sea of Amy-rakia no more than a river bed—and over it all the great south wind blowing and the sky red with dust, the sun half-obscured.

Back to the camp then to wash the red dust off in the cold fast-running waters of the Asprocalico, and as we left, goats were being milked under the Roman arches and the tinkle of the sheep bells sounded across the river. The bright little huddle of tents beside the river, the Teddy bear lying on the ground where Higgs's young wife sat with her baby, the students squatting on the ground eating their evening meal . . . the scene suggested a holiday camp rather than an expedition intent on wresting one more small grain of knowledge about man's past from a Greek hillside. The sun was setting as we left the mountains behind. Everywhere Greek peasants were returning from the day's toil in the fields, the village kaffes full of men drinking coffee or ouzo, the streets crowded with carts, horses, even cattle, and near Preveza the great ruins of Nicopolis standing black against the pale evening light.

One day of rest and preparation, and then we motored out past Actium's crumbling fort, hoisted sail and started on the 365-mile voyage back to Malta. All that first day out from Preveza we watched the storm clouds building up astern, great anvils of cunim rising high above the Pindus Mountains, the sky black. And as night fell heavy sheets of lightning flashed. The stars above us were diamond bright, but we wondered what it was like now in the Asprocalico gorge. The little camp had looked so pretty, the setting so perfect. How would it be with the rain thundering down, the roar of the river increasing as the flood waters rose?

The sea was lumpy, the wind increasing. By morning it was blowing force 4 from the north-west. Dolphins came to keep us company, the smaller, darker variety in the morning, larger ones in the afternoon. They were surfing on the forward surge of the waves, gathering in fours and fives to make concerted mock attacks. From the bows we could see the skin valve on the top of their heads opening as they vented, could see the way they gathered speed with a muscular up and down thrust of the last third of their bodies, the big black tail fins beating. Their large eyes stared as they rolled, watching us curiously, their underbellies gleaming white. We saw swordfish jumping, the occasional flying fish, and then as the sun sank the wind left us.

We were lucky—we had been able to sail 128 miles. Away from the coast, June is a month of little wind, and the previous year on the Pylos-Malta run we had only managed to sail 28 miles. We motored all the night and all next day, except for a short period under spinnaker when we were nearly run down by a coaster. She was the *Sta Maria del Pina* and all the after part of the ship was festooned with socks. We could only suppose that the skipper had done a salvage deal! The heat haze was so bad that afternoon that we were seriously concerned about our landfall on the coast of Sicily. I have noted before, however, that haze in the Mediterranean is very like the gauze curtain in a theatre, the sun acting as the footlights and rendering it impenetrable. As the sun set the cone of Etna appeared, suddenly and very dramatically, on our starboard bow, the whole volcanic mass of the mountain lit from behind. Visions of a quiet night anchored in Syracuse were soon dispelled by the night and a series of unidentifiable lights. Charts are one of the many hazards of organising a voyage with the boat laid up 1,000 miles from home. I had thought that chart 187, Palma to Catania, was on board, but though I searched the chart table drawers, through the two hundred and more charts that I have accumulated there, I could not find it. I had the small-scale chart of the Eastern Mediterranean, but, whilst answering the purpose for coastal navigation in daylight, this omits to give the lights. As a result we spent a frustrating and sleepless night motoring from one unidentifiable headland to the next. There was not a breath of wind, the surface of the sea like a polished mirror, so smooth you could have skated on it.

Dawn found us in a milky void of intense humidity searching for the coast. We eventually found it off Cape Passaro, the south-east corner of Sicily, with yachts drifting limp-sailed in the heat. This was the Syracuse-Malta race in which we should have competed if the fascination of early man had not delayed us. We lazed and bathed our way across the Malta Channel and the following morning we entered Grand Harbour, the stone of the great fortresses warm and yellow in the sunlight. We cleared Customs and headed north-west to the little island of Comino, which lies in the channel between Malta and Gozo, washing the salt off sheets and blocks as we sailed. There are very few places to anchor on the sea-eroded limestone coasts of the Maltese archipelago, but in the north-west corner of Comino there is a little sandy cove full of grottos and strange fish where the shallows are a brilliant emerald green. There in the peace of this perfect spot, with the bells of Gozo's many churches ringing across the narrow channel, we dealt with the rest of *Mary Deare*'s gear, preparing the ship once again for her long ten months' lay-up at Manoel Island.

VI

TO THE GOLDEN HORN

Crew for Istanbul—1966
Major C. R. Stirling
Captain Ian Peradon
David Hare
Richard Ballantyne
Freda and Raymond Hughes
David Stokoe

For those who sail in the Mediterranean, the problem of Turkey has to be faced sooner or later. I knew the difficulties —but having seen the Turkish coast from the Dodecanese two years before I had to go, I had to see Troy and the ruins of Ionian cities; above all, I wanted to sail my own boat through the Dardanelles and across the Sea of Marmara to Istanbul, to see the Golden Horn and the Bosphorus. We left Malta on Monday, May 2, 1966. Bob was with us as usual, and Ian, who had helped sail the boat out from England in 1963. Our major problem, as it turned out, was to be our engine. This failed us almost immediately after we had slipped from the marina. I got it going again, but 27½ miles west of Malta, it packed up with a cracked cooling box and a blown gasket.

The gods were kind, however; a breeze came in from the nor'nor'east, backed to north, then to north-west, finally to west. For 2½ days and nights we ran continuously under our cruising spinnaker, only handing it at 1300 hours on the Saturday when we were in the channel between the west end of Crete and the island of Anti Kithera. It was a most perfect passage—by night a full moon and the blue-and-white striped spinnaker bellying out in front, the occasional grunting vent of a dolphin; by day, stripped to the waist, bright sunlight sparkling on the ever-empty sea. Our enjoyment of these days was only marred by nagging concern about the lack of engine when we closed the windy shores of Crete and by the arrival on board of tired, bedraggled birds—linnets mainly—all solitary stragglers trailing the main migratory stream north from Africa. Most of them died in the dawn, their little matchstick legs turned stiffly upward. Few would touch the food we offered them and those that had the strength to take off again seemed to suffer from the movement of the ship, circling many times before recovering their sense of direction; some never recovered it, disappearing in the wrong direction.

The only ships we sighted were a squadron of the 6th Fleet. An uncanny experience this. At 0215 on the Thursday night I was sitting alone at the helm, in a hazy void of opaque, moonlit water, when I was jerked awake by the sight of mast-head steaming lights bearing down on me. I had just checked through the glasses that the vessel would pass close under my stern when more steaming lights appeared over the horizon; first one, then another. Finally there were five ships spread out in a great fan, and every one of them steaming almost directly at me. It is not pleasant to know that you are cast in the role of radar mouse to five destroyers playing cat-pounce, even more unpleasant to see looming up dead ahead a series of red vertical lights topped by what looks like the gas flare of an oil refinery. Slab-sided in the moonlight at a half-mile range this monster looked more like a floating dock than 70,000 tons of carrier. Their mission of frightening the life out of me completed, the five escorting destroyers put on double flank and slid with uncanny silence and speed over the horizon astern, leaving *Mary Deare* wallowing in a confused sea that was badly cut up by their wake and the carrier's cumbersome manoeuvres to avoid us. The only comfort I got out of the whole rather disturbing half-hour was the reflection that my steel-hulled boat showed up on their radar screens. This does not, however, entitle anybody with a steel hull to infer that they can take liberties with some other radar-equipped ships, particularly tankers—some 100,000 tonners now have only 11 officers and men on board!

Dead reckoning can never be accurate in the Mediterranean

since the current factor is a matter of guesswork, and it was important to know our exact position as we closed the islanded passage between Kithera and Crete. Ian is a professional navigator, but this had one disadvantage—his enthusiasm for sextant work often coincided with his deck watch. On entering the Kithera Channel we made the customary libation to Poseidon and all Saturday sailed Crete's northern shore, the sea bright, the air crystal clear. To starboard jagged cliffs streamed down from volcanic, knife-edged ridges, and beyond loomed great snow-clad mountains. At dawn next day the wind switched suddenly to south, came whistling down the gap between Mount Ida and Mount Krapi. We reefed in a hurry, and then a few minutes later rolled them out and hoisted genoa again. Crete is a dark, windy place, but by mid-afternoon we were becalmed within sight of the main port of Heraklion. If the engine had been working we could have been in port in time for tea and snug in our beds that night instead of fighting the elements.

The calm ended at about 1730 with a light breeze from the south-east. We got under way with full main and genoa, but almost immediately it was blowing force 5 and we were reefing. We stood out to Standia Island, expecting the wind to drop with the sun. Instead, it increased, gusting furiously across the narrow waist of Crete and down the mountain-spined valleys that run towards Heraklion. We hove-to, bows-on to the lights of the port, *Mary Deare* making steadily to windward so that forty minutes later we were off the entrance. The wind, funnelling straight out of the harbour mouth, made entry impossible. We handed No. 3 jib and skidded off down-wind, rounded-to and jogged to windward under main alone. It was now gusting force 8. This went on for three hours. Finally, fearful of the strain on the mainsail, we hoisted storm jib and beat very fast up to the harbour mouth. There was shelter here, but a racing boat will not heave-to without making to windward. In the end I decided to risk anchoring, jilling to the east and letting go about 300 yards off what looked like a sandy bluff. We were quite snug here under the lee, but two hours later the wind switched abruptly 140°. The main was up in very quick time, but even so the seas were already quite big, the boat snatching at the chain so violently

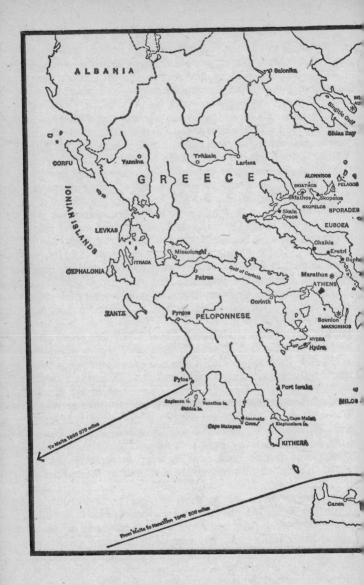

we could not fetch our anchor. The chain was almost certainly jammed in a rock crevice, for whilst we were preparing to buoy it and let slip the whole length, it parted. *Mary Deare* immediately began to blow shorewards. After anchoring we had rolled in more reefs and even with the jib up, she had not enough sail to claw her way off against the breaking seas. I tried to gybe her round, but she had no way on her and would not answer to the helm.

We were now sailing sluggishly level with the coast and falling steadily down on to it. I remember thinking—this is it, we are going to be blown ashore. Ian suggested gybing again. 'She'll come round if you let the main fly,' he said. There was no alternative and so I turned her towards the shore, now very close indeed, with Bob slacking away the mainsheet. This moment is very vivid in my mind—the shore, now revealed as a mass of rocks, coming nearer and nearer as the boat gathered way, and myself at the helm waiting, tensed, for the moment when her bows would crunch against the rocks. Slowly she began to answer to the helm. And then suddenly we were round and over my shoulder I saw black rocks sliding away, so close they almost seemed to be touching the keel. 'It's all right, everything's under control,' I heard Ian say in a quiet, matter-of-fact voice to Dorothy, who had appeared in the hatch with life jackets and passports, the two things necessary to make our entry into Greece!

It was the nearest I have come to losing my ship. That I made the mistake of anchoring under the lee was partly due to my East Coast training and partly to the fact that I was a stranger to this island of vicious down-draughts. I should have run down-wind, but that would have meant abandoning Crete, and after a week of sailing, with Crete as our goal, we were not inclined to accept defeat. The log records: 'Got away fast then, sorting out the tangle on the foredeck in flurries of spray, the remains of the chain and the nylon ropes and the buoy with which we had tried to save the anchor. Jilled between Standia Island and the harbour entrance until dawn. A temporary lull then; let out three rolls and lay for the harbour working on the engine. Finally it fired and gave just enough power to get us in to the old Venetian port, where we lay to our second anchor stern-on to the quay opposite the castle. Very tired and a little battered. Just turned in and the Customs arrived.' After a long sail Dorothy makes straight for a haidresser and it was the girl operating the drier who told her that there had been a severe earth tremor during the night!

Next day, instead of seeing Crete, we stood watch over a dirty and very puzzled mechanic. The basic trouble was finally diagnosed, the cooling box repaired, a new gasket made, valves reground. He was on board all the following day, the after part of the ship stripped out, everything filthy, and in the end the engine worked, but with smoke coming from the exhaust—not a good sign. The charge for this first mechanic was about double what it should have been, and he was the dirtiest. This may have coloured our feeling about Crete, for we did not fall in love with either the country or its people the way we had with the Cyclades. The Cretans are quite different from the rest of the Aegean islanders—a harder, more violent people. Their character is no doubt bred of the harshness of their island. It is a volcanic place, the terrain more hostile than any I have seen in the Mediterranean, except perhaps Santorin, 80 miles to the north. They talk endlessly, and always about themselves, which is perhaps why they make good politicians—the present Greek Government is full of Cretan ministers. But they do not regard themselves as Greeks. They are Cretans.

In some extraordinary way Evans's reconstruction of Knossos matched our feelings and gave us the sense of racial continuity. Knossos is not beautiful, but it is strangely powerful, which is true also of the unreconstructed palace of Minos's brother at Phaestos. Even the remains of the king's summer palace at Aga Triada on the southern coast have the same sense of power built into them. The whole island is very important archaeologically, for, unlike the rest of Greece, it has never been mulcted of its treasures. The Cretans have sensibly insisted that nothing of the past should be taken out and, as a result, the archaeological museum at Heraklion, which is large and very well laid out, has one of the finest displays of pre-Christian indigenous art in the world.

The port of Heraklion is crowded to overflowing in the raisin season, but at any time the main quay is interesting, full of inter-island caiques and beat-up relics of the steam age. When we were there a new flagpole was being erected over the Customs House for the ceremonial return of the skull of St. Titus, the first Christian to spread the gospel in Crete. He died in Venice and the Venetians had finally returned the skull to the Greek Government, who were sending it by warship to Heraklion. We had seen the ruins of this saint's church and close by a concave wall constructed of tablets recording the laws of Phaestos's king in the ancient script. This is on the road across the narrow waist of Crete. I would have liked to have visited the wild north part of the island, but our route lay eastward. The sun was shining when we left, and out beyond Standia Island in the evening light we could see the snows of Mt. Ida behind us, and in front, more snow-capped mountains, the grizzled head of Dicta, where Zeus was raised. It was pale moonlight when, in the early hours, I closed the rocky headland that guards the entrance to Spinalonga and jogged quietly, waiting for the dawn. And when it came, we motored in through the narrows below the empty ruins of houses and the massive fortress that stands on Leper's Island. It was here that the engine failed again. We anchored quickly in the still glass fjord, and six hours later, whilst I was still working on the engine, we reefed and hoisted sail in a hurry, for this is a bad place for down-draughts and from utter stillness it was suddenly blowing half a gale. The little port of Ayios Nikolaos was close by and we had a fast sail in blattering down-blasts. It blew all night, the trees bending to the weight of it, and in the morning we slipped, lay to our anchor whilst we reefed 4 rolls, and then sailed out, bound for Rhodes.

The sea-bright morning faded to winter grey, the waves were 12 ft high and we had a bumpy ride of it out to the bare rock islands that lie off the eastern end of Crete and through the narrow passage between Dragonera and Pexamada; grey seas, cave-gapped rock, and large flights of sea birds skimming. The wind increased as night closed in, our last sight of Crete a dark, impressive line of mountains hanging over the horizon astern against a violent sky. By morning we had raised the west tip of Rhodes and the weather was improving. We shook out the reefs two at a time and hoisted No. 2.

Under the land the wind came astern and the sun shone again as we searched for the only hazard—Khina Rocks. We located them eventually, a tiny, dragon-toothed bit of rubbish lying alone in the empty sea and I was glad we were not sailing this coast at night, for they were unlit. We closed Lindos in the evening, the re-erected pillars of the acropolis standing clear and bright in the sunset, and all the rocks a warm, golden colour.

That night, massive above us in the moonlight, loomed the great castle of the Knights, the town at its feet glimmering white, and in the morning sun we rowed ashore, climbing intricately patterned cobbled paths to the great stone staircase that is the castle's only entrance. Here, in the rock face, the ancient Greeks had carved out a seat in the form of the prow of a 'black ship'. The ruins of their acropolis stand above the castle and include many large curved seats and the well-heads of rock cisterns, but it was the site rather than the ruins themselves that staggered, its sea vista almost as breathtaking as Sounion.

As the mule-borne tourist hordes moved in, we went down into the town to sit in a quiet little taverna under a lacing of vine and eat plates of octopus, cooked in oil over charcoal with garlic and herbs. Lunch down in the bay at a beach-side restaurant that was invaded by a bus-load of Swedish youths—overblown nymphets and boys of doubtful gender; it was like a teenage film. By afternoon thunder clouds were building up, a swell coming in. We had anchored in 33 ft about a cable off the end of what passed for a jetty, and though we rolled heavily that night and I was up anchor-watching in the small hours with rain falling and lightning flashing, we did not drag. The dawn was heavily overcast, with seas breaking in the narrow entrance. The engine just took us out before it began to smoke. The wind died and we lay for twelve hours making little progress with sails slatting to the roll. A breeze came in with the darkening of night and in the middle of Dorothy's dinner of stuffed aubergines we were suddenly doing 6 knots under ghoster; we had very fast sailing then, well-reefed, so that we were off Rhodes by midnight. The sea was unpleasant, and remembering the tragedy of *Trenchemer*, I waited for the dawn, when we berthed ourselves in Mandraki harbour between two sailing boats, both American and both round-the-worlders. *Neophyte II* was replacement for a boat that had been cut in half by a merchant vessel off Sydney; Lee Quinn, a journalist, was sailing her round the world with two girls. *Kismet* was jointly owned by two couples from Boston, who had worked desperately hard for 5 years to save enough money to purchase a boat and make the voyage—they were now reaching the end of the 3-year circumnavigation they had planned, and very sad about it. They particularly attracted us, for they were not escapists— they had done it as a way of seeing the world, an exercise in the excitement of living whilst they were young enough to enjoy it.

Bob and Ian both left us at Rhodes, the boat stripped out again and more mechanics on board, and the sun in total eclipse, a darkening gloom at midday that was extremely eerie. It was here that David and Richard joined us from England. We now had two good dinghy sailors aboard, which was just as well, for when we left the engine was still far from healthy and Istanbul over 600 miles away, a dead beat against the prevailing wind. Just north of Rhodes is the island of Symi and we put in to Panormittis for the night, a little harbour in the cliffs with a huge monastery sprawled along almost the entire length of the waterfront. Monk Margaritis greeted us, bearded with bright twinkling eyes and a person- ality that bubbled with vitality. The monastery had over 200 rooms, owned all the country round, even the harbour itself, and this monk, who lives alone there with his old abbot, was virtual lord of a great estate. He invited us in, up the broad steps to a gleaming white courtyard where cleaning women, going home, came to hand him their keys. The church was on our left, dim inside, the gold paint of icons gleaming faintly, the glint of many silver lamps, and pictures of the Archangel Michael to whose services the monastery is dedicated. Most beautiful of all, six short slender columns of great antiquity, part of a temple to Poseidon that was incor- porated in the Christian structure. In a room overlooking the harbour he gave us glasses of grappa which he had made him- self from the monastery grapes and flavoured with figs, the naked light bulb shimmering on old books, and as I pushed the shuttered windows open and stood looking out across the steel-grey water darkening to night, I was thinking of the monk's story—how during the war they had been evacuated to Rhodes, the caique had been overwhelmed by a storm and nearly everyone drowned—he had sworn then that if he survived he would devote himself to the service of God and later he had studied theology at the great monastery of Patmos. I was thinking, too, of this monastery, how once a year, at the time of the festival of the Archangel Michael, patron saint of fishermen, it was overrun with a thousand pilgrims, at all times open to men who wished to study and meditate. It was a strange, placid world, quite removed from modern life, and yet, coming from the sea, from the sight of the heavens at night, the rocks and the water by day, the elements a part of our daily existence, it did not seem either incongruous or remote.

The monk came down to the taverna especially to order our evening meal for us and when he said goodbye he did a very strange thing—he handed me his card; it was printed in English and read—Monk Gabriel Margaritis, Monastery of Panormittis, Island Simi, Dodecanese-Greece. We left at first light, a little before five in the morning, with three rolls down and No. 3; a long beat out to Cape Khrio, and then slow headway north, beating all the time against the Meltemi back and forth between the islands and the Turkish coast. The wind increased steadily throughout the day and it was fast sailing in bright sunshine, the salt of spray caking on our faces, burning like a chemical and gritty behind tired eyeballs. We drove hard like this for 86 miles to make good the 50 miles to Kos, a bumpy, tiring ride, and there was no let-up in the wind until we were inside the sheltering arms of the old harbour of the Knights; sudden peace then as we glided in under sail to anchor in the still black waters under the lee of the castle walls. And in the morning, after breakfasting ashore off charcoal grilled meat sandwiched between hot bread, we sailed for Turkey.

Bodrum is only a dozen miles from Kos, a deep inlet on the south side of one of those great peninsulas which stretch predatory fingers out to the Greek islands. This was once the Greek city of Halicarnassus. It was here Mausolus built his colossal tomb. There is nothing left of this first mausoleum, one of the Seven Wonders; it was all torn down by the Knights who used its stone and marble to build the great castle which still dominates this little Turkish town. We anchored under its bulk, careful to avoid the 'secret port' which once sheltered the Knights' guardship and is now a submerged pattern in the harbour water marked by a rusting buoy. Ashore, we went through the whole long bureaucratic rigmarole of entry, helped by a woman who spoke English—the harbourmaster first, then Immigration, then Customs, finally Security Police. How long do you stay? What time do you leave? 'It depends on the wind. My engine is not working.' How do you explain the problems of sail to people who have never been out in anything but a motorboat?

Bodrum's single narrow street seemed composed almost entirely of souvenir shops selling sponges and the products of a local shell craft that included necklaces made of coiled mollusc shells that we had seen nowhere else. The castle of St. Peter towered above the town, the red flag of Turkey with its star and crescent flying from its towers, a startling splash of colour against the cloudless blue of the sky. It is a strange place, more impressive even than the great castle at Rhodes, since there is a tower for every *langue* of the Order, some of them incorporating round column drums from the Tomb of Mausolus, the English tower in particular; marble from the same source was used for carving the escutcheons of the Knights in a material resistant to the weather, so that there are many more of these heraldic shields than in Rhodes or Kos or Lindos. The little chapel of the Knights is now a museum containing the largest collection in Turkey of ceramics of the Mycenean period, and higher up there is another museum, a most unusual one exhibiting a collection of underwater finds from two sunken ships; old stone anchors, amphorae, eating tables, Bronze Age ships' gear going back to 1300 BC, together with photographic records showing how the American aqualung divers organised the 'dig'.

In our first evening ashore we walked inland with a copy of the old archaeological chart, a survey made by Cdr. Thomas Spratt of HMS *Volage* in 1847. These old charts have recently been released by the Admiralty and I had arranged for

he whole series covering the Turkish coast to be brought out
o me from England. The Bodrum chart showed the old walls
of Halicarnassus climbing up to the heights above the modern
own. It must have been a huge city, but since the chart was
made the walls have largely disappeared. Up above the old
Greek theatre we came upon camels grazing, and higher up
he slope we could see the cave mouths of old sepulchres where
he Greeks had placed their dead. Below, only a few hundred
yards from the harbour shore, a Danish archaeological expedition was making the first exploratory dig on the site of the
Mausoleum; they had uncovered a section of the outer wall,
and in deep trenches, the stones immediately above the bed-
rock, which had been protected by 5 metres of accumulated
topsoil, were as white and smooth as the day they had been
laid.

Late that afternoon, a breeze having at last come in, we left
in a hurry, not realising that the whole round of officials we
had visited on arrival had to be repeated on departure. As a
result, we had no certificate of health. We would have liked
to put in to one of the ports of the Gulf of Mandalya, but
with no engine, time was already pressing and we had a
wind. It was very beautiful that night and, as always when we
are driving through a kindly sea, Dorothy sat alone in the
bows for a while before turning in. From where I stood at the
helm I could see just her head, very still, in silhouette against
the stretched white Terylene of the genoa. Later the wind
died and we glided in a moonlit world past the island of
Pserimos and north along the shores of the Greek sponge
island of Kalimnos. Dawn found us amongst off-lying islands
of bare rock, but soon the Meltemi came in again from the
north-west and we gathered speed—Leros, Lipso, Arki. a
whole chain of islands disappearing into the heat haze. The
wind backed, no longer the Meltemi, but becoming southerly
—sirocco weather, humid and heavy. We eased sheets and
sped north, a distant glimpse of Patmos with its great monastery high on the island's summit, and then the bulk of
Samos coming clearer, towering higher in the haze. A difficult
decision then—whether to go the long, safe way round, or to
risk being becalmed without an engine in the narrows between
the island and the Turkish mainland? We held for the Straits,

praying that the wind would stay with us. Dim in the dusk the rocky entrance to the port St. Paul had used slid by. We were committed then to the dog-leg passage with the lights of a cruise liner showing at the far end. We met her at the most dangerous point, between the lit rock island in the middle and the Samos shore, and behind us blazed the lights of Pythagorion where we had lain two years before.

It was dark when we emerged from the Straits, the wind still with us, carrying us quickly north to Kus Adasi, the port for Ephesus and our next objective. With only one irreplaceable anchor left and no engine, I baulked at entering this unknown port at night. We sailed off and on till the first pale light of dawn crept over the Turkish mountains, then we exchanged No. 3 jib for No. 2 and headed in. A gunboat put out to meet us, swung sharply round with a great roar of engines to lie just ahead of us, indicating that we should come alongside. No doubt they wondered what we had been up to, sailing back and forth all night close off the Turkish coast. However, when they realised we were going in to Kus Adasi, they gave us leave to proceed. The wind fell light and we changed to the ghoster, feeling our way in gently past the castle with its lighthouse and into the small boat harbour close against the shore. It was very shallow, the weedy bottom clearly visible, and the wind died completely. However, it had been dredged close up to the quay and a kindly Turkish fisherman gave us a pluck in.

The Customs officer here was more than friendly—he waived the entry procedure. The Governor himself came down to welcome us, and when he realised our engine was out of action, he sent his inspector of municipal diesels to examine it, together with the Professor of English at the local Lycée to interpret. The engine was absolutely essential to us if we were to make up against the currents of the Dardanelles to Istanbul, where David and Richard had air passages booked to England and three other friends were flying out to join us. The inspector worked on it himself, got it going and we motored out into the bay for engine trials with half the officials of the port on board. We were then free to explore, and the following day we left very early on one of the longest taxi drives I have ever made—over 500 kilometres. We went south to Priene through a lush green country, some of it irrigated; great plantations of fig trees, olives as well and some fruit. There were horses with foals, fluffy donkey babies beside their dams, and big, flat-headed dogs with shaggy white coats. Storks were nesting, the young straining their necks for the food their slow-flapping parents brought them. It was Sunday, yet women in baggy trousers were working in the fields. The men, dark and solemn in their black clothes, were gathered in the shade of the cafés. The ruins of Priene lie fantastically set under a towering cliff with the great Meander plain stretching away to the south. It was once a port and you can still see the old boat harbour, now many miles from the sea.

Out into the plain, along a straight dirt road, we crossed the yellow, almost orange slash of the silt-laden Meander by a rickety wooden bridge. Bee-eaters and rollers flashed brilliant colours above the reeds and then we were on the south side of the plain, at Miletus with its great theatre climbing the slope of a hill. The ruins of the old city, spread over a great area, lie half buried in a jungle of growth, half-water-logged in swamp land, truncated columns thrusting out of reeds, cattle and horses grazing and a young farmer in a broad-brimmed hat offering us Roman oil lamps—or were they modern reproductions? Didyma is only a little further south, a village dominated by the great temple to Apollo, massive, towering columns and the secret sacrificial court unroofed but otherwise virtually intact. Apart from the Parthenon, this is perhaps the most impressive of the ruins of ancient Greece, and after climbing to the walls above the court of the twelve pillars we sat in a café gazing at this astonishing spectacle, drinking beer and ayran, which is yoghourt whisked up with salt and soda water, a local drink to which I had been introduced by the governor of Kus Adasi—'It is very good for the stomach.' It was certainly refreshing in the heat.

We went back across the Meander plains by another road, cut up to the fast north-south highway, and two hours later struck off on a cobbled road that took us through pine-clad slopes and rock gorges to Aphrodisias. Storks were nesting on the high tops of columns, and in a stretch of swamp land, noisy with the croak of frogs, a little white marble odeon lay basking in the sun, so fresh and new-looking that, seated in one of the dolphin-carved marble chairs, I could almost believe that the actors would appear at any moment. The ruins of this temple city are spread wide. Most of it is still below the earth that has hidden it for centuries, American archaeologists having only recently started work on it. Yet this, I was told, might one day be more impressive than Ephesus. We went on to the village, where carved sarcophagi stood paraded outside a long wooden cattle shed in the dark interior of which lay the treasures, the finely-sculpted figures, the carved column heads that the archaeologists had dug up. There was a café opposite and we sat under an enormous plane tree on a marble seat 'borrowed' from the odeon and drank coffee and water. It was evening as we started back, and on the cobbled road we ran into a wedding party that looked more like a picture from the Russian Revolution—the men, arms linked and very drunk, a bottle of raki going the rounds and minstrels playing, a balalaika and fiddlers, and over their swaying heads the blood-red crimson flag of Turkey flying in the sunset. We had two near misses on the main road back, for these peasant people are not yet mentally geared to the speed of modern travel, and after the second our driver, who was badly shaken, stopped at a garage pull-in for long-distance buses, where they dispensed ayran, coffee, moussaka, and the peanut vendors did a roaring trade. And so to the quay where our boat lay and a late meal in a restaurant overlooking the water. Next to it was an open-air café covering almost an acre where families in from the country on a day's outing sat round samovars and the men sucked smoke from the mouthpieces of hookahs hired from the management.

We went to Ephesus, of course, but after what we had seen that day the ruins that bring Hellenic cruises from half across the world seemed less impressive. It was the sheer size of it that staggered us. Cdr. Richard Copeland had surveyed the walls for the chart he drew in 1836, but at that time little else apparently showed above ground. Now the exposed ruins cover more than a mile, spanning two millennia of time, and when we were there the work of opening it up was still going on, for only one-eighth of it has so far been exposed. The temple of Artemis, which for 1500 years was the raison

d'être of the old pagan city, was nothing but a hole in the
ground the size of a large field—nothing there but the top
of a column standing out of the water, another amongst the
reeds, and children bathing. But the greatness of Ephesus was
that it spanned both the pagan and the Christian eras, for it
was here that St. John wrote his Gospel. He died there and
the ruins of the great church erected to his memory still stand,
grand and magnificent, near the Turkish fort beyond the little
town of Selçuk. High above, on a hill, a sanctuary stands on
what is believed to have been the last home of the Virgin
Mary, whom Christ had committed to his care. Because of this
Ephesus became a place of Christian pilgrimage, a city of
200,000 people, and the trade that flowed through its port to
the interior of Asia made it second only to Alexandria as the
entrepôt of the East. In the swamp land formed by a tributary
of the Cayster river we could still see traces of the stone dykes
built in a forlorn attempt to keep the port from silting up,
and on the long ridge of the hills above there were still
vestiges of the great protecting wall that Copeland had surveyed. But in retrospect, it is the charm of the little sanctuary
of the Virgin Mary that has left the deepest impression, the
quiet peace of its shaded spring and the fine view from the
hairpinned road that leads up to it.

For the first time in her life *Mary Deare* was watered by
a fire-engine, and after an exasperating 3-hour wait whilst
the local agent cleared us, we got away at 1800 hours. The
wind died and we motored hour after hour through the night,
and in the morning we had reached out to the end of the last
long Turkish peninsula, to the narrows between Anatolia and
the Greek island of Khios, the sea flat calm and the engine
occasionally missing on one cylinder. By evening we were
heading out to the westernmost tip of Mytilene, better known
by its old name of Lesbos; the sea was glassy, the heat heady,
and as night fell the curve of *Mary Deare*'s bow-wave spattered drops of liquid phosphorescent light, her wake a glowing line of white streaming astern of us. We worried about
the engine and kept going—there was nothing else to be done.
A second dawn, and still motoring, but the scene had changed
—gone were the high islands and headlands; instead, the coast
was low, fringed with the white of limestone. Was that flat

land the plains of Troy? We passed close by the island of Bozca Ada, long shelves of rock white in the sun, and ahead were steamers in the haze pointing the entrance to the Dardanelles. We rounded Tarsan Adas and saw the long barrels of guns on the distant headland overshadowed by the 70-ft obelisk of stone brought from England, the memorial to men who died in a war that began over half a century ago. Beyond it, on the first point inside the entrance, stood the massive, four-legged, almost Martian monument to the Turkish dead.

We had only five gallons of fuel left as we entered the Dardanelles, motoring close under the lighthouse and the war memorials, so close, to avoid the current, that rock showed under our keel. It was slow work and Chanakkale nearly 20 miles away, but once past the half-way headland we moved faster, helped by a counter-current. The shipping was thick in the confined waterway, big new Russian tankers, incredibly old freighters—the Black Sea traffic was a very mixed bag. Only 3 gallons of fuel left now, but we could see the narrows, and at 2 o'clock we were off the northern fort and turning into the stream, where big ships, clearing for Istanbul, were being drifted backwards as they lay with engines stopped. The Customs launch came out to us, ordered us into the Control Port, and as we closed the quay, the agent's boat piloted us in to anchor in 15 ft close off a jetty just north of the main port. We were cleared very quickly, the matter of our lack of a health certificate left to the authorities in Istanbul, but I had trouble over refuelling, the Customs requiring proof that I had changed sterling for Turkish pounds—a not unreasonable demand since all fuel has to be imported and Turkey is short of foreign currency.

By 1730, fuelled and cleared, we motored out, and in the soft evening light struggled up against the sluicing current, heading north for the Sea of Marmara. As night fell, we came up with a Turkish tug standing by an old Greek Liberty ship which had gone aground—lights blazing on the steamer's bridge; presumably her captain was spinning out the price-fixing argument to give his engineers time. Later the vessel got off under her own power and overtook us, going very slowly, her engines in no better state than ours, the tug shadowing her hopefully. I did not like the Pilot's description of Gelibolu

and so crossed to the southern shore and felt my way in on the
echo-sounder to anchor close off the pier at Lapseki in 41 ft.
This pier has been extended now to form an L and the port
dredged, but it is still in the prohibited area and you are not
allowed to land. A boat put out to us in the morning and a
man speaking French asked us if we needed anything, but
whether he was a security official, an agent, or just a kindly
citizen we did not discover.

At 1100 hours the wind came in from the north-east, blowing straight down the Dardanelles. We hoisted main and No.
2 and started out on a filthy day of beating back and forth
to clear the current in the northern entrance. The clouds were
low and it began to rain. The seas were short, steep and
breaking. We reefed, tacking through the steamer lane, an
endless flow of ships with only the Russians meticulously
giving way to sail. The prevailing wind is always contrary
in the western part of the Marmara, the seas always steep.
It did not let up until dawn the next day—a grey dawn with
rain squalls. We were through the narrows between the islands
and the northern shore then and had sea room. Gradually the
day improved, but not until the afternoon were we able to cut
the motor. Fast sailing then, and as night fell we came abreast
of San Stefano light with the glow of Istanbul's three cities
reflected on the low cloud base. Not wishing to enter the
Bosporus in the dark, we spent the night sailing close in to the
shore between San Stefano and Seraglio points, clear of the
steamer lane and just outside the route taken by the numerous coastal caiques. Rain fell in sudden showers and strange
smells wafted to us on the wind, not all of them pleasant. And
as the first grey luminosity of dawn touched the sky, we heard
the muezzins calling the faithful to prayer from the dim-seen
needle-points of minarets. We headed for the entrance to the
Bosporus and soon the pattern of domes and minarets began
to emerge, vague outlines dominating the long peninsula of
the old town—St. Sophia, Sultan Ahmet, Bayezit, Suley-
maniye, all the mosques that stand above the Golden Horn.
The domes were huge, the bulk of the buildings staggering,
but it was the minarets I remember, tall, pencilled shapes that
seemed to prick the underbellies of the clouds; ethereal in the
grey dampness of the dawn, they seemed to belong to an

Arabian Nights world and not a part of the bustle of a great port. Stemming the current below the old Seraglio, now part of the rich Topkapi museum, we entered the waterway that gave birth to Constantinople, daylight dispersing the clouds and the Golden Horn opening up to port with ferries lying thick by the first bridge. We located the sprawling bulk of Dolma Bahce Palace and by a little garden of trees found a shallow patch where we could anchor.

Fortunately I had been given the name of a shipping agent, an Englishman. Without his help I do not know how we should have managed the formalities, or even understood what was required of us. In answer to my phone call he came out in a huge launch with all the necessary officials on board—even the Chief of Intelligence was there! Why? 'Because nobody can understand why a yacht should visit Istanbul except to spy.' This sense of insecurity, of suspicion, is understandable. Our agent moored us at Bebek, half-way up the Bosporus, and in the week we spent there we watched the shipping moving through, the preponderance of Russian vessels. Ataturk created Ankara as the political and administrative capital of Turkey, but God created the narrow gateway between the Black Sea and the Mediterranean, and this makes Istanbul the natural, physical centre of Turkey's life. Here you talk about the Anatolian and the European shore. Here trade flows and the great nation to the north is forced to bow to the regulations of a much smaller power every time she wants to pass a cargo or a warship into the Atlantic or south through Suez. It is a powerful position that the Turks have inherited from the old Byzantine empire they destroyed. No wonder they guard it jealously.

That first night we lay at Bebek the rain came down in torrents, the air was cold. Ferries slid incessantly past our stern, their searchlights sweeping the black waters, the warning peep of their steam whistles urgent in the darkness. The Bosporus is 171 miles long, most of it less than a mile wide and the current flows perpetually south at anything up to 5 knots as the Black Sea rivers pour their waters down across the Marmara and through the Dardanelles to feed the sun-evaporated Mediterranean. Boats proceeding north must hug the shore close; even so each point is a rip of fast-flowing water. We had passed through two of these rips in the six miles to Bebek, but though the navigation is tricky and a pilot advisable, the beauty of this unique waterway, with the white of palaces and houses standing out against the lush green of the hills on either side, the constant movement of caiques and ferries, and the great ships in the fairway remains unforgettably in the mind.

Waking to a Sunday morning of soft European sunlight we watched the little resort of Bebek come slowly to life, a shimmering curve of restaurants and houses reflected in the water. At midday we went ashore for drinks on the private quay of one of these houses. David and Richard had to catch a plane back to England. They also had to have a Customs officer to see their baggage landed from *Mary Deare* and to see it out to the airport. Inevitably the Customs officer was late and this tiresome piece of red tape caused us considerable anxiety. The engine was our next problem, for we were nearly a thousand miles from Malta and on previous experience I anticipated having to motor most of the last 400 miles. For the rest of the week Dorothy and I divided our time between the owner of the local shipyard, a diesel expert, and visits to Istanbul. The diesel expert was a man of over sixty, very slow, very meticulous. Half a day was spent poring over the engine. He then insisted that the boat be moved to his yard at the far end of the Bosporus. He arrived to pilot us up at 0740. It was a morning of pure enchantment as we hugged the European shore, old wooden houses and abandoned consulates, as strangely constructed as Dulac illustrations to a fairytale, sliding past, gardens bright with flowers, restaurants and cafés and boats and coloured awnings, all gleaming fresh in the morning sunlight. He showed us the house, still half in ruins, where a Russian ship had put her bows, running ashore in a thick fog. It was about here that he began to mop his brow and turn pale. I thought perhaps he was suffering from sea-sickness, for our exhaust was smelling and in the rips *Mary Deare* had a strange uneasy movement. Ahead of us now we could see the entrance to the sea that is called Black in every language; I had been strongly warned against sailing into it on account of its violent, unpredictable storms and its lack of harbours. The headlands that form the gateway to the Black Sea were steep and rocky, the sea beyond lost in a dark murk, uninviting. We were now crossing a large, sheltered inlet with ship repair yards lining the further shore. Having seen us moored to a buoy close under the bows of a ship that was stern-on to the shore, the old man left us. Time passed. Finally a boy came out in a boat, muttered in bad French something about 'hôpital' and 'très malade'. I went ashore then to find the old man closeted with his doctor in a dingy office. His son, Mettim Bey, told me he had had a stroke. But after the lunch break he was still there, issuing instructions to the engineer who was recalibrating our injector nozzles, a job that had been done in every port where we had had mechanics. Finally we went back down the Bosporus, keeping to the middle of the channel, the current tugging us fast and the green shores and the pretty dolls' houses sliding by; in no time at all we had reached the narrows, Rumel Hisari's guardian bulk looming over us as we made for our mooring. The mechanic, who had come with us to change the oil and remove the filter, left us only just time to clean up before rowing ashore for a party at the Naval Attaché's house, high like a look-out above Bebek, a fabulous view down the Bosporus. Mettim Bey came out to us next day to say that his father had not had a stroke after all, he was just overtired, and that he had not been able to find new oil and air filters. He would try again tomorrow. He failed, but it did not matter; I don't know what that old man did to the engine, but though it remained difficult to start, we had no more trouble with it. It had, however, wasted a lot of our time in Istanbul.

Nevertheless, we managed to see a great deal—St. Sophia, of course, and the fabulous treasures and pavilions of the Topkapi; also that little gem of a church Kahriye Cami, the only one of the mosques we visited where the hideously-painted Moslem plaster had been removed to reveal the beauty of the Christian mosaics below, and Yerebatan Sarayi, the great underground cistern with its 144 fat columns; we had toured the colossal walls of old Constantinople, seen the Golden Gate, and on the evening we were due to dine with Raymond and Freda, just arrived from England to join us, we ran into

them by an inconceivable juggling of impossible permutations
in the alley maze of Kapoli Carsi, the world's largest covered
bazaar. We had also seen an election, many of the polling
stations being set up in the courtyards of mosques. Menderes's
old party, now called the Justice Party, had been returned to
power, and later in the week we had a meeting with Kemal
Aygün, who had been Menderes's Chief of Police and the
Mayor of Ankara and had spent four years in prison after
Menderes's fall from power and his execution. This meeting
took place in his flat—Turkish coffee with chocolates and
then glasses of tea and rich cakes, and Kemal Aygün showing us endless pictures of himself and Menderes and Nehru,
Nasser and other eastern leaders. He gave me a letter to
Istanbul's Chief of Police, just in case, and a phone call he
made brought a police launch all the way up to Bebek the
following day to bid us welcome and ask whether they could
assist us in any way. But when I suggested that they might
waive the matter of Customs formalities for my crew joining
the following evening, the result was a blank look, a bundle of
tourist brochures and many handshakes.

Actually, the Turks have done their best to relax some of
the regulations. There is an archaic law which makes it obli-
gatory for boats under 500 tons to be entirely sealed with
wire whilst in Istanbul, or alternatively to have a Customs
officer on board throughout their stay whilst members of the
ship's company have to pass through Customs formalities
every time they go ashore or return on board. This would
have made our visit to Istanbul impossible.

Saturday evening, June 11, we attended a party in the
gardens of the British Consulate to celebrate the Queen's
birthday. It was as cold and damp as any outdoor party can
be in England and in the midst of it I was informed that the
young man who was joining us direct by air from England
was not on the plane. This upset the whole carefully organised
arrangements for a Customs officer to see him and Raymond
and Freda on board at the same time. He turned up on another plane, but the agent and I spent a long and very trying
evening telephoning all over Istanbul before all three, with
the Customs officer, had been brought together at the house of

our kind friends at Bebek. It was almost midnight before we were all on board and well past before an unnecessary amount of luggage had somehow been stowed away.

We left at 1100 in the morning and had a fast sail across the Sea of Marmara, anchoring at Lapseki again, just inside the Dardanelles, at 1445 the following day. Tuesday we were up at first light, at Chanakkale by 0715; a quick clearance, a taxi, and by 0925 we were standing on the grass mounds that mark the walls of Priam's Troy. Here storm-foot Iris, the messenger of Zeus, had come like the wind from Mount Ida in Crete, here the old king had stood and watched the Myrmidons, the Hellenes and the Achaians beach their ships on the Hellespont shore, had watched the bloody tide of battle flow back and forth on the flat plains below, had seen his son killed by Achilles and the great wooden horse of the wily Odysseus brought to the gates. It was all there in our minds, the whole epic of Homer's *Iliad* which we had been reading on board; but little remained of that city or of the eight other Troys that had been built there before and after—a few walls, an ancient ramped gateway, a sacrificial well, and the whole circumference marked by grass-covered mounds, slashed by Schliemann's rather hasty tunnelling. It was the site, not the scattered stone remains, that gripped the imagination, for the nine walled cities reaching back into the dim past of more than 5,000 years ago had been built on the end of a spur of higher ground, and from the mounds that marked their walls we looked down across the dark tree-ed green of the plains of Troy and beyond to the distant blue of the Hellespont with ships moving in and out of the Dardanelles. Standing there we could still visualise the black ships coming, imagine how the Trojans must have felt as the camp and its protecting wall grew and the tide of the invasion began to envelope them. . . .

So all this host went sweeping over the earth like a conflagration. . . . So under their trampling feet the ground loudly groaned, and quickly they passed over the plain. The unearthed ruined traces of Troy still stand, but of that ancient war no vestige remains, not even an earthwork mound to mark the walls and moat the Danaäns erected to protect themselves and their ships. The *Iliad* claims they forgot the sacrifices that were due to the gods:

While Hector lived, and Achilles nursed his anger, and the city of Priam was unsacked, so long that great wall stood. But when the best men of Troy were killed with many of the Achaians, and those that were left sacked the city of Priam in the tenth year and the Achaians had sailed away, then Poseidon and Apollo determined to smother the wall. All the rivers which flow down from Ida to the sea . . . where shields and helmets have fallen in heaps and the bodies of brave men —all these rivers they led upon it, turning their streams together. For nine days the flood poured over the wall and torrents of rain fell unceasing, that the sea might sooner swallow it up. Earthshaker himself guided the waters with his trident, until he had swept away all the foundations of logs and stones which the Achaians had laid with such labour; then he made smooth the shore of the Hellespont, and covered it over with sand again.

I had now seen the greatest of the archaeological digs— Troy, and Mycene, where, with Dörpfeld as his assistant, Schliemann had proved that Homer's work was not just myth but a great writer's statement of history, and Knossos, where Evans had proved an island civilisation that matched the Egyptian in age and culture. Now in the fading light of that bright evening we had a distant glimpse of Troy as Menelaus and his captains must have seen it first, from the sea as we sailed west from the Hellespont towards the island of Limnos. The strong south-west-going current that sweeps across this northen part of the Aegean carried us through the night, and in the misty morning sun we lay off the castled entrance of Merini Kastro for a swim and a leisurely breakfast of bacon and eggs. Next day, Thursday, June 16, we left Limnos very early and by midday the high peaked shape of Mount Athos was growing out of the haze. The wind that had blown hard all morning now eased, we shook out the reefs and sailed in close to the vast bulk of the Holy Mountain, searching through the glasses for the monasteries that cling to its slopes. We located three of them on the steep south-east face, jilled in close to the rocks, searching for the smaller hermit cells of anchorites, and found a few perched like oversized boulders above the outriding headland of the southern end, one high up in a gulley like a lonely mountain refuge and some ruins on the shore. And then suddenly the calm sea was ruffled by the wind coming round the south side of the mountain. We reefed quickly and pulled away from this windy corner where the current-borne water was now dark and poppled. No question of visiting any of the monasteries that fringed the Singitic Gulf; we ran for the little bolt-hole of Sikias on the further shore and over our shoulders, across a rising sea, we watched the cliff-hanging monasteries of Dionusiou and Simon Petra and all the high-perched hermit dwellings fade astern.

The pictures you see of Mount Athos all seem to show the monasteries in close-up, so that the impression they leave is of the mountain dominated by religious buildings. The reverse is true. Seen from the sea it is the mountain that dominates, 6,000 ft of scoured rock rising almost sheer to a single peak, a gigantic pyramid, in fact, with the monasteries that cling to its skirts and slopes completely dwarfed. The solitude of the place, the isolation, is overwhelming, so that one can grasp the reason for the peninsula's inviolability through 14 centuries of war. The monks, once more than 20,000, are now fewer than 2,000, but the mountain, with its head in the clouds, its feet in the sea, its whole bulk exposed to the great air currents that flow between Asia and Africa, is as near to God as any place on earth, and though we passed without landing, it left a deep impression on us all.

From Sikias we sailed south to the Sporades, to Skopelos, which was being dredged, to Skiathos, which was beautiful, and then west into the inner lead that runs for over 100 miles between the long island of Euboea and the mainland. Here for the first time in the Aegean we had to work our tides, and when the flood came against us we put in to the little port of Skala Oreos, where we sat under the trees by the water's edge and ate fresh-caught baby lobsters, watching the manoeuvres of the fastest waiter any of us had ever seen as he crossed the road and ducked beneath the trees, running with trays piled with food, glasses and bottles. We left in the morning very early to catch the tide, and at 1700 that afternoon we passed through the narrows at Chalkis where the tide can run 8 knots below the low-slung sliding bridge. We hit the sluicing millstream just beyond it, a crowd watching as we skidded sideways, flung over by the rip, and then we were driving for the dog-leg of the second narrows, below the belching chimney of a cement factory. Rain and wind greeted us on the far side as we navigated by chart the shallows of a broad reach of water to the old tower and the sand spit with its lighthouse that mark the final exit. Beyond the spit we got the full weight of the wind funnelling up the straits from the east. It was wind over tide then, a steep, breaking sea, the stream against us and night closing in. We reefed and had a dirty three-hour beat until, at midnight, we crept in through the rocks to the sunken breakwater of Eretri, anchoring close against the shore clear of the ferries. The wind dropped suddenly. The night was still and black, and in the morning we motored out, the sea like glass, hot sun and the green hills, instead of the high limestone mountains north of Chalkis. A bathe in the beautiful spit-protected pool of Port Buphalo, where a few fishermen's cottages stood shimmering in the heat and there were boats and donkeys on the beach, and then round a headland and a small island to the deep fjord of Potamos. The wind had come in again by then, still easterly, and we stayed there the night, anchored close in to the rocks.

We left at 0400 next morning, for it was now June 22 and time was pressing—we had to be in Malta, almost 600 miles away, by July 2. The smell of breakfast cooking wafted into the cockpit as we opened up the plains of Marathon, searching in vain for the mound where the Athenian dead were buried, seeing behind the sheltering headland the bay where the Persian fleet had lain at anchor. By 1030 we were toying with the spinnaker and the south end of Euboea was dropping away on the port quarter. By midday we were under genoa, the water chattering at our bows, headed for the narrow straits between the prohibited island of Makronisos, with its grim penal camps, and the great iron factory sprawl of the mainland hot and red in the sunshine. An hour later we could see the temple of Poseidon on Sounion's cliffs high above us, and all that afternoon we watched it fade away astern as we motor-sailed across the calm, oil-slicked waters of the Gulf of Athens. At the far end Aegina was just visible and over the bows the island of Hydra appeared like a jagged promontory jutting out from the hills and rocks of the Peloponnese coast.

The sun was setting and the wind rising as we entered th straits. A bad place this for down-draughts, a breeding plac for squalls and seamen. The trees that brought down moistur and so gave it its name were cut down centuries ago, no trac of them left on the barren tops. We turned a corner of roc and there in the dusk was a glimmering cascade of house pouring white down the folds of hills to ring the secret water of a small harbour. From this drowned volcanic vent th Venetians had once monopolised the east-west trade of th Aegean. And at the beginning of the 19th century there wer 10,000 Hydriote seamen, fleets of ships, and the wealth tha flowed in to the great trading families built the big house that still remain, monuments to the past maritime greatnes of the port of Hydra. That night Dorothy and I explored th furthest reaches of the paths and steps that climbed the hills and from the topmost group of houses, high on a crag, looke down into the lit basin of the port far below, and on the peri phery of the town the bare hills stood silent and watchful i the starlight. It was very beautiful, strangely tragic, fo Hydra was nothing now, just hostels and restaurants an souvenir shops (rather good ones), the tourist trade in place o the real trade of the sea.

We had a lazy day there and left in a red dawn with th sun coming up like a flaming ball, the sea all fire and th islands standing black to the east. We lunched with ou anchor down in 21 ft in Port Ieraka, a narrow dog-legged gu in the cliffs that ran back into hot sun and shallows, to sleeping honey-coloured village crawling with vines. Th Aegean is full of such surprises, but sadly we were no leaving it. By 1700 we were close under the rugged cliff of Malea, with the lighthouse and the monastery above u and the whole peninsula in silhouette against the afternoo sky, jagged and grand. We were very close in-shore, followin in the wake of a deep sea trawler, and it was here, in th Elaphonisos Channel between Kithera and Greece, that th first zephyr of a breeze came in from the west. It was no mor than a ruffling of the surface, a gentle warning, and it ha gone by the time we reached Matapan, the low, lit finger-ti of the Mani Peninsula. The moon set a few minutes after mid night, just too soon, so that I had nothing but the stars an the swinging beam of Cape Matapan to light me in to the little cove of Asamato. It was hard to find and distances were deceptive. We used the spotlight and anchored in 20 ft off a beach that appeared to be part of a grass bank.

It is always strange to wake in broad daylight and see the place you have entered in the dark. The beach was not a beach, nor was there any grass; it was a most appalling dragon-toothed collection of sea-eroded rocks, and they were much closer than I had thought. A breeze came in, bringing with it the scent of thyme from the slopes above. Three women were dunking sheep in the shallows and picking off the ticks, donkeys stood with their foals, the world dripped sunshine and peace out of a blue sky. We made a warp fast to one of the rock teeth and hauled stern to the shore, and then we walked to the lighthouse. By the time we got there it was blowing force 6, the sea seething white below the Cape. We drank ouzo with the keeper and his wife, saw over the light and stayed to share their meal of fish caught that morning and cooked as a rough bouillabaisse. There is a cave at Matapan which some regard as the gates of Hades from which the dead rose up to talk to Odysseus. The lighthouse keeper, speaking Italian, said it was 'piccolo' and that only a good underwater swimmer could enter it. He also said that Churchill had twice come to look at it—one can almost hear the old man saying, 'I always like to know where I'm going!'

It blew very hard that afternoon and *Mary Deare* trembled to the down-draughts with three warps out, all bar-taut, as she strained at the rocks The lighthouse keeper, who came on board with his wife for drinks that night, said the westerly would last five days. We set the alarm for an early start at 0345, but it was still blowing and we did not get away until five hours later, a big swell and no wind as we motor-sailed out past the lighthouse. The sea sloshed at the sloping slab that marked the 'gate to Hades'. The wind came in again. By evening it was blowing a near-gale and we had a hard night of it, beating into a heavy sea out beyond Venetico Island. The dawn was grey, but we were clear of Sapienza Island, sailing north and just able to lay the entrance of Navarino Bay. At 1035, very tired, we dropped anchor off the jetty at Pylos.

We left Greece at 0300 on Wednesday, June 29. In contrast to our experience in Turkey, the only formalities on leaving had been the handing in of the paper of identity issued to us at Limnos. The gale had blown itself out in the day we had spent shopping and resting in this friendly port, but it had left a big swell and the motion was unpleasant. Twice we hove-to for dinner, fresh food from Pylos and the last of the delicacies we had brought from Malta. By Friday we were sighting ships—first, the Suez-Messina lane, then the Matapan-Malta Channel vessels, and in the evening tankers coming up from the new oil-fields in Libya. By Saturday the sea was calm, the haze thick and we were motoring past Sicilian fishing boats, through great circles of nets marked by plastic floats that stood out white and yellow in the sun. Gozo beacon was loud and clear on the direction-finder and in the afternoon Malta showed up over the bows, a blurred shadowy outline, no more substantial than a smoke trail. For the fourth time we entered Grand Harbour to be welcomed at the Customs Quay as old friends. That night, berthed at the marina, sleep was made impossible by the machine-gun crackle of firecrackers. Sliema was en fête, the church outlined in fairy lights. Tired though we were, Dorothy and I both got up to watch the final set piece—golden rain shooting up from the roof of the church, cascades of light illuminating the waterfront, the yachts, the whole fortress shape of Manoel Island. We were indeed back in Malta.

PART TWO

The Islands

INTRODUCTION

Whilst the first part of this book is essentially the 'logs' of voyages and should be read as such, this second part is more in the nature of a collection of journeys, even though *Mary Deare* provided the means of travel for two of them. These journeys, which range across the northern hemisphere from 60°N to the equator, were undertaken for a variety of reasons: several for the American magazine *Holiday*, one for the *Sunday Times*, and two formed the background of subsequent novels—the three visits to the Outer Hebrides and St. Kilda were the basis for *Atlantic Fury*, and the journey to Addu Atoll in the middle of the Indian Ocean for *The Strode Venturer*. They are arranged chronologically and, because of their widely differing backgrounds, will, I hope, complement the first part of this book by indicating the effect of the sea upon the lives of a variety of people. The conditions described are, of course, those existing at the time the journeys were made.

In the second part of the book there is no mention of crew who sailed on the three voyages that were the basis of 'The Breton Coast' and 'The Danish Islands', and, of course, there were other races. I would like, therefore, to mention the following: Brigadier Miles Smeeton (well-known in the sailing world for his two attempts to round the Horn, recorded in his book *Once is Enough*), Ronald Ramsay (who built a sister ship to *Mary Deare*, which he later sailed to his home on Vancouver Island), Lord Riverdale (then Commodore of the Royal Cruising Club), Colonel Ian Battye, Martin Wharmby, Rupert French and Michael Sabine.

I
DALMATIA

The Dalmatian Coast—the charm of islands, a sunlit sea, the beauty of a dead past; some instinct told me to avoid the obvious route by sea and to surprise it from the rear, from the heart of Yugoslavia. And so we flew to Belgrade, a white, defenceless city on the edge of a great plain, moated against the march of invasion by the Sava and the Danube rivers. Approaching it from twenty thousand feet, the Alpine ranges of Austria fell away behind us as we crossed the frontier, the Danube plain rolled out before us. We looked across to Hungary, to Rumania, too, with never a change in the flat fertility to mark the frontier line between Yugoslavia and these satellite states—and ahead, almost visible to the pilot beyond its mountain screen, Bulgaria.

Seven land frontiers, and four of them—the four longest—Russian dominated. . . . Yugoslavia is all but ringed about by satellites. Four days later I stood on the wild, deserted frontier of the fourth satellite—Albania. Sixty thousand Albanian troops, I had read in an English newspaper, stood ready, poised on this very border. But all I saw there was the mellow peace of the beautiful monastery of St. Naum standing deserted by the side of a great lake and a handful of Tito's border guards sprawled rifleless on the grass playing with some peasant children.

Nowhere that I could find was there any sign of tension, any mood of fear or uncertainty. In ten years, President Tito told me, we will have done this, we will have done that; and the confidence of this staunch man is reflected in his people. There is conscription, of course. In Zadar, whilst watching two walnut sellers as nut-brown and wrinkled as their wares, a group of youngsters passed me, led by an accordionist playing national songs and accompanied by weeping relatives. It was a new intake going to board one of the steamers that belched black smoke across the ruins, going to serve their

173

country. A common sight, and the Navy active along the coast, troops in the towns and in lonely, barbed-wire cantonments—a general air of readiness. But no sense of doubt or uncertainty.

The key to the country's mood is Tito. He is a hero, even to those who are opposed to the regime—and only a small proportion of the population are actually members of the Communist Party (I was given a figure as low as 5 per cent.) To the people as a whole he is the man who stood firm in 1948 and manoeuvred the Russians out. As a result the ordinary citizen no longer goes in fear and spontaneous criticism testifies to the freedom of speech, and to the confidence of the regime. Through the fires of invasion, civil war and finally of the Revolution, Yugoslavia has at last become a real country, so that now one has the feeling that nothing short of a cataclysm could break it up again into its component parts.

And what a beautiful country it is! I have dabbled my hands in the Danube where it runs through golden miles of maize corn reaching from horizon to horizon, and a hundred miles away driven through country so green with oak and poplar that, but for the gay-painted peasant carts and the round Serbian caps, the up-turned pointed shoes, I could have imagined myself back in England. And fifty miles beyond, the mountain ranges, the land all rock and dusty with drought—limestone drinking the precious water and giving nothing. And beyond the stony tops of the Karst, the hot sun beating down upon the waters of the Adriatic, an island world with a wealth of history. A changeling country this, the coat of its scenery made of many colours; and the people singing all the time their national songs. Like Shaw, who loved it in his last years, I will plead—Go there now before it is spoilt; beg, borrow or steal time or money, but go, and go quickly before the new roads and mass means of communication have taken the edge off the uniqueness of it.

What is so special about it? Perhaps I should follow the example of Tito's old friend, Nehru, and count from one to six the strangeness of its social pattern. It is one country—Yugoslavia, which means the land of the South Slavs. It has two alphabets, Roman and Cyrillic. The latter looks just as convincing read upside-down and makes complete nonsense of the most obvious sign or the name of a street, even one's own name becomes unrecognisable—mine is XAMOHA NHC! It has three religions, Greek Orthodox, Roman Catholic and Moslem. It has four languages, Serbo-Croat, Slovenian, Macedonian, and Dalmatian, this last reflecting the Italian influence. It is composed of five different races, Serbs, Croats, Macedonians, Montenegrins and Slovenians. It is a federation of six republics, Serbia, Croatia, Slovenia, Bosnia-Hercegovina, Macedonia and Montenegro.

Having said all that, and emphasised the complexity of the social structure, I feel I should add that the people are uniformly well-behaved and well-intentioned to the stranger, embarrassingly hospitable, overwhelmingly friendly, and fascinated by any contact with the outside world. As one person said to me, who had suffered much from Russian victimisation: 'It is a good place to live. The people—they are so kind. They are poor, but they will share anything they have.' You don't need to be in trouble to discover this, particularly at harvest time. Typical was Nada, a big, smiling motherly soul who thrust two figs into my hands in her excitement at discovering that I was English. 'Momento! Uno momento!' In a moment friends and neighbours surrounded us, and we were seated on the rock path on clean linen, loaded with figs and grapes. 'Eat! You must eat!' As always, somebody was found who could talk to us, interpret all we could tell them about the world outside. . . . This was Vinka, a student who loved Shakespeare, but could not continue her English studies because her family were too poor. 'My father, he is only a little clerk—12,000 dinar a month—it is not much—Now I must work. . . . Please write. Please send English books so that I can teach my pupils.' This is the poorest quarter of Sibenik (Shibenik), with the sun setting and the lizards crawling over the crumbled stones of the thirteenth century walls. The nice thing about Yugoslavia is that you can wander, day or night, through the poorest and most overcrowded districts of a city without ever feeling that you have strayed on hostile ground. Indeed, you are welcome.

From Belgrade Dorothy and I flew south into Macedonia, with the promise of grapes and a harvest moon. It was September. Three hours later we stood on the ramparts of an old Turkish fort looking out across a city of mosques. This was Skopje, the capital—the ancient Scupi of the Romans where the route the legions took to Greece crosses the Vardar river. Skopje before the earthquake with nine minarets thrusting their pointed tips, spear-like to the blazing sky. The rounded humps of Macedonia's mountains ringing us round, making a natural basin of which the fort was the hub, and the heat was the dry heat of near-desert country, thinned to sparkling wine by the altitude. This was the land that saw both the beginning and the end of Turkish domination, for at Kosova Polje in the hills to the north Serbian feudalism died a bloody death almost 600 years ago, and it was at Kumanovo in the arid plains to the north-west that the Turks were finally flung out, a bare 50 years ago. They were in Macedonia a long time and there is a Turkish flavour about it—Turkish coffee, Turkish architecture, the people themselves marked, as in Greece, by Turkish blood. But it is all in the past now. Even the religion is dying, killed by the searing wind of Revolution, so that the mosques are little more than empty monuments for the curious to stand and gaze at.

We were shown round one of these mosques by a young Macedonian whose sallow, full-lipped features revealed his Turkish blood. It was a strange experience for me to walk inside a mosque, stranger still for my wife to be admitted. Yet here it was just a show place—a *cultural monument*, our guide insisted—with a caretaker wanting a tip and visitors' books in three languages. The childish delight with which our guide got down on his hands and knees and bowed his head to the carpet and then looked up at us with a jeer on his face was oddly unpleasant. It was a renunciation of his own God, as crude as though he had cocked a snook at the Prophet.

Close by was another 'museum', the little underground church of Sveti Spas (St. Saviour), as proof that Christianity existed cheek-by-jowl with the Moslem faith. Our young Macedonian friend could not refrain from climbing up with a smirk and seating himself in the ornately carved bishop's chair, just to make the point that the religion here was as dead as that in the mosque. However, he thought highly of the fantastical wood-carving with which the church was literally festooned, a fifteen-year labour of love by the Filipovski brothers a century ago. I could not help feeling that our young friend's sense of values was sadly astray for, having wasted our time in this wood-carvers' nightmare of the baroque. he walked us right past the entrance to the Kurčumli Han (Kurshumli Haan).

There is another of these great caravanserai on the coast near Sibenik, but it is difficult to reach, and anyway I cannot believe that it would have the same impact as this monolithic giant of a building squatting amongst the little houses of Skopje's old bazaar. The near-dozen stone cupolas give it the air of a mosque, the massive stone walls embedded with lines of tiles the look of a Roman fort; the half-circle loose tiling of the sloped roofs is Roman, too. So solid and grandiose is this structure that I had to remind myself more than once that nothing Roman had withstood the shattering blow of the earthquake in AD 518. In fact, the Kurčumli Han is Turkish built, probably with Dubrovnik funds, for it is nothing less than a fortified market place surrounded on all four sides by arcades of two storeys, the great stone pillars bonded with lead from Macedonian mines. Here Turkish and other eastern traders met the rich Ragusan merchants of the coast, did their business in the ground floor arcades and slept the night in the 'hotel' rooms of the upper storeys.

Everything is conveniently to hand. Behind the main structure were stables for horses, a parking lot for camels, and the stone granaries that now house the harvest archaeologists have reaped from the tumbled cities of Scupi, Stobi and Heraclea were full of fodder. The Keeper held the gate fast in the mornings until every merchant reported his goods intact and nothing stolen. Flanking the Han stands the mosque on one side, the public baths on the other.

The Turkish bath—so reminiscent of British Edwardian opulence—was proof again of the Roman influence on Turkish architecture through the Byzantine Empire. It was squat and solid and surmounted by cupolas. Inside, the stone walls were lined with hessian and bright with the paintings of Vangel Kodzoman, a local artist. It was there, in that unusual art gallery, that I had my first glimpse of the bursting vitality of Slav art. It was not so much that his pictures were

good; it was the sheer ebullience of them, the strength and
the colour. Paintings like these are everywhere, for Government, the Party, State enterprise have replaced Church and
merchant as the patrons of art, and pictures by local artists
hang in factory, hotel and office. The urge to express themselves in form and colour seems to go deeper even than their
love of singing and dancing, as though in painting they can
capture and hold the turbulent violence of their moods.

This urge is not new. It goes back many centuries and it
was this that had drawn me to Macedonia. Talk to anyone
who knows Yugoslavia and sooner or later the word 'frescoes'
is mentioned. They are to be found in the old monasteries, they
say, in places that are unfortunately somewhat inaccessible.
My mind had pictured grim stone edifices perched on towering cliffs, a retreat for men who had renounced the world. I
was not prepared for the sudden breathtaking beauty of St.
Andrew in Treska. Hidden in a limestone gorge, we came
upon it suddenly, walking a narrow path hewn from the cliff
face. The blind, concrete face of a dam blocked the valley
below us, water shimmered in the hard sunlight—an artificial
lake. We turned a corner, half-arched by a rock overhang, and
there it stood, a little gem no bigger than a chapel. No monastery this in the accepted sense, rather a hermitage, the
stone of its fourteenth century walls mellow as corn at harvest
time, picked out with the red of brick and capped by the
warmth of loose-tiled roofs from the midst of which a solitary
tower burst forth to give form and balance to the whole.
And in the dim interior I stood transfixed before the work of
three men in the year 1389, the year of Kosova and the
Turks.

All the walls were a deep azure blue and from floor to roof
they surrounded me with saints and martyrs and Biblical
scenes, a flood of colour so rich, so full of the urge to create
that it was breathtaking. No matter that these were not the
finest frescoes I was to see, nor even the oldest; no matter
that the plaster had fallen away in places and the damp eaten
into the scenes—they were original and untouched frescoes,
and my first. And remembering the turbid history of Macedonia, the wars, the long occupation by a race that worshipped
another God, it seemed incredible that they had survived,

even tucked out of sight in the lost seclusion of the Treska gorge.

An hour later we were climbing a parched track to the village of Neresi and another monastery. Grapes were ripe in the fields and the walls of houses were festooned with strung lines of tobacco leaf drying in the midday heat. The yellow of gourds, the brilliant red of pimento—the little peasant settlement was as full of colour as Kodzoman's paintings. As I stopped a moment to wonder at a wooden building of unusual design, verandahed and with a small wooden tower at one corner, a boy who had fed us grapes on the way up hawked and spat. 'Pardon the manners of the country people,' our French-speaking companion apologised. 'They respect their mosques.'

I had never seen a wooden mosque before.

A small tree-ed dell, an arched gateway, and then we were faced with the mellow beauty of St. Panteleimon. Our young Neresite hawked and spat, thereby indicating that his tastes in religion were catholic and he regarded us simply as foreigners. The squat main tower was set off by smaller towers at each of the four corners, the loose-tiled roofs, sloped in places, arched in others, gave a haphazard appearance to what was architecturally a structure of perfect balance. Inside, the place was a shambles of dust and rubble and scaffolding. Great cracks split the ancient walls, whole sections of fresco were missing.

The present regime in Yugoslavia does not encourage religion, but it does give high priority to culture and fully appreciates the value of the old Orthodox churches and their frescoes. Josif Trajkovski was in charge of the reconstruction at Neresi, a blond giant with the head and features you see on ancient Greek friezes. Looking like a labourer, in dirty singlet, his face white as a miller's with the dust of centuries old plaster, he took us into dark recesses behind great baulks of timber and showed us with the pride of an expert mural treasures dating back to the twelfth-century building of the church—the Mourning of Christ, the Visitation of the Virgin, the Birth of Maria, the Descent from the Cross, the Resurrection of Lazarus and the Entry into Jerusalem. All these have the formalism that gives to the mural painting of the period that quality of mysticism that makes them such an important art form, for through formalism these early painters achieved something nearer to a visual expression of God than any of the later, more realistic works. Moreover, in the three-dimensional quality of their painting they were two centuries at least ahead of the Italians.

Neresi is particularly interesting, for not only is the formalism relieved by a touch of humanity, particularly in the Mourning of Christ where the Mother is in tears, but side by side with these old frescoes are others from the sixteenth and nineteenth centuries so that the harshness of colouring and the crude realism of the latter is emphasised by comparison. 'There is so much to be done to preserve these ancient things and so little money,' Trajkovski said, a cry that I was to hear everywhere in Yugoslavia. It is not the fault of the Government. Considering how poor the country is and how much they have done and are doing by way of industrial expansion, it is surprising that they have been able to devote as much money as they have to the preservation of a rich past.

It was here at Neresi that we were shown how the frescoes are handled during reconstruction. They are first coated with a washable adhesive to which a special cloth is applied. A wood stiffening is glued to this and the whole fresco, together with the plaster on which it is painted, is then chiselled from the wall. Mounted on canvas and wood, the first stiffening is washed from the face of the painting and the fresco is returned to its place when the wall itself has been repaired. The finest example of complete restoration is St. Sofia in Ohrid for which UNESCO provided the funds. Fortunately the Turks in their haste to convert the church for use as a mosque merely painted or plastered over the frescoes. Now this huge eleventh century church, so massively built that it is at one with the earlier Byzantine basilica it has absorbed, is a blaze of colour, the frescoes all wonderfully preserved by the centuries of plaster that covered them. Standing incongruous in the middle of it is the Koran-reader's pulpit.

Ohrid (pronounced as a Scot would pronounce it—Ochrid) is the Mecca of the fresco-gazer. It is an old Turkish town built on Roman foundations. Its ancient wooden houses jut over, and sometimes bridge completely, the narrow alleys that wind up the hill to the church of St. Clement, and it looks out over one of the most beautiful lakes in the world. Three thousand feet up and ringed with mountains, the Albanian frontier running down the middle of it, Lake Ohrid has more than fifty monasteries, some of them smaller than St. Andrew in Treska, scattered along its shores. This was the cradle of South Slav culture, here Christianity first reached them through the teachings of St. Clement of Ohrid and St. Naum nineteen miles away to the south. *Face-en-face* at each end of the lake, as Vasil Lahtov put it, these two missionaries blazed a trail that reached out as far as Russia. In order to make the scriptures available to their converts, they invented the Cyrillic alphabet. They introduced medicine, veterinary practice, too, and because they also encouraged the Slav aptitude for painting, so that their churches were beautifully decorated, Ohrid Lake became a centre of pilgrimage.

Vasil Lahtov, burly, friendly, intense over 'peens' (brooches) and other archaeological matters, was curator of the local museum and one of six gentlemen of Macedonia who insisted on trying to show us the whole of Ohrid in a single day. We began at a market in Struga, bright with the colour of national costume and harvest produce, and we ended up at midnight in the echoing halls of a workers' hostel that was almost as big as the new Palace Hotel, where the tourist now lives in fantastical marbled splendour. It was a very Balkan day, full of argument and information in four languages. I remember a water melon cut so that at a tap it fell apart in slices. We ate it in the sun, dripping juice and watching a clumsy boat full of stones crabbing the current of a river where it flowed like pale green silk into the dazzling shimmer of the lake. There were grapes, too; we carried them with us all day and ate them in the cool of evening on the Albanian frontier, beside a small lake that was deathly still and surrounded by willows dappled with the white of egrets' wings.

I shall always remember that evening. As we walked up to the monastery of St. Naum, the vast expanse of Ohrid Lake was like a sheet of glass with the mountains of Albania, reflected, coming across the waters to meet us. The monastery itself was all honey and russet red in the sunset, a symphony of colour so quiet and restrained that it was like a benediction.

And inside, St. Naum himself looking out from the wall above his couch-like tomb, dark and primitive and strangely calm in the yellow light of a taper. The sun had set by the time we left and all the warmth was gone from stone and tile, leaving a dark silhouette, a crouched mass that still retained its symmetry and its sense of repose. What a culture it must have been, before the Turks came!

I was thinking about this as we drove back along the dirt track that bordered the lake, and then we stopped in the little fishing village of Pestani and I saw a sight that staggered me, children crowding eagerly round our car, faces pressed excitedly against the windows. 'It is Boris they have come to see,' I was told. Boris Bojadziski was one of our six gentlemen, an author and a poet; a tall, very vital man, so intense in argument that beads of sweat gathered on his brow. 'They read his work in the schools, so now they like to see him.' I had never before seen a writer treated like a film star by village children; but then I had never before been in a country where illiteracy was being wiped out in a single generation.

In the morning, as we flew out of Ohrid bound for the Dalmation coast, we were shown one final monastery, St. John of Kaneo. Pinned to our wing tip as the pilot made a tight turn round it for our benefit, it stood on a promontory jutting into the lake, a whirling pattern of browns like some beautiful butterfly asleep in the sunrise. It was there for an instant, and then it was gone and we were climbing into the mountains, ridge upon ridge, seen so close that I could make out the old parachute drops of partisan days and the trails they used above the tree line. And between the ridges, with their sudden limestone cliffs, their thickly-forested slopes, lay deep-gouged valleys with here and there the pale ribbon of a track, the small pattern of a settlement. Seen from the air like that, it required no feat of imagination to understand what it must have been like to be a partisan and fight a war from those ridge-tops, parched by the waterless heat in summer, frozen by the bitter cold in winter.

From Ohrid to the Dalmatian coast is a four-day journey by bus, through Pec (Pech) and the arid highlands of Montenegro. It is a very spectacular journey, and there are bears in those mountains, wolves, too, and the people still maintain their murderous family feuds. But the road was very bad and as an alternative Jugoslovenski Aerotransport (JAT) had much to recommend it. It still had something of the dash of pioneer days about it, but its old Dakotas were comfortable and well-flown, and because they flew through the mountains you could see a great deal of the country in a short time. It was also very cheap—about 15 dinars (just over ¼d) a mile!

In fact, all transport in Yugoslavia was ridiculously cheap. It had to be, otherwise the country would grind to a halt, for a man's wages were then less than 10,000 dinars (about £9) a month and seldom more than 20,000 dinars a month, plus child allowance. But though travel is cheap, the Government makes it pay by using it to the maximum, and this is the snag —steamers, trains, buses are all overcrowded. There is no queuing for places. It is every man for himself and the weak go to the wall and have to stand.

Land communications are the country's chief problem. The roads in the south are some of the worst I have ever seen, and for the State enterprises that run the public transport it is a major headache. Vehicle factories are too small to be geared to mass production. The result is that a long-distance coach costs a fortune; Split, to solve its transport problems, had bought a fleet of secondhand double-decker buses from London—an incongruous sight. Heavy import duties to conserve precious foreign currency had raised the price of a single bus tyre to an astronomical £150. Wear-and-tear of vehicle and tyres is shattering. The road from Kotor to Cetinje, where it climbs 6,000 ft over the Lovcen, gives some indication of the problem. I saw it from Tivat airfield that afternoon and counted twenty-four hairpin bends zig-zagging up the limestone wall of the mountain.

For the sum of 200 dinars (less than 6d) a JAT bus took us a three-hour journey to Dubrovnik along dirt roads so narrow that we seemed to be shouldering our way between the stone walls. Darkness fell. The air was suffocatingly humid after the dry heat of the mountains. The strays we picked up on the way had no Turkish strain in their blood: instead they chatted in the liquid accents of Italy. The bus was filled to overflowing and all I remember of that journey now is the dust, the smell of diesel oil hanging heavy in the humid heat, the walls of rock coming up at us out of the night on the endless bends, the lurching and jolting and the persistent cries from the rear for paper bags with which all buses are equipped—the sweet, alcoholic reek of *rakija* (plum brandy) mingled with the sicklier smell of vomit.

There was one interlude, however, right at the start, when the sun was setting and we had to wait half an hour at the little port of Tivat for our turn on the ferry that bridges the narrows of Kotor Bay. For that half-hour I would make that journey a dozen times; the bay that I had seen from the air, looking like a Norwegian fjord burnt brown by eternal sunshine, had all the charm of an Italian lake seen from the water's edge. Its surface was mirror-smooth, its old stone houses dripped honey in the sun's last rays, and down the still glass cut of the narrows, where white-painted lighthouses winked their warning, a glimpse of island churches, looking like dream palaces, tantalised. If I were planning another visit to Dalmatia, I would start by exploring that bay.

And so, jaded, we came at last to Dubrovnik . . . a sudden blaze of lights, the looming bulk of old stone towers, a street jam-packed with tourists. Gone was the peace, the cultured splendour of Ohrid. Here at the JAT office was only the bedlam of tourism, the Putnik travel offices crowded, the buses besieged and no sign now of the old town we had come to see. Our hearts sank, and sank still further when we learned that the hotel booking that should have been made for us had not been made. A French-speaking Yugoslav found us a room at the Excelsior for one night only. The taxi that took us there was two-and-a-half times more expensive than the long drive from Tivat. The Pearl of the Adriatic! We fell into our room, disillusioned.

And yet, less than an hour later, refreshed, we were two people touched by the wand of enchantment, utterly bewitched. We sat on a terrace, soft-lit in the velvet warmth of the night with a bottle of Zhilavka, Mostar's famous wine. It was green in the glass, dry as shaved ice on the palate. Branzoni, our first Adriatic fish, was brought to us, grilled whole and cooked superbly. Distant music drifted across the water from the lit shape of a passing steamer, a warm breeze stirred the palm fronds, whispering, and a late-night bather dived into the sea below us, breaking with a splash the monotony of water lapping. And laid out before our astonished gaze, compact and entire, stood the whole walled city of old Dubrovnik, luminous and beckoning.

The call of it was so insistent that we seemed to have no option. As the last strollers left the streets, we dragged ourselves as far as the gates—just a glance inside, we thought, just a quick look to see what it was that had drawn so many people to this old walled city with its merchant adventuring tradition. A wooden drawbridge, a dark abyss descending between towering walls, a glimpse of steamers idle at a quay framed in a stone arch, and then we turned sharp right, came out from under the Clock Tower gateway and stopped a-gasp, transfixed by the sight that met our gaze. We were suddenly back in the past, back in the seventeenth century, and we had the city to ourselves; not a soul was there. But it wasn't entirely the emptiness that cast the spell. I saw Venice first in wartime, late at night and deserted. It hadn't this quality at all. This was different, something quite unique. This had the fragility of an ivory chess piece. Pisa has that same fragility, but Pisa is all wedding-cake, a cold, white marble. This was warmer, softer, more beautiful than anything I had ever seen.

Stretched out ahead of us was the great empty thoroughfare of the Placa (Placha). It cuts the city right across, from the Pile to the Ploce gates, and it is built where once the sea separated Ragusa, island settlement of the Greeks, from the Dubrovnik of the mainland Slavs. There is no street like it in the world, for seen like that, deserted and at night, the lights catch the gloss of the worn stone paving blocks so that they gleam like yellow ivory. A kind of marble, I thought, and then I knelt to touch their surface. They were stone—a particular type of limestone, so polished by the daily thousands of feet that scuffed across them that they had that peculiar gloss that the bare feet of Arabs can give to hard plasterwork.

Spell-bound we walked the city, up past the church of St. Blaise and the Rector's Palace, up to the cathedral and through a narrow way to the Jesuit Monastery, and on through alley after alley, airless with the day's heat trapped—a glimpse of a little garden, a shadow moving across a blind, the sound of a man snoring, alley cats bustling and screeching about their business, geraniums dripping from carved stone balconies high above our heads—and all around us, every stone, the past of a republic that had defied Venice and appeased the Turks. We couldn't stop; exhausted, we went on walking.

I can declare now that everything everybody has ever said about Dubrovnik is less than the truth. But steal up on it secretly, at night, when each alley springs a new surprise, and squares and little courtyards burst upon you without warning like the fragments of a dream. By day it can never be quite the same, for enchantment does not survive the company of thousands. Dubrovnik is in business then, tourist business— and business is so good you can hardly move on the Placa when the shops open after the siesta.

What it is like now that the new coast road has been completed I shudder to think. With little more than a thousand hotel beds and about three thousand rooms in private houses, Dubrovnik was even then bursting at the seams. A woman we met, who rented an apartment above the market place in what is really her own house, said she was dreading it. 'Everyone in Dubrovnik is dreading it. But it is necessary. Tourism is important so that we can import the things we need from abroad.' When I reminded her that it was a long coast and the road not yet started, she looked at me with frank astonishment. 'But of course we shall have the road in five years. Tito has promised it.'

Tito had said it would be so. That was enough for her. And she was a descendant of one of the old patrician families!

There are very few people in Dubrovnik today who can trace their family back to the great days of the Ragusan Republic, and thereby hangs a tale. Go into the city early, about six, when the market is really busy, and you will see women in their national costume as beautiful as you have ever seen. They are tall and straight and fair, with fine-boned features and an aristocratic mien. These are the women of Konavle. Greek and Roman patrician blood dominates the peasant Slav in them, for they are heiresses to a great past— a past that goes back to the seventh century.

At Cavtat (Savtat), a half-hour's steamer ride to the south, you can see the place from which their forebears came. It is very beautiful asleep there in the sun beside the still waters of an inlet, and seeing it, looking so like a little patch of Greece tossed down at the foot of the bare Dalmatian hills, you can imagine how it must have been when the Croats and the Serbs came down to the coast on the tide of the Slav invasion. For Cavtat stands where once the Greco-Roman colony of Epidaurum stood. Overwhelmed, the survivors took refuge on the rocky crags of the island of Dubrovnik. Highly civilised and clever, both politically and economically, they absorbed their Slav neighbours, and for eleven centuries trod a diplomatic tight-rope that maintained the independence of their tiny republic through the rise and fall of Byzantine, Norman, Venetian, Hungarian, Croation and Turkish power, their sailors fighting at sea, their diplomats in the courts of Europe. And in the long centuries of Turkish occupation they paid their tribute and went their way, not even the terrible earthquake of 1667, which brought down in rubble almost all the city but the walls, shaking their faith in themselves. That was left to internal dissension and the march of Napoleon's armies.

The patrician leaders bowed then to force of circumstances and handed Marshal Gauthier the keys of their city. A glance at the remains of Gauthier's forts, which still frown down from the surrounding hills, and it is obvious that they had no alternative. But so appalled were they at the disaster that had befallen them that they swore to a man to leave their wives alone and breed no children into captivity. But though they mostly kept their fine oath, they did not consider it applied to any women but their wives and they spent their virility on the peasant girls of their farms on the Konavle plain, so that the strain of their aristocratic blood is no longer Dubrovnik's heritage.

Nevertheless, capitulation preserved the city so that it stands just as it was rebuilt after the earthquake. Here and there you can glimpse the older, richer city—the Sponza Palace survived, so did the Rector's Palace and the fountain of Onofrio and Roland's Pillar. The walls, too, are the original, dating back to the eighth century, with many improvements and huge forts and bastions added. Walk the top of them at sunset, a two-kilometre circuit of the city that is unique; I saw it then as I had first seen it in the Belgrade studio of a famous artist, saw it suddenly with Pedja's eyes, a fairytale city, all warm stone and deep-cut alleys and battlements, with fantastical towers and domes toppling in the confusion of earthquake against the blue of sea and the distant blur of islands.

And from the eastern side, where the Bokar tower falls sheer to the water, you'll look across to the Lovrjenac fort. It stands on a crag and the battlements, where Shakespeare's *Hamlet* is played each year at the Festival, rise in steps to a lofty prow that faces towards the mainland like the bows of a battleship. Something about its shape took me back to the dry uplands of Macedonia, to the plain of Kumanovo. High on a hill overlooking the battlefield stands a monument of megalomaniac proportions, a fortress almost, that contains within its stone walls the bones of all the Serbs who died in that Balkan War. It is shaped like the bows of a ship, and the bows point straight towards Turkey. Was Lovrjenac the architect's inspiration or is this unusual design traditional?

War, disaster, occupation—has the country ever been free till now? As you proceed along the coast each hilltop almost testifies to the unending struggle for control. Turkish fortresses predominate. But the French had forts, so did the English out on the islands. And everywhere Venetian power has left its mark, its trademark you might almost say, for at places like Hvar (Hwar) and Korčula (Korchula) the Venetian lion, the Lion of St. Mark—a little chipped sometimes by hostile elements—still stands in all its winged insolence over fortified gate and patrician palace. Mark these lions well. Each has his paw on a book. If the book is open, then peace reigned when the sculptor chiselled the stone. If the book is closed . . . but almost always the book is closed. Only once, on a well-head in Hvar, did I find the book open.

And when the power of Venice finally faded, there were still the French, the Austrians, the Italians; a brief interlude as a young country under a Serbian king, and then invasion, the Germans, civil war, revolution. There is hardly a village in all Dalmatia that hasn't at least a plaque recording the names of its partisan heroes, and the scars are still there. In Korčula roofless patrician palaces are almost indistinguish-

able from the ruins of the bombed-out houses and a start has
only recently been made to put these empty shells to use as
lodgings for the shipyard workers. In Trogir, too—another
Venetian stronghold—we came upon sudden gaps and piles
of rubble. But it was at Zadar that we really came face-to-
face with the war. To get the Germans out of this vital port,
Partisan H.Q. called for some seventeen separate raids, almost
80 per cent of the town was destroyed. After fourteen years
it still had the look of a town just captured from the enemy,
all rubble and dust, with the eyeless windows of bombed-out
buildings staring across acres of emptiness.

In Trogir, in front of the great Venetian mass of the
Kamerlengo fortress, stands the statue of a partisan in the act
of throwing a grenade. It has something of the quality of
Mestrovic's work, the same strength, the same almost megalomaniac expression of dominance that produced the Gregory
at Split or the ark-like tomb of the Unknown Soldier at Avala;
it expresses fearlessness and ruthlessness. It should be remembered that Tito's partisans fought two wars at one and the
same time; the war against the Germans and the civil war
against the Cetniks and Ustase. This last was the Revolution;
it was from this that Tito's Yugoslavia, the Yugoslavia of
today, sprang.

The memory of that revolution is carefully preserved. In
Belgrade, in the grounds of that gigantic Turkish fortress of
Kalemegdan, there is a war museum that is, I believe, the
only one of its kind in the world. Surrounded by kilometres of
walls that go back to the pre-Roman Celtic settlement and
from the battlements of which you look down upon the
bridge that carried the Russian hordes in the wake of the re-
treating Germans, guns and tanks and aircraft of all nationalities lie scattered amongst the streets. There is even a reconstruction of Tito's cave headquarters in Bosnia, complete with
his personal effects. And housed nearby is the Partisan history
of the Revolution, told in documents, photographs and
weapons. It catches and holds the atmosphere of the times; the
cold, the misery, the fearful reprisals—mass execution, men
strung up on lines, a hero in the moment of having his head
severed by an axe. It is all there, the leaders, too—a potent reminder, a warning. And it is not only in the capital that the

story of the partisans is preserved. Even Korčula, so wrapped up in its ancient past, sets a room aside in the Gabrielis Palace to tell the Odyssey of her partisan citizens as the struggle see-sawed up and down the coast. I was there on September 13. The red of the partisan flag flew over the gatehouse tower, maroons banged from the battlements. *Lest we forget!* It was the anniversary of their liberation. The phoenix fires of the Revolution are as carefully nurtured as the flame on an unknown warrior's tomb.

If I had to pick one place on the Dalmatian coast, it would by Korčula. It looks like a rustic, rather battered little Dubrovnik; but its beauty breaks the heart. It stands on a fist of rock thrust out into a narrow strait, all honey-coloured stone rising steeply to the pinnacle of St. Mark; seen at sunrise as a golden city, or as a black silhouette at sunset, it has a sort of tumbled splendour. Dr. Arneric showed it to us first —the place where Marco Polo was supposed to have been born, the scene of the traditional 'Moreska', the walls that an ancestor of his had torn down in a misguided enthusiasm for hygiene, the fort that General Roven built against Napoleon, looking exactly like a larger version of the martello towers that the English built along their coasts for the same reason. A patrician, still with a palace of his own, this was the same Dr. Arneric who figures as the 'cardinal' in Rebecca West's classic *Black Lamb and Grey Falcon*; a jovial, priestly figure, still enthusiastically talking of his pipe-dreams of a proper water system, for water is the crying need of all these limestone islands.

The Greeks came to Korčula in the fourth century BC. In the vineyard walls of nearby Lumbarda there were found after the war the fragments of the tablet on which the 180 Greek families recorded the laws by which the settlement should be governed. Preserved now in the museum of the Gabrielis Palace, it is the oldest relic in Dalmatia. Korčula the Black, the Greeks called this island—but little is left of the great umbrella pine forests that gave rise to the name; the trees went to build Venetian galleys, to warm the stony hearts of successive invasions. Close by on Vrnik island the quarries that provided the stone for the old Greek city, for the present Venetian town, for Dubrovnik, too, are still worked. But it is its situation that gives it life; steamers from everywhere along the coast, from Rijeka to Kotor, call at all hours of the day and night, and across the three-mile-wide straits the mass of the Peljesac penisula towers, grey and stony. Vis, Lastove, Mljet, a whole archipelago—the charm of an island world steeped in history.

It was in Korčula that Dorothy and I attended our first church service, climbing on a Sunday morning to the little sun-drenched square at the top of the town. Above us the bell of the thirteenth century cathedral rang its summons, fantastical gargoyles peered down at us from a brilliant sky, the smoke of a steamer drifted across the roofless palace opposite. My spirits sank as we entered the cathedral, for it was almost empty. But just before eleven o'clock the people of Korčula began to pour in—and they went on pouring in, even after the service had begun, until the whole place seemed packed. Sunlight picked up the colours of the Tintoretto half-obscured by the altar candles, spotlighted the beauty of Andrijic's great stone ciborium; music and the sound of young voices singing filled the whole stone edifice. It was a strangely moving experience after the empty 'museums' of Macedonia.

I was told that the Catholic churches of the Dalmatian coast were fuller than they had ever been. 'At Split they are so full that old people faint in the crush on Sundays.' And the same informant added: '*It is the only means of protest they have.*'

What exactly was meant by this I am not quite certain. One is conscious, of course, that it is a Communist country, but it was not the Communism of Stalin. Indeed Yugoslavia was a compromise between Communism and Capitalism, already pointing the road that Russia would later be forced to tread. When we were there private enterprise was permitted on a small scale, the limit then being five employees—above that it became a co-operative with everybody, including the State, sharing the profits. One man told me that as a result of co-partnership his income had risen from 18,000 to 30,000 dinars that year. Admittedly President Tito's picture looked down on us from every office, every restaurant wall, but it was a very un-Big Brotherly picture, more like the pin-up portrait of a well-known film star. In fact, we became so accustomed to that strangely attractive face that a wall without it looked quite naked. As for police, they were chiefly remarkable for their absence.

It seemed to me that the packed churches represented not so much a protest as a spiritual need. How else explain the spectacle that I saw at Trogir?

We had come north from Split, along the coast of the seven castles, where Greek, Roman and Venetian antiquities are being slowly smothered by the sprawl of industrial development. Trogir is a walled Venetian city with the water-encircled atmosphere of Bruges, and we had come, as everybody must, to see the thirteenth century cathedral of St. Lawrence, and in particular the great entrance door—Radovan's masterpiece. It is a superb piece of carving; the Nativity, scenes from the Old Testament, saints, animals, grotesque shapes that include a merman even, all flanked by the two great heraldic lions supporting the giant figures of Adam and Eve, and set in a little stone square that seems made to match, as though the Middle Ages, with the narrow alleys, its palaces, had all been petrified and preserved for our benefit.

As we stood before the great portal, carved by the cathedral's architect in the year 1240, the verger appeared beside us, a bell-rope in his hand, and began to toll. Candles were lit in the dim interior and from alleys deep in shadow came the sound of a brass band. People appeared at windows, blocked the mouth of converging streets, and then, slowly, into the square came the procession. Whose funeral it was I forgot to ask, I was so amazed. Behind the catafalque and the priests and the band walked an unending stream of people. The men came first, the town's dignitaries, and then more peasant types with faces that might have been taken down from Radovan's stone carvings, and after them the women, a line of slow-marching figures in black that seemed as though it would never end. I could not believe that Trogir, which is still no larger than it was in the heyday of its Venetian masters, could hold so many people.

The temporal power of the Catholic Church has been broken, its lands and riches confiscated. Its priests, except those that are the paid caretakers of ancient monuments, are

Dorothy at the helm – a smiling sea in the Bay of Biscay

The northern end of the Bosporus – in the background is the gateway to the Black Sea and Russia

Our meeting with Tito

The South Ford, between the islands of Benbecula and South
Uist in the Outer Hebrides

A landing craft loading for St. Kilda in the South Ford – this
ship was the 'hero' in *Atlantic Fury*

The old village – St. Kilda

'The Treasure Seekers' – Bob Restall and his wife with the stone dated 1704

This small Adduan boy is older than he looks – the effect of centuries of a limited coral island diet

"Moth-balled" dhoni shelters on the island of Midu

The dhoni park – Gan Island

My first look at the vedis – the most pathetic sight in the Indian Ocean

Launching a typical dhoni built almost entirely from materials
grown on the atoll

The sunset scene when the bats fly home like crows to roost

a charge upon the community they serve. This is back to the original conception of the Church as a servant of the people, and though the more tractable Serbs may pay lip service to atheistical materialism, peasant Dalmatia in its poverty still has need of its priests and finds a funeral oration by a Comrade an unsatisfactory end to the drama of life.

I asked President Tito whether he thought his people could live by bread alone. To this he replied with a chuckle that he had managed very well without religion all his life. That may be. All his life he has been fighting for a positive goal; he has always had something to reach up to. But for the people . . .

Whilst I was picking autumn narcissi for my wife on the top of Osjk Island, off Velaluka, with all the islands out to Vis in black silhouette against a flaming sky and the sickle of a new moon climbing above hills dark with carib trees and vines, three men were rowing a boat towards the black line of the horizon. They would go on rowing that boat for twenty-four hours or more until they reached the shores of Italy, seventy-odd miles away. They were not the first to use this escape route. I was told that in Italy there is a camp and a complete organisation for sending them on to the States.

Why do they go? They're not persecuted. They're not in danger. The young man in the crowded bus, looking very smart and rather conspicuous in the new suit sent him by his uncle in Australia, shrugged his shoulders at my question. They hear stories about what it is like outside, he said, and because they are not allowed to go they have a great desire to go. As a book-keeper he earned 14,000 dinars a month, less than a construction worker. He, too, wanted to go—but only on a visit, he said.

To keep the people happy whilst building a new country . . . it is a problem, for industrial expansion is slow without foreign capital; it is also unspectacular. The answer is to give them amenities they never had before. Take a little village like Lumbarda. From its vineyards comes the heavy, cider-like wine called Grk; from its fishing harbour the silver spoils of the Adriatic caught at night by acetylene lamp. A peasant community without much thought beyond the day's work.

Doubtless they were pressed into giving their labour free for the community, but the result is that there is a good quay where before there was rubble, a small park planted with palms and other trees, a 'Culture House' with a bar, an excellent restaurant, a cinema and games room, all imaginatively decorated, beautifully clean.

All along the coast you will find the quays new-built and extended into promenades, with trees and flowering shrubs and modern lighting. It may look pretentious against a background of poverty and over-crowded housing conditions, but it is based on a Yugoslav habit which I will call the *Titova Obala*. This is the evening promenade, when the whole village or town turns out after the day's work to stroll in twos and threes, in family groups, until it is time to go to bed. On the coast this promenade takes place on the Titova Obala —the new quays named after Tito. In the interior it is the main street—the Marsala Tita—and there for two hours or more no vehicles can pass, the people so pressed together they barely move. And in Macedonia it is black hair, black clothes, the whole street in solid black.

But in Dalmatia it is different. There is more colour; and in encouraging each community to build its Titova Obala the State has been very astute, for the result is that every evening a man and his wife, the young people, the children, too, can see the shape of things to come, can glimpse the future that hard work can give. Sit with me a moment in a café on Zadar's fantastic mile-long waterfront where the huge rebuilt museum, neatly incorporating the remains of the old, stands grandiose in splendid isolation. It is evening; a water cart is going round the town in a gallant attempt to lay the dust, and the people are coming out from the rubble for their nightly stroll. At first they are just black shapes against the sunset, which has suddenly flared up, setting the water of the straits on fire and showing the flowing shape of the island opposite all purple like the hills of Scotland. And then the lights come on, close-packed and brilliant like the footlights in a theatre, and suddenly the water is black and the people stand revealed like characters when the curtain has gone up.

They should have been dusty and drab, these people from the ruins of a bombed-out town. Instead the women were elegantly dressed—so well dressed, in fact, and with such taste, that they would put to shame many a rich city of the West. The children, too, bubbling with vitality and health, their clothes new-laundered, starched and ironed, as though every day were a Sunday, little girls' hair gay with ribbons, little boys scrubbed and well-behaved. Prams were standard, low-slung, of the latest pattern. The men, too, were carefully dressed, though new suits were few, for a new suit costs the better part of £40—perhaps three months' wages. We were told that everybody in Dalmatia had relatives abroad who provided them with money and clothes, but not every woman in Zadar could be dressed by a rich uncle in San Francisco or Sydney. The truth was, of course, that whilst good dresses were almost unobtainable in the shops, material was getting easier and there were fashion magazines everywhere. And since there was not a great deal as yet on which to spend money, clothes and dressmaking for the Titova Obala was the nearest many Yugoslavs get to the idea of keeping up with the Joneses.

In Split, where the monumental remains of the Emperor Diocletian's palace seethe with the thousands that have made it their home, there is a bathing beach where people can forget the crowded conditions in which they live; the water is warm, the view fantastic, an open-air cinema, changing cabins, a restaurant. I went there once at sunset. A man sat fishing upon a rock, his little son jumping up and down beside him at the sight of a dolphin plunging through the still water, the islands dark whale shapes along the horizon. And at Sibenik, out beyond the protecting narrows, another elaborate people's beach—cabins, picnic beaches beneath the pines, a boat service. And in the mountains, workers' hostels so beautifully set that they would reap a fortune if developed for the tourists.

These amenities help make life bearable for people who are sacrificing the present for the future. Water polo, too. . . . I remember a match played under lamps that shone brilliant on the boatloads of people massed on the seaward side of the pool, everybody yelling themelves hoarse as at a football match. And everywhere there are cafés in which, for the price of a single coffee, you can sit all evening listening to music pumped out over the radio, thumped out from bands and amplified by loudspeakers to ear-splitting volume.

Music, music, music—it goes on and on. And in the cities, first-class cultural entertainment run by the State, and so cheap I couldn't believe it was true. Four stalls for the Opera at the National Theatre in Belgrade cost me 1,000 dinars (just under £1). I listened to the music of David Oistrakh's violin at the opening of the concert season; from the West they had had Yehudi Menuhin, most of the big names—and the seats the same ridiculous price.

But it is the past rather than the practicalities of the present that makes this country so beautiful—so incredibly, hauntingly beautiful. The sudden glimpse of Hvar at night; that lovely Venetian piazza, that ivory campanile. Hvar—the old Pharos of early Greek settlers—is full of treasures . . . *The Lord's Supper,* painted by Rosselli in gratitude to the Franciscans who nursed him back to health, that little gem of a sixteenth century theatre built into the old Arsenal that housed the town galley. And at Zadar, the huge ninth century church of St. Donat standing in solitary splendour amongst the ruins, the whole of its great weight resting on the paving stones of a Roman forum, its foundations the fallen Doric columns of Empire. Even Split, unlovely in the dust of ages, the smoke of steamers, seething with crowds, industrialised—even Split has its moments; at night, in the ruins of the palace that was the inspiration of Adam's Georgian designs, every twist of the narrow, crowded alleys is a potential film-set for something as epic as *Ben-Hur,* and to sit at a table in the terrace cafés of the Peristyle or in the arched seclusion of Srebrena Vrata is to bridge the gap of centuries, the past and the present all around you. And beneath the ruins, beneath all the houses with which the palace has been honeycombed, lie vaults newly-excavated by the enthusiasm of the brothers Marasovic; there you will find the stone blocks that have supported the teeming life of centuries so well preserved by a thousand years of filth that they look like a reconstruction.

There is no end to the list. One final glimpse of the unique an art gallery run by my publishers in Novi Sad—the Galerija Matice Srpake. Here in the heart of the rich province of Vojvodine, Radivoj Kovačevic, the English-speaking cus

odian, will tell you the story of icons painted in the early
ighteenth century that have the same formalism that is char-
acteristic of the early Ohrid frescoes. Yet they are not deri-
vative. In 1690 the Austrians were defeated by the Turks and
oo,ooo Serbian families fled north into what was then the
uninhabited swamplands of the Danube. Within fifty years,
cut off from all contact with the south, they had recreated
out of their cultural need an art form that went back beyond
the Middle Ages. And at the same time they were painting
pictures that were typically eighteenth century. It is all there
in that gallery, an extraordinary mingling of outside influence
and the inborn need of mystical expression.

It was after visiting this gallery that I went to see the man
who had made Yugoslavia as it is today—Tito. In a residential
district of Belgrade, dappled with plane trees, the official car
that had been sent for us stopped with its bumpers against
the blank pine face of wooden doors. Number Fifteen. A
wicket opened. The drab of a partisan uniform, a quick glance
and the doors swung back. A short drive, roses blooming, a
white portico; we were received by black-coated officials of
the household, the doors of the cabinet room opened silently,
the President stood there to greet us.

No one who has ever met Tito has failed to be impressed.
Short, burly, with the compact body of a fighter, it is still the
head that draws one's gaze; it is a fine head, strong, with the
planes of the cheeks still firm, the hair thick and scarcely
touched with grey, the blue eyes, clear, compelling. The im-
mediate impression is of a born leader, and the impression remains, indelible—a man of implacable will, of great courage,
alone, still fighting. He was then sixty-five, yet he looked no
older than those film-star-like pictures we had seen in every
public place. Perhaps it is his sense of humour, his obvious
enjoyment of life, that has kept him young.

Coffee was brought, *rakija*, glasses of tomato juice. I hadn't
expected tomato juice; it was occasioned by the fact that he
was suffering from rheumatism, legacy of his penchant for
cave-dwelling during the war. Nor had I expected the conversation to be conducted in English. He had learned it in
prison, he said, in order to read the footnotes to English engineering books—in each case the text had been translated,

but not the footnotes, and these he had found vital to a proper study of the subject. That had been between the wars; he had spent a lot of time then in Yugoslav gaols, on the run, in exile, for he had come back from Russia a convinced Communist.

Tito is not his real name, of course. It is a partisan nom-de-guerre derived from his insistence on telling people to do this, do that—*ti to, ti to*. He was born Josip Broz, the son of a Croat peasant. He fought on the Russian front in the first world war, was taken prisoner, volunteered for the Red Army at the time of the Bolshevik Revolution. In the fourteen years since the last war his inherent nationalistic instinct must have been at odds with his Russian indoctrination, so hard and so repeatedly have the Russians struck at him.

He was amused when I said that, as it affected the ordinary people I had been meeting. I didn't see all that much difference between his method of government and our own bureaucracy, except perhaps that his government, through State ownership, taxed the people before they earned their money, whereas ours taxed them afterwards; smiling, he said he thought there were still some fundamental differences. And then he added, with a twinkle in his eye, that I might be interested to know that authors were encouraged and taxed at a specially low rate! Nevertheless, the fact is that Yugoslav Communism—Tito's communism—was even then very different from Russian Communism—much less harsh, much freer, more fluid and with a strong element of nationalism running through it. The State's willingness to compromise suggests that Tito had accepted human nature as the key to successful government.

Two things in that cabinet room are important; very prominently placed is a large teak and ivory map of India slung from a pair of gold-banded tusks mounted on a block of ebony. Tito pointed it out to me. 'A present from Nehru.' He might just as well have said: '*India and Yugoslavia, we think alike—we are neutral.*' I was reminded that between Nehru and him stood the United Arab Republic and that Nasser had been a recent visitor to his island retreat at Brioni. Behind the cabinet conference table, at the far end of the room, opposite the french windows, the whole wall is taken up by a huge battle picture painted by Kreto Hegedksic in

1572. The subject is the peasant uprising of the previous year; the scene, Hrvatsko Zagorye, close by Tito's birthplace. 'It was like your Wat Tyler's rebellion,' Tito said. 'It is the part of the country where my ancestors lived. I like to think they may be among the people in the picture.' It impressed me very much, that picture of a past struggle hanging there on the wall, and this burly man, who had fought his way from peasant outlaw to the presidency of the new country he had created, standing there, his feet slightly apart, his head thrown back, staring up at it. I couldn't help wondering if that picture, the fact that it hung there, always before him in moments of decision, were not the key to the difference between this country and other Communist countries.

II

THE DANISH ISLANDS

We sailed to Denmark direct across the North Sea, to the
Limfjord, that series of brednings, or broads, and dredged
channels which cuts right across the north of Jutland. This
was in 1959 and it was *Mary Deare's* maiden voyage. Three
and a half days out, in the quiet of a still dawn watch, the
first zephyr of the land breeze carried on its breath the stored-
up smell of the country, a warm, rich, earthy smell, a mingling
of dry grass, heather and cow byres. And then the light came
and we saw the fishing boats and the line of the sand-dune
coast, low as a desert strand. And as we sailed in across the
bar, past the little port of Tyborøn where the masts of the
fishing boats stood thick as spears against the brilliant blue of
the sky, a new smell—the sickly sweet smell of fish oil.

Limfjord! Wherever you go in Denmark you find that
name—in the shops, in the restaurants, on the tongue of every
gourmet—for it is from Limfjord that the oysters come;
not Portuguese oysters, but the real thing, the equal of the
Colchester native. Caviar, too—that false caviar that is cod's
roe specially treated; it cannot be compared with the roe of
the royal sturgeon, but it is nevertheless popular as a garnish
for the endless smørrebrød.

The consumption of smørrebrød in Denmark is fantastic,
involving more man hours, it seems than any other occupation. Every hotel, restaurant, inn or café, even the pavilions
where people go to dance, have their smørrebrød *kart*, the list
long or short according to the catering facilities. Smørre is
butter and brød bread, and this is the foundation for every
imaginable garnish. At Andersens in Copenhagen it reaches
the peak of variety with a *kart* that is more than a yard wide
in several different languages. *Sild*—usually a marinated form
of herring—is vital to almost every meal, and much of it
comes from the Lim.

Doubtless to encourage the consumption of Pilsener and

Schnapps—or perhaps simply because Danes seem to enjoy sitting in the cafés—the waiting for this simple, easy-to-prepare food is endless. Its appearance is always attractive, designed, one feels, to appeal to the eye rather than to the palate. It tends to be over-rich and very filling. Even more filling is the *anretning*. This crops up all over Denmark. It is not a dish but a whole meal, a blend of hot and cold, of fish and meat and vegetables; it is, in fact, everything a restaurant has to offer bar the kitchen stove.

The most fabulous *anretning* I came across was, very properly, in the Limfjord, at Aalborg where Denmark's gin is distilled. The Royal Hotel described it as their *luxus anretning* and here it is direct from the *kart* in Danish: *Luxus sildeanretning—fersk, røget laks—kaviar—stegt al røget, al—stegt fiskefilet—salater—saltanretning—sma boeuf—kalvefilet met rist. champignons—lever—champignons à la crème—kylling eller andesteg—osteanretning eller desert.* It is only served for an order of two or more. When it arrives you understand why. One portion would be fully sufficient for four people. . . . To do justice to such a rich and gargantuan repast you need to have starved yourself for at least three days.

It is not easy to describe an area as unique as the Lim. With all that water it should be flat and marshy; it has the wide skies, the distant horizons of a marsh country, yet there are hills and small cliffs and moors covered with heather. There is strangely a touch of the Highlands about it, and the long evenings, the cold, clear air, remind one of places much further north. It has, in fact, an Arctic tang . . . the sense of remoteness, almost of hostility, the same milky look as dusk comes down; and yet give it a gleam of sunshine and the water, the shores, the little hills positively smile at you.

But without that smile it wears a grim visage, the waters leaden, thrashed to a steep breaking fury, and all the country round dour and wind-torn. You realise then that this is not the Denmark that produced Hans Andersen—this is the Viking Denmark, the land that cried in its cups 'Skaal' and downed its drink out of the broken skulls of English victims. 'We are the only true Danes,' said the man from Aarhus in Jutland, which he pronounced Yuland. 'These people from Fyn and Zealand and all the other five hundred islands—we

accept them as part of the family, but they are not true
Danes.' This with a twinkle, for his wife was from Copenhagen on the island of Zealand. This man whom I met in the
little fishing port of Snapton was putting into words what I
had already begun to feel. The people of Jutland *are* different—harder, more independent, their features unsmiling,
their eyes coldly blue; seafarers who still live by the seas that
surround their strangely-shaped, north-pointing peninsula,
farmers who have forced a hard land to give bacon, eggs and
cheese to the world. They made me very conscious of the
history of my own country, the waves of invasion by these
hardy, violent, cold-blooded folk who had peopled England's
northern lands a thousand years ago.

Here in the north, buried or partly buried in the heath-
land soil, lies much of Denmark's earliest past. Four hundred
round barrows, dolmens and stone circles can be counted on
the little hills of Mols Bjerge, and near Aarhus in the bog at
Borum, were found the remains of men and women of the
Bronze Age, saved from disintegration through three thousand
years by the marsh. They lay in oak coffins and one of them
can be seen in the National Museum at Copenhagen, complete with its Bronze Age occupant all marvellously preserved.
There, too, is the famous sun chariot found at Trundholm
Moor in the north of the island of Zealand, the work of early
Iron Age craftsmen, its great silver bowl with its figuring now
Copenhagen's greatest treasure. On a hill near Aarhus, where
they once worshipped Thor, stands Thorsager's round church.
Only seven of these round churches still remain, four of them
on the island of Bornholm out in the Baltic far to the east.
They were dual-purpose churches built to the glory of God
and for the protection of the community against the raids of
the Wendish pirates.

At Nykøbing, a third of the way through the Limfjord,
where old-fashioned lanterns stuck on posts lit us through the
dredged channel at dusk, I caught a fleeting glimpse of that
traditional Viking thrust into northern lands. A landspektor or
chartered surveyor called Jarby sought me out, having read of
my arrival in the Mors Island evening paper. With typical
Danish hospitality he swept us all off to his home, which stood
on a bluff overlooking the fjord.

It was long and low like a Canadian ranch house, the walls of the big living-room painted red and lit by the soft glow of candles and firelight. There were pictures on the walls painted by a Greenlander who could neither read nor write and who could only express himself through his brush. There were Eskimo walrus-tooth carvings, executed with the same strong, primitive force that I had seen in similar carvings in Hudson's Bay. He and his wife had both spent some time in this huge glacial slice of Danish territory. They had been in the Faroes, too—there was a set of rough, painted cottage chairs from these remote islands standing, not incongruously, amongst the bright-coloured modern Danish furniture. There was also a razor-sharp whale knife in a brass-banded sheath: 'Though I was from the outside, I was still given my portion of a whale at the day of the Killing—everybody is given their portion, you see.'

It was difficult to picture our neat, elegant hostess in these circumstances as she sat dispensing the coffee that is always a part of Danish hospitality. Brandy, and wonderful little wrapped delicacies from some pâtisserie and the glow of firelight in a room that she had planned herself, and her fair, delicate-featured daughter of ten serving us with such seriousness, and with that same natural politeness with which she had bobbed her little curtsey as she greeted each of us in turn.

Thirty thousand people live on Mors, this island stuck in the middle of great stretches of water in the far north of Jutland, live by fishing and agriculture. Our reception at Løgstør had been very different. We sailed into this tiny little fishing harbour at the head of the great Løgstør Bredning in a heavy downpour and when I had thanked the man who had kindly taken our warps, he stared at me out of those cold, china-blue Jutlander eyes and, nudged by his companions, came out with the only English words he seemed to know. 'Da-nish bacon,' he said thickly. It was a crack at the British for cutting down on our imports which had hit Jutland particularly hard.

Northern Jutland is worth seeing, once, for the feel it gives of a land open to the sea, scoured by the elements. There is nothing anywhere to obstruct the wind. The cold in winter. . . . I could feel the threat of it even in August. And the Pilot

Book for the passage through the fjords referred constantly to buoys and broom markers that were removed from their position before the ice formed. East of the North Sea coast there is little salt in the water and the ice forms quickly; no weight in the water either, so that given the slightest wind the whitecaps spit in your eye . . . a pretty, twinkling sight in sunshine, but when the water is as leaden grey as the sky, then the white has a wicked, cruel look and one thinks of the waves piling in on the western coast, the fishing boats drawn up on the sands and the women standing, pathetic, windblown silhouettes, watching for their menfolk still at sea.

South it is different. South of Aarhus, it is more wooded and the land has a tidy, cultivated look with barely a frown on its visage, even when the weather is bad. The people, too; softer, more easy-going, feeling safe for generations behind their water-maze defences. Builders of ships—yes; sailors—yes; but not the people responsible for that incongruity of northern colonialism, Greenland. Only when you are in the north of Jutland, when you talk to men like Jarby, does Greenland as a Danish dependency seem to make any sense at all.

But south, as you walk through walled lanes of green, you are made conscious—as all Danes are conscious—that here, too, the winds drive across the flat land without let or hindrance. The highest hill in Denmark is only 565 ft and every well-managed farm, the homesteads even, have their windbreaks of poplar, beech or some other tree. And everywhere the wind machines. They stand on the islands, gaunt as huge pylons, with bladed arms spread to the skies, pumping water, making electricity; these are the modern versions of the old windmills, of which there still seems one in almost every small town.

South, too, you become suddenly conscious of history, the sense of an old-established people with a long tradition of pleasant building. I still remember the excitement I felt when I came to the island of Ærø and in a moonlight exploration of the little port of Søby stumbled upon low, timbered houses —houses that were several centuries old and reminded me of my own East Anglia. Excitement, I say, for I had come south through the narrow waters of the Little Belt and in every town and village I had been conscious of the past lacking. Even the ramparts of Fredericia's old fortifications proved to be only eighteenth century earthworks, grass-grown and made over to a public park. One of the oldest buildings in all those northern towns, and the most attractive, was always the Apothek, doubtless because the Borgmester was usually the apothecary.

Maybe if I had pushed inland, to the remoter agricultural towns; maybe if I had gone to Viborg, scene of the old ballad, *The King Slaying in Finderun*—they told me Viborg was an old town. But I never got to Viborg, and so I was left wondering what in the world had happened to the old houses of Jutland. Had they built them of softwood, like the Norwegians, so that age and decay had obliterated them? Or again, like the Norwegians, had they suffered the devastation of fire? More likely, I thought, they had torn them down in a period of new-found prosperity to replace them with the present nondescript architecture.

Whatever the cause, their absence elsewhere in the north gave to the island of Ærø the added enchantment of the un-expected. The little port of Ærøskøbing, capital of the island, is a dream, a doll's house town of cobbled streets and single-storeyed houses so miniature, so exquisite as to have a sense of unreality. Here are timbered structures standing shoulder-to-shoulder with little gay-painted houses of a later period, some so small that they seem no bigger than an over-size kennel—a door, a window and a sloping pantiled roof. It is all very precious, very self-conscious, a show place full of tourists.

It is not quite true that I saw no old houses in the north of Jutland. At Aarhus there is the old town—*Den Gamle By* —a complete reconstruction of a medieval village, all brick and timber and leaning gables, with water running through it and the willows hanging green. In the evening you can wander alone there, peopling the deserted cobbled streets with your imagination, drinking from the fountain in *torvet*, the big market place that lies under the shadow of the four great houses brought from Aalborg in the Lim. But it is all dead, as dead as the old farmhouses on exhibition close by Horsens-jord.

Very different is the boom town of Kalundborg in the north-west of Zealand. Great modern grain silos tower above the port, floodlit and displaying as fine a line of modern concrete architecture as you will see. Lit at night in blazing colours, they stand as symbols of Kalundborg's pride in its industry. The townspeople claim that in ten years they will build a city as big as Copenhagen, which holds a quarter of Denmark's four million people. This is a slight overstatement, but American millionaire Paul Getty has already acquired land for the development of an oil terminal, and my friend Niels Norlund of the *Berlingske Tidende*, Denmark's most influential paper, assured me that the town would double its population within that period.

We sat in the glassed-in pavement café of the Jernbane Hotellet consuming smørrebrød and Kalundborg-brewed Pilsener under the shadow of the newest silo and watching the world go by, which seems to be Denmark's chief leisure occupation. There was a constant stream of people coming off the ferries, and the cadets from a great four-masted training ship, whose yardarms stood black against the night sky, hung about eyeing the girls. The *kart* at this café translated each item of smørrebrød into English; *Dyrlaegens natmad* was translated 'The Vet's night food.' 'You know what a veterinary is?' The waiter said carefully as we asked him to explain. 'Like a doctor, but for the animals.' We said we knew what a vet was. 'Well,' he said triumphantly, 'it is what he eat before he go to bed.' We never did discover why a smørrebrød composed mainly of pâté maison and onions should be regarded as the stuff of which veterinary suppers are made.

Before coming to Kalundborg I had read the legend of how Vor Frue Kirke—the Church of Our Lady—had come to be built. It was erected by Esbern Snare, a Danish nobleman, in 1170, and the design is unique in Europe, for it is five-towered and based on the old Grecian cross. According to the legend, Esbern Snare fell in love with Helva, the daughter of Nesvek's lord, who demanded a church at Kalundborg as the bride price. Whereupon Snare sold his soul to a Troll, who for the price agreed to build the church, the only escape clause in the contract being a declaration of the Troll's name which nobody had ever heard. The church went up at a great rate whilst Esbern Snare's men searched the countryside for a clue to the name. It was Helva, lying beside her lover, her ear close to the ground, who heard—just in time—the Troll's wife far below crying the Troll's name to her baby.

A strange story, and a strange church. From where my boat lay I could see the great brick structure and the five towers surmounted by green copper steeples standing flood-lit on a hill above the town. It looked more like a fairy castle than a church; it had that remoteness, and the barbaric, un-earthly quality of something taken straight from the illustra-tions to a fairy-tale. When we came to it that night the floodlights were out and the great brick structure towered enormous and gloomy against the stars. But in the lantern-lit street leading up to it, we came across old brick and timbered houses, a whole street unexpectedly belonging to the past.

There is much to see in Kalundborg, and it has the added charm of the old world living cheek-by-jowl with the new. The church itself has been so lavishly restored that it is diffi-cult to find even traces of the original brickwork. But the huge central tower gives a marvellous view of the country round, and particularly of the fjord where the ships come in. The structure is huge, but all towers, for the church inside is no bigger than a village church. Opposite the main entrance is the District Museum. It is housed in a rambling, early-seven-teenth-century mansion that looks more like a huge farm-stead with its open courtyards full of doves and chickens and dogs and babies and its long, low, barnlike stone buildings.

Museums do not greatly attract me and this was full of the town's bric-à-brac. But wade through a dozen nondescript rooms and you come to the largest exhibition of traditional costumes in Denmark. And just beyond, in an enormous, earth-floored room, where part of the stonework of Esbern Snare's old fortress has been excavated, is a display of old-time native country craft and its primitive machinery, the like of which I have never seen anywhere else. And outside, taking up all the space of an open courtyard, is a fine model of Kalundborg as it was in 1600 when the waters of the fjord surrounded the old walled town.

Places that surprise one with the unexpected are always

more rewarding than those much-publicised places that one feels one ought to visit; I suppose because of the sense of discovery. I remember particularly Kerteminde—what a lovely name! We sailed in at night and exploring beyond the modern façade of the town, came upon streets of old one-storeyed Lilliputian houses—houses that had not been self-consciously dolled-up for the world to gaze at, houses that were part of a working town. And Karrabakaminde, a little place all white in the moonlight, with bleak waters sluicing in and out, a tidal movement in a world where tides are not supposed to exist.

Just south of Kerteminde, where the Great Belt, coming down from Samsø Island and the more open sea of the Kattegat, narrows to a waist, you can see at a glance how water has shaped the Danish way of life, what a problem it has been. Every major land artery crosses water, not once, but many times. Now everywhere there are bridges, some of them of immense length for such a small country. But the Great Belt is a problem not yet solved. Every train, every truck, every car bringing foreigners and foreign goods into the big island of Zealand and the capital, Copenhagen, must cross the Great Belt. There is talk of a tunnel one day, or perhaps a bridge, for it is not deep and the island of Sprogø would make a half-way break.

Nevertheless, this gap is almost as wide as the Dover Straits and train and car ferries were taking one hour and forty minutes to make the 18-mile crossing. When we sailed through the narrows between Nyborg and Korsør I counted ten big ferry steamers visible at one time, and the knowledge that this was normal, that it went on night and day unceasingly, made me realise how great is the transport problem in a country split in three by two major waterways and then split up innumerable times again by a mass of inland waterways, channels, fjords and brednings.

I had been conscious of it on the islands, of course. Every little port, it seemed, had had its station for faergen—for the ferries. And in hundreds of miles of sailing through enclosed waters I had benefited from the many dredged channels, some of them no wider than a town street and marked on either side by broomstick markers surmounted either by a brush of twigs or a twist of straw; channels that would not have been kept dredged if they had not provided the essential ferry artery between island and island.

This is why, in exploring the country, I had been convinced that my own boat was the only possible means of transport. And so it proved, for we covered some two thousand sea miles and visited more than forty different towns and ports, two dozen different islands. All are accessible to the more conventional traveller, but it takes longer. Three of the smaller islands I particularly remember, islands so off the beaten track that only the more enterprising Danes and a handful of foreigners ever visit them.

Romsø, smallest of the three, is an hour's motorboat ride from Kerteminde, a Robinson Crusoe place, all grass and woods, with cattle grazing and horses seemingly running wild. A few campers, some day visitors, a timbered farmhouse in a woodland clearing and the proprietor of the island shooting pigeons with his son. He shook my hand, warmly extended to my party the freedom of the island, and there we were in that little lost world, in a beechwood on an island that was barely a mile across. Another lonely timbered cottage in a clearing and then we were out of the woods and climbing a grassy slope to a look-out which gave us a view of ships ploughing their way up and down the watery artery of the Great Belt. The sun shone, the sea was calm—we waded through the shallows collecting mussels. A moment of utter tranquillity quite set apart from the hurly-burly of the outside world. One could vegetate, rusticate, become 'bushed' on Romsø.

And then there was Sejerø, very difficult to pronounce— Seyroo; a little port blazing in a raucous sunset and bare hills as abrupt as giant burial mounds standing along the back of the island. A white church peered above the yellow of the cornfields, its gabled ends climbing, crenellated, like an Elizabethan mansion. We left the fishermen lying snugged in their little gut, climbed a road winding past stone farmhouses and fields stooked with corn, and suddenly came upon a lake with swans and a kitten chasing ducks. The village of

Sejerø lies around this pond on three sides, and the villagers, with rare perception of beauty, have made of the fourth side a little garden.

The church is whitewashed and the wall that surrounds the graveyard is whitewashed, too. It is this startling white that gives it a strangely Eastern quality, almost Moorish. Two women tending graves told me it was built in the eleven hundreds. It is very beautiful. The pews are painted, as they are in most Danish churches, and there is the inevitable model of a ship hanging from the roof. There are galleries, too, and a painted ceiling and the general air of a place much loved.

But it is on the graveyard that the eye lingers. Never have I seen a churchyard so beautifully kept. A profusion of flowers and flowering shrubs was offset by a variety of dwarf cedars, junipers and cypress; not a weed to be seen, the tombstones chosen with an instinctive awareness of the dignity of stone and each grave tended daily it would seem, so careful was the effect. Later, in the south of Zealand, I saw churches of the same unusual design, but none with quite the same Eastern charm.

Walking back, still filled with the enchantment of the place, we called at the inn, which in Denmark is called the *kro*. There in the dark of an old cottage room we sat over our Tuborg lager watching Danish television, a newscast that confirmed the swarms of ladybirds we had encountered as something peculiar to this brilliant August. In Denmark the holiday season really finishes at the end of July. In August we had been told we might expect high winds and a great deal of rain. But it was 1959, an exceptional year, and we had neither—only sunshine.

The third island is Nyord in the south of Zealand. I had asked Niels Norlund what out-of-the-way places we ought to visit, going south from Copenhagen. After consulting an expert on the staff of the *Berlingske Tidende*, he gave me Rødvig, Nyord, Vordingborg, Fæmø, Fejø Agersø, and Omø.

We saw them all.

At Rødvig cement works have torn the white cliffs to shreds, yet people come from all over Denmark to the famous *kro* above the little port, to sit no doubt as we did, under the trees, driniking Pilsener and gazing out over the shallow waters of the Fakse Bugt; it was hot and very still, and the trees arched to frame a sea that was as calm and heat-hazed as an Italian lake. Vordingborg is dominated by its Goose Tower, all that remains of the great fortress of the Valdemars. It is the Runnymede of Denmark, but there is no evidence that the liberty of the subject was established here and a Constitution signed. Instead, the eye is caught by the first Valdemar's defiant goose. No longer gold, but gilded copper, it stands spotlighted against the night sky with its open beak still shrieking scorn and hate at ancient Hanseatic enemies. Fæmø is all apples with a little church sleeping amongst the orchards, its doors kept locked by a lazy priest. Agersø and Omø lie open to the winds funnelling down the Great Belt; they are dominated by wind machines.

But Nyord—Nyord is something special.

Arne Petersen, an eel fisher, who towed us off the shallow, weed-grown bottom of the Bøgestrøm after I had missed one of the dredged channels, warned us that the entrance was narrow, the little harbour shallow. The population, he said, was about two hundred, inbred as a result of isolation and with only about three family names. In fact, the wood-piled entrance to the *havn* was 20 ft wide, not twice the width of my boat, and inside, the shallow, soft-mud bottom was being dredged by an old black barque fitted with a grab. The smell was overpowering and we got out with difficulty to lie at anchor in the fairway with small freighters from Hamburg and Rotterdam trundling past.

At dawn we rowed ashore to find an old-world settlement of timber and thatch clustered about an octagonal church, the whole place over-laid with the good earthy smell of cow dung. Migrating swallows were thick on the telephone wires. Sugar beet fields ran out to flat, marshy grazing. A man passed us with a string bag squirming with eels. There was peace, absolute peace.

The eel is as important to the Danes as it is to the Dutch, and smoked eel is a great delicacy. The shallows of the Bøgestrøm are cluttered with the stakes of the eel fishers, as are the shallows of most of Denmark's enclosed waters. On these stakes the nets are hung. Arne Petersen said he had made nearly £1,500 the previous autumn operating for only three months with two small open boats. Now he had purchased a third. Sitting in our saloon, drinking Jamaican rum and talking excellent English, he told us of a retired sea captain at Røvig who had become an eel fisher and was now earning in three months more than he had ever made in a year with all the responsibilities of running a merchant ship.

Arne, like so many seafaring Danes, had travelled the world in sail, in those black, two-masted barques with the long bowsprits that we had seen everywhere, accompanied now by the tom-tom beat of their diesels. He had been to the Americas, to Portugal, Spain and France, and into most of the main ports of England, a small, weather-beaten man, blue eyes in a nut-brown face. Before coming on board he had removed his wooden clogs, his dirty overalls. He had the natural good manners, the dignity and warm friendliness that is typical of most people whose livelihood is the sea.

'The season for eel is only just started. You must go aground here later in the year, then I give you eel for your *middag*, after I have towed you off.'

But it isn't only eel that you find in these ports. A building housing the Fiske Export and the Fiskehus stands on every quay, and when you go to buy your fish, it is not frozen fish. Wooden traps lie off the Fiskehus and from these your meal is fished out with a net, alive and flapping, to be gutted and filleted according to your requirements. Buying dabs at Rødvig, I was told that this little fish port exported to Germany and even to the States.

The waters that separate the islands have in the past meant more to the Danes than fish; they have meant security. With the Little Belt separating Fyn from Jutland, and the Great Belt again separating Fyn from Zealand, their only concern for almost a thousand years was the land defence of the mainland peninsula, and here they had the Maginot Line of the Danevirke, a battlemented wall of brick extending across Holstein from the North Sea to the Baltic. It was planned by Gudfred, their king in the days of Charlemagne, built by Queen Thyra Danebod and strengthened by Valdemar I in the twelfth century. But when Bismarck invaded in 1864 General de Meza abandoned it without firing a shot.

One cannot help feeling that the sudden realisation of their vulnerability in a new age had a profound effect on the national psychology. Their aspirations became internal, rather than external, so that their energies were concentrated on their own economy and on education. Schools for adult peasants speeded the development in a classless society directed by a liberal-cum-socialist government. Neutral in the Kaiser's war, they believed they could maintain the same state in Hitler's war.

Standing on the grass redoubts that surround Kronborg Castle at Helsingør, I looked across the narrows to the Swedish shore and wondered how they must have felt after April 9, 1940, their country blacked-out by the second German invasion in a century and the coast of Sweden four miles away a blaze of lights. Is this why the Danes, like the Norwegians, do not love the Swedes, even though all are a part of the Scandinavian bloc? Or does it go back further, back to the Swedish wars of the sixteenth and seventeenth centuries, when Christian IV lost the struggle for the command of the Baltic?

There has been a castle at Helsingør since the days of Erik of Pomerania and you have only to stand on the old earthworks and look across the Sound to realise how dominant its position was. The Sound is the third and most important natural sea exit for the otherwise land-locked Baltic. For two hundred years, until 1660, the Danes exacted toll. Ships had to dip their flags. The word of Denmark's king was law to Baltic ports depending on trade with the West, and the Hanseatic League itself bowed to the threat of blockade tactics backed by the guns of Kronborg Castle.

The present castle was built by Christian's father, Frederik II, in the years between 1577 and 1585. It is a disappointment to those who come to it with preconceived ideas of grim battlements based on Shakespeare's *Hamlet*. Shakespeare never saw Kronborg and the ghost of Hamlet's father haunts a Norman, not a Danish keep. Kronborg is a Renaissance in style, a relatively light and dainty building of sloping leads and many-windowed grey sandstone walls. It has little cupolas, coppered spires, gables, a lighthouse even.

The approach is impressive, for it is triple-moated, and the entrance to the castle is through a covered passage. Almost every great Shakespearean actor has played *Hamlet* in the courtyard of Elsinore, and surrounding this one courtyard stands the whole edifice of the castle. It includes a church, the Nautical Museum, the huge hall of the Riddersal and the Rigeraadsal with its Gobelin tapestries depicting early kings.

But what struck me most at Helsingør was a freighter thrusting its great flared bows against the castle entrance, towering fresh-painted above the garden where swans were gliding through moats full of water lilies. The humming shipyard of today is neighbour to the past and the slips run down into a busy port crowded with innumerable ferries carrying Denmark's land traffic across the last sea gap to the rest of Scandinavia and the north. Beside this bustle and the shipyard's roar, the tall windows of the Prinz Hamlet Hotel give an almost bizarre glimpse of riches and evening dress, bizzare because the castle is dead, Hamlet dead and nothing there that's alive to see but the port and the shipyard.

Next day I did a thing I had always wanted to do. I sailed my boat into Copenhagen. A strong breeze had swept the clouds away and there it lay with all its copper spires standing green against a blue sky. I was seeing it then as Nelson saw it in 1801, from the sea, and we went roaring past the grim fortress of Tre Kroner to lie in Langelinie within a stone's throw of Hans Andersen's little mermaid.

The Danes have so publicised this statue of the mermaid seated on her boulder that everyone visiting Copenhagen seems to be possessed of an overwhelming urge to see it. They stand in queues to photograph it. It is small, quiet and placid; it has serenity. Very different is the great column beside the Raadhus supporting two winged-helmeted Vikings, their cheeks puffed out as they blow their great curved Bronze Age *lurs*. It is a powerful statue, full of ebullience and the pulse-beat of war. Why the mermaid, and not this, as a symbol of Copenhagen? Or even that other huge bronze group in Langelinie— Gefion the Asa-Woman who, granted as much land as she could plough between sunrise and sunset, turned her four sons into bulls and ploughed all Zealand. It has power and purpose, standing there above the cascading water of the fountain. So, too, has Sinding's Valkyrie close by.

Why, then, the little mermaid? Hans Andersen was a great

writer. But that hardly seems sufficient explanation. Is it perhaps that the mermaid symbolises Denmark's national mood since the defeat of 1864?

Symbolic, too, is Tivoli, the pleasure gardens close by the Raadhus. The night we went it was packed—and not with tourists, with Danes. It is Coney Island, the Bois de Boulogne and Soho all rolled into one. There are dozens of restaurants and eateries there, and you can get anything from a hot-dog at a stall to the finest dinner in town. It has its charm, for amongst all the blaze of lights, the fun fairs and the fruit machines are little oases of quiet where delicate traceries of lights swim mirrored in quiet waters.

But there are other Danes in town whose idea of amusement is very different. You find them in Nyhavn, that narrow canal that runs up to the great square of Kongens Nytorv, the cultural centre of the city. I had been told that every building in the street was a sailors' dive. To my astonishment it was true. We went there late at night, threading our way slowly along a pavement crowded with drunks. On our left there were the honky-tonks; on our right the canal, black-watered and mirroring the stately façade of rich business premises on the far side. Nobody molested us, nobody seemed surprised at our presence there. It was a street that strictly minded its own business.

Its business is, of course, the business of any such street the world over. An Englishman, who had made his home in Denmark, told me that you could go into any of the dives and sit over a Schnapps and watch the fun and nobody would give a damn—so long as you didn't try and talk to a girl. Live and let live is the street's motto. He should know, for he had a flat at one time over one of the dives. His Danish wife, Grethe, showed us pictures of it out at their present home by the Royal Danish Yacht Club's basin at Skodshoved. It was a luxury flat covering the upper storey of two houses of the sixteenth century with the old wooden beams exposed.

'It was a wonderful place to live,' he said. 'Nobody cared whether you were rich or poor. You lived there; that was sufficient.' He described how once they had trouble and all the bums of the waterfront had rallied round. 'These people belong here,' they said. 'Leave them alone.' And once there was a society wedding, the reception in one of the flats and the guests rolling up in Rolls-Royces and Cadillacs and half the riff-raff of Nyhavn invited, too.

Copenhagen is København Havn, and København Havn means merchants' harbour. In the old days Nyhavn was the hub of it all. The buildings remind one of Amsterdam, for they belong to the same period and were built for the same purpose. But where Amsterdam is a merchants' city, København Havn belongs to kings, is dominated by the royal palaces of Christiansborg and Amalienborg. Nevertheless, the merchants have one fabulous monument, the Dragon Spire. It stands on the Børsen, a Dutch Renaissance building that is the oldest original Bourse in the world, and wherever you get a glimpse of the city's skyline, there are the four dragons with their tails fantastically coiled to form a spire. It is, oddly, a piece of Danish loot, for the spire was captured by a warship whilst being transported from Holland to Sweden.

Traces of the shipyards that gave Denmark mastery of the Sound can still be seen on Christianshavn canal, and opposite the Citadel by Langelinie stands Nyholm Old Crane, a direct link with Nelson's day, for this wooden crane on the old square tower set up the top-masts of the warships that fought at the Battle of Copenhagen.

But it is all past history. More than a century of determined anti-militarism has left its mark and now Tivoli seems to epitomise the mood of Copenhagen—a gay, unenergetic search for amusement. And though there is nothing like it in the rest of Denmark, there are the pavilions which serve much the same purpose. Pavilions are to be found in most Danish towns, particularly by water, and if you want to see the Danes at leisure, this is where you go.

A combination of café and palais de danse, the pavilions are the meeting place of the young. Here you can sit by the hour watching, fascinated, the Danish technique of pick-up. Generally speaking, the girls keep together at their own tables and the boys at theirs. The band striking up is the signal for a mad scramble for partners. But once a girl has moved to a boy's table, then she is his partner for the evening and the other males lay off. Surprisingly, the pavilions are places where the family also goes for an evening out, eating and drinking side-by-side with the business man on a night out with his secretary. It is all very democratic, very Danish—and so is the food; beer and Schnapps and smørrebrød.

Eva Knud, a Danish countess we met in Copenhagen, talked of Svendborg Sund where she had once lived—'The most beautiful place in Denmark.' We came to it from Langeland in the quiet of a hot afternoon, and from Troense on the island of Taasinge we looked down on the narrow waterway where there were lawns and gardens and beautiful houses, and the only traffic was the ferry steamers and yachts gliding their white sails against the green of tree-ed banks. It had the lush peace of a river scene. Below us a little shipyard gave off the resinous smell of wood shavings. Behind us a village of old houses and gardens lay asleep, with coloured umbrellas shading visitors over their tea and cakes.

From Troense the Sund curves to reveal Svendborg sprawled on its shallow hill. Big vessels in for repair were framed in woods that reached right down to the water's edge. This place has a long history of ship-building and these same woods once provided the materials of which the Hansa fleets were constructed. Beyond, the sun was sinking behind the islands that guard Svendborg from the more open seas of the Little Belt. The flat, unruffled water blazed, then turned to milk, finally to lead, and as night fell we came to Faaborg, mooring beside the white hulks of two half-completed barques.

Faaborg is another of those places to be explored at night, it is so full of surprises. At first glance a modern town, the shops are brilliantly lit, the cafés full of people; but just behind the church are streets of old houses and above the port we came suddenly on a little square that was surrounded by gabled, timbered buildings, a little slice of medieval architecture with the house names in gilded lettering hung out in the old manner on wrought-iron signs.

Faaborg was our last port in Denmark. Next day we sailed out across the Little Belt, round the top of Als and down into Als Sund, the narrowest of all the Danish waterways. For five miles we were crowded by small freighters in a cut no wider than a minor canal. It is something to have seen Als Sund, for when you have seen it, knowing that it is a natural seaway, you realise to the full what an extraordinary land this is, so cut about with water lanes, so full of islands.

And at the end of Als Sund is Sønderborg.

It lay beyond yet another of those low swing bridges, a line of mellow old merchant houses, all yellow in slanting sunlight. Their feet, it seemed, were in the water, their gables stood shoulder-to-shoulder behind the masts of ships berthed at their doorsteps. Nobody ever had a lovelier last look at Denmark than we had that afternoon as we hoisted sail again and beat out past the last brush marker, just as countless sailing ships had before us down the centuries.

III

THE BRETON COAST

I came to Brittany first on the tail-end of a gale, new to navigation in a boat I had just bought called *Triune of Troy*; the waves were like downlands pitching forward, the first rock island a roaring welter of foam. Eight miles of rock from the seaward buoy to the estuary mouth that led to Morlaix and the big following sea gradually subsiding as we plunged in through the *Grand Chenal* until the low-tide rocks, showing a 30-foot band of black weed-growth, stood like a huge harbour wall between us and the gale-torn English Channel. I thought then what a coast this must have been for men seeking refuge from their enemies long ago when there were no buoys marking the entrance channels, no beacons set up on submerged rocks, no charts, no Admiralty Pilot to describe the leading marks by which the off-lying dangers could be avoided.

Lézardrieux, Tréguier, Tregastel, Trebeurden, Morlaix, Roscoff, L'Aberwrac'h; I have now sailed into them all, and they all have this in common—rock-strewn entrances that are a navigational nightmare. Lézardrieux is a favourite of mine on this north coast because the Pontrieux River is the first of the Breton oyster rivers and the Relais Brenner makes the long, difficult entrance abundantly worth while. The first time I sailed in I missed the *Grand Chenal*; I was down-wind and down-tide of it, night was closing in and we were tired. Ahead of us the grey granite tower of Les Heaux rose slender as a needle from a jagged litter of rocks. The Admiralty Pilot only gives directions for the *Grand Chenal*. It adds: 'There are several other channels of approach but as none of them should be attempted without local knowledge no directions are given.' One of these channels was the Moisie Channel and this we decided to take.

Here is the description of the Moisie Passage given by Hasler in his sailing directions: 'First make a position from which *les Heaux* lighthouse bears 280° magnetic, distant 1¾ miles. From here the leading marks on the *Ile Bréhat* will be in line: *Rosédo* white pyramid and *St. Michel* chapel bearing 170° magnetic. Before following this line, check that it passes about 160 yards east of *roche Moisie* red-and-white beacon tower surmounted by two cones, bases together. Then follow it closely, leaving *roche Moisie* beacon tower 160 yards to starboard, *Nougejou Bian* red-and-white beacon, surmounted by two cones bases together 60 yards to starboard, and *Pen ar Rest* white beacon tower 4 cables to starboard. Then quit the leading line and steer so as to leave *Vielle du Tréou* black beacon tower, surmounted by a cone 1 cable to starboard. . . .' And so on. We were hard on the wind and in the midst of this piece of intricate navigation we had to shorten sail in face of a squall.

I give these sailing directions in detail just to illustrate how wonderfully protected the people of North Brittany have always been by these sea approaches. Some, like the Malouine passage into L'Aberwrac'h with its rocks fashioned by the waves into witch-like faces are no more than fifty yards wide, others have submerged reefs and unmarked rocks that are only to be avoided by keeping exactly to leading marks, transits and bearings. In heavy weather the coast is deadly. The tides are enormous (30-40 ft rise and fall) and the sea pours back and forth through the rock gaps with the force of a mill race.

Turn the corner at Ushant and you are in an area where the Atlantic and Continental weather systems meet; fog or strong winds with a low murk of cloud. Twenty miles of reefs here, the marker beacons standing thick as headstones in a sailors' graveyard and a furious tide running. And on the west-facing Biscay coast two great bays full of lobster and sardine, an inland sea full of oysters, the Raz de Sein where the tide roars like the rapids of a great river, and to seaward great rock estates, acre upon acre of submerged reefs that show their fangs as the tide recedes.

Every rock, every beacon, has its name—names of affection, of hate, names full of local meaning: La Jument, Le Dragon, Basse Devel, Petit Cochon, Basse du Chariot, Le Grand Coin, Les Chats, Les Fourches, men ar Groas, Basse Jaune,

Castel Bihan, La Voleuse, La Vache, Les Errants—thousands upon thousands, their names as much a part of the lives of this seafaring people as the street names in our cities and towns.

But here on the Biscay coast, where the sun has a sea-washed crystal brightness, there is a bay more beautiful, I think, than any in France—the Baie de Douarnenez. It faces west towards the Atlantic, its beauty enhanced from the sea-man's point of view by the grim perils of the Chenal du Four and the Raz de Sein that lie like Scylla and Charybdis either side the narrow entrance. It is ten miles long and eight miles wide, and the silhouette of the surrounding hills has a gentle roll.

At the head of the bay, terraced on the slope of a hill, stands Douarnenez itself, bone-white in the sunshine.

At least, that is how I saw it first, sailing in with the sun full on it after a night of stress. And in the morning I went ashore to buy croissants, and walked into a fisherman's world. It was only eight o'clock, yet the waterfront road was crowded with men; Bretons in smocks of faded red and blue, blue trousers, dark blue berets, clogs on their feet. They came ashore from their fishing boats in little groups, walking with the slack roll of men more accustomed to a heaving deck than the land-bound asphalt.

All one side of that waterfront road was lined with bistros. It was a street of drinking places and hotels. And the seaward side was decorated with the fine-meshed nets of the sardiniers. They hung in festoons from wires specially rigged, and they were all shades of blue, for the Finisterre nets are dipped in a dye preservative. And beyond the nets were the boats. They packed the fish quay, three, four and five deep—small local boats moored side-by-side with the big tunny fishers. And from the mast of every boat blue nets hung drying in the sun. Only the tunny fishers' masts were bare, their 100 ft long whips, or fishing rods, standing like the antennae of giant water beetles.

I asked for croissants in bistro after bistro, and they stared at me as if I were from another world. Croissants belonged to the big, wonderfully stocked pâtisseries higher up the town. The waterfront bistros were doing a roaring trade in Pernod and Dubonnet. I settled for *café seul*, feeling conspicuous, for though I was dressed in seagoing rig, it was perfectly obvious I hadn't worked all night on a heaving deck out amongst the rocks of the fishing grounds.

Where had they come from, these men who needed strong drink for breakfast . . . these men who sat so still and word-less with gnarled hands clasped around their glasses, their stocky, heavily-muscled bodies slack with weariness, their eyes alert and long-sighted in nut-brown, weather-beaten faces? I walked along the fish quay, amongst the slippery scales and the slime, and found the answer in the numbers painted on the bows of their boats, the letters before each number giving the port of origin—Dz for Douarnenez, B for Brest, C for Camaret. They had come from as far south as Ile de Groix, from as far north as L'Aberwrac'h. There in the Port de Rosmeur I saw boats from most of the fishing ports in Brittany unloading the work of a night, two nights, perhaps a week at sea.

The bay stretched smiling in the sunshine. It looked so easy then, such a pleasant, healthy life. But the fish are caught out beyond the bay, along the coast to north and south where the tides roar in white overfalls and the rocks lie thick, great sub-merged reefs spilling seaward. And the sun does not always shine!

Take the road west from Douarnenez, out to the Pointe du Raz—then you can see it, understand the dangers, the rigours of the life. Stand on the point there and look across the Raz de Sein. Ahead of you, on a rock, stands the grim, grey light-house of La Vieille; and beyond it, and a little to the left, is Le Chat. Between lies the Raz—the most dangerous tidal race in Europe. The mass of rock you see beyond Le Chat is the Ile de Sein; half-submerged, it runs westward ten miles and more to the Ar Men Buoy, a jagged reef that acts like a huge natural breakwater to the tides running north and south. The only gap through which the piled-up mass of water can flow is the narrow gap of the Raz de Sein. See it when it is blow-ing hard against a full spring tide; then all the area below you is white like a cascade and the roar of the water spilling through the gap is the roar of a gigantic rapid . . . whirls and eddies, and waves springing up from nowhere and bursting

with a sound like gunfire, and all the cliffs and rocks rever-
berating to the crash and roar of breaking water.

Once seen, this white hell of tormented sea can never be
forgotten, and the noise of it lingers in the ear, a reminder
that the Breton works in a world that is both fruitful and terrible.

To the north, hull-down on the horizon, you can see the
faint outline of Ile d'Ouessant—Ushant. On a clear day, that
is. But mostly Ushant is shrouded in its own peculiar murk,
or by the drifting smoke of burning kelp as the seaweed-gath-
erers convert their marine harvest into fertiliser. This area, like
the Raz, is a menace in fair weather, an inferno in bad. Two
hundred square miles of reefs, with rock corridors between.

Ushant, the Chaussée de Sein, and further south the Glen-
nan Isles; these are the three great rock, reef and island
groups, a world apart, the sea dominating the people's lives so
that even today Brittany is not really France. Like the Welsh,
to whom they are akin, they have preserved their language
and a proud independence. These men crowding the bistros of
Douarnenez, coming ashore from boats in dozens of smaller
harbours tucked inside the natural protection of tide-exposed
rocks, are basically Celts. Their Celtic ancestry goes back to
the fifth and sixth centuries, when the Britons, fleeing from
Cornwall and Wales before invading Saxon hordes, crossed the
Channel in their boats to settle in the estuaries and bays that
were so wonderfully protected by nature. They were welcomed by the Armoricans, and Armor became known as Brittany, or Little Britain.

They brought with them the legend of King Arthur to comfort them with the superiority of their own disrupted civilisation. They invented a counterpart to the legendary lost land of
Lyonnesse, which is supposed to lie submerged beneath the
waves where the lighthouse on the Bishop Rock blinks a greeting to ships from across the Atlantic, and set it in the loveliest
bay of their adopted land. It is as typical a figment of Celtish
imagination as any Cornish legend and quite my favourite
story from Breton folk-lore.

The Baie de Douarnenez, according to the legend, was once
dry land, sealed off from the Atlantic by a four-mile *digue*

(dyke) across the entrance. Here, surrounded by rich grazing, stood the city of Is. It was a magic city, lovely beyond compare—so lovely, in fact, that they used to say it gave France's capital her name, Par-Is . . . as lovely as Is. Sluices carried the river water to the sea, and the silver keys of the *digue* gates were worn by Princess Dahut round her neck.

She was the daughter of Gralon, a saintly king, and in this it is the story of Lear all over again. Dahut was a witch, wicked as sin. She enslaved the sea's dragons, giving one to each citizen, and these brought wealth to the city of Is. They were pirates, in other words, and wreckers, too, and Sodom and Gomorrah weren't in it for their wickedness. Dahut magicked all princes and nobles who came there, drawing them to her and strangling them; a black horseman carted the bodies away, flinging them into a chasm where, of course, on stormy nights they say you can still hear their pitiful cries.

One night a prince arrived, bearded and with flaming eyes. He offered to teach the court the dance of the seven deadly sins, and having entranced them all into action fatal as a whirlpool, he seized the keys from Dahut and was gone. Gralon, like Lear, was living alone and neglected in his own palace, and to him came the pious bishop of Quimper, Corentin, warning him of disaster. Gralon mounted his black horse, and as he took off into the night like a Pegasus, he saw below him the Devil himself opening the gates of the *digue*, saw the Atlantic pouring in, the city overwhelmed, the dragons drowned in the first rush of water.

Traditionally correct, he tried to save his terrified daughter by hauling her up on to his steed, but the load of her sins weighed them down, and Corentin, seeing that the besotted father was incapable of throwing the witch off, struck her from the saddle with his bishop's crook. She, like her fabulous city, lies drowned below the blue waters of Douarnenez Bay, and naturally there is a rock with the print of a horse's hoof to show where Gralon's steed, relieved of its burden of wickedness, made the first giant leap to safety.

When I sailed into the Baie de Douarnenez that first time I sought shelter under the cliffs of Morgat on the north side. I had the dawn anchor watch and I sat alone in the cockpit as daylight came creeping down the bay. Above me on the cliffs a solitary menhir leaned like a watcher turned to stone. I had a strange feeling then, as though this were a place of the dead. Perhaps it was the knowledge of the Raz de Sein so close, or perhaps just the dead feeling that comes with the first grey fingers of day, for at that time I had never heard of Is.

But now I can never sail those waters without picturing in my mind that story and thinking of the lost city there below. It may only be a myth, but the fact is that up until the time of the Revolution the priests from all the surrounding churches collected in the fishing boats once a year to say a Mass over the dead city.

And the story itself is so revealing of the Breton mentality; their fear of the sea, their superstition. It mirrors so exactly their obstinate, sea-born puritanism, their certainty that the wicked shall perish.

There are other stories, dozens of them, but mostly connected with the menhirs, for the hills above Douarnenez are littered with megalithic monuments. In fact, this part of Brittany holds the richest collection of late Stone Age and early Bronze Age stones in the world. Certainly the people of Armor did not need to go far for their material; it lay scattered all about them.

My first sight of these megalithic remains was on one of the out-islands at sunset. We moored in the new harbour that this tiny community had built to replace the one destroyed in a gale and walked up through their doll's-house village and out on to a tableland of grass where the village street became a rutted wagon track. All around was the sea, water on every side, still and blue, with the whole long chain of the Presqu'Ile de Quiberon standing out of the flat surface of it in a petrified line.

And there in front of us, in the sheep-cropped grass, was a great pattern of stones. It took the breath, for in that place, with the sun setting and sea and rock all round, time had no meaning, and I could see it, understand it—the need of a primitive people, alone and isolated on that island with the wrath of a god they feared always beating at their door, a god upon whom they depended for food, for life itself.

Ile d'Houat and Hoëdic and the other out-islands of Quiberon Bay are not easy to reach, but Carnac, close by on the

S.A.I.   H

mainland, is, and the stones of Carnac are quite fantastic. There is first the Menec series of megaliths, a thousand menhirs drawn up in eleven ranks and extending more than half a mile to Menec village, which is itself half surrounded by seventy more. There are another thousand menhirs in ten lines at Kermario, and six hundred more at Kerlescan. See this extraordinary gathering of stone men drawn up, rank upon rank, like soldiers on parade, and you need never again suffer from the urge to launch out into some wild piece of country because it is marked *cromlech* on the map and you feel you ought to look up the gods of your prehistoric ancestors.

The origins of this megalithic cult are largely a matter of conjecture. The positioning of some of the stones is certainly based on astronomy, which is hardly surprising among a seafaring people accustomed to rough astral navigation and in an age that had no other means of telling time or even season. The connection with the sun is particularly marked and this led to its worship, along with other minor deities, and the elevation of the wise men to the status of priests. Beginning with one stone to mark the position of the sun at the season of the sowing, with a watching point for the elder protected by stones and with a spring or well at hand to slake his thirst, it is not difficult to see how the whole thing developed as more and more stones were set up and the whole business of prediction became more complicated. But by the time the Romans reached Gaul, the Druid priests were little better than magicians, and in time of stress were indulging in human sacrifice. By then the stones themselves were being worshipped and Christianity had to be grafted on to this Cultus Lapidum so literally that some of the menhirs still show the mark of the crucifix that surmounted them.

At that time the Bretons believed that the great stone menhirs went down to the water at times to drink and that anyone who saw them was mesmerised and crushed under their moving weight; that a race of black dwarfs inhabited them and that if they caught a human at midnight they would make him dance in circles in the moonlight till he dropped down dead from exhaustion; and 'Les Soldats de St. Cornely' are supposed to be the petrified forms of the soldiers of a pagan king who chased Bishop Cornely into Brittany. The stones stand in three great rows cutting off the saint's retreat, and since the bishop was borne in his flight by two oxen, he became the patron saint of cattle, the date of his festival coinciding with that of the Celtic god, Hu-Gadarn, whose two oxen dragged the crocodile responsible for the Deluge out of the deeps.

The theory was put about in some places that the Devil threw the stones down from the moon, in others that the Virgin Mary had brought them in her apron! On tiny Houat, where nuns run the village store and priests play skittles with the fishermen, you would not be at all surprised to find these stories still believed—or in the isolation of Hoëdic and the lonelier isles to the south like Ile d'Yeu, or in old fortified farmsteads and lonely châteaux and in the narrow-streeted, grey little villages far up the estuaries where the stone houses have stood for centuries. But not in Douarnenez. Douarnenez is a modern, practical town and everybody is making money— good money by Breton standards.

They say Douarnenez is built on sardines. But the shoals are moving further south and bigger catches are made off the North African coast. Nevertheless, there are still a few 'confiseries' left and there you can see the dexterous beheading, the speed with which they fill the wire baskets and rush them to the boiling oil. Dipped, the sardines are quickly machine-packed in tins, sealed in with the best olive oil and stacked in racks to be turned regularly for a period of three years; the longer the better, for they mature like wine, and are treated with the same respect.

But though hundreds of boats put out during the long season from June to November, it is not easy to get fresh sardines in the restaurants. That first evening we climbed two terraces up from the waterfront to a street where the sign of La Caravelle hung, but there were no fresh sardines. Instead, we had cockles, a speciality of Brittany. They are served unopened—neat, shiny shells, grey as pebbles—and your hunger mounts as you wrestle with them. And after the cockles, we had mackerel, caught only a few hours before.

Nobody but a barbarian would bother with meat in a land where the sea is harvested the year round. It was at Mère Armande in Concarneau, a few miles to the south, that I first discovered what it was to eat fresh sardines. They were big, hand-picked fish—much larger than tinned—and they were grilled, their scales crisped to brown, with melted butter, herbs and lemon. A dish to dream about.

Go north from Douarnenez to the wild, rock-strewn coast that faces Ushant, and at the Baie des Anges in the little port of L'Abertwrac'h you can feast on the produce of the rocks that stand like dragon's teeth beyond the window, cooked as it would be cooked in Paris—but much fresher; your lobster or your langouste has come from the concrete tanks by the quay, tanks that, in fact, supply the Paris restaurants. And opposite these tanks, at a much simpler hotel, I once had a gargantuan meal, beginning with an hors d'œuvres for two that included a crab whose shell measured almost a foot across.

And oysters! Brittany is described geologically as 'worn-down ribs of ancient Hercynian folds'; this means that the marked passages through the off-lying rocks almost all lead to river estuaries, some steep-banked and narrowing to rocky gorges like the Tréguier and Auray rivers, others widening to broad acres of mud. Farmers may struggle to get a living from the rock-based land, but these mud estates yield a rich harvest. Here, carefully staked out, carefully cultivated, are the *parcs aux huîtres*. The great inland sea of the Morbihan is thick with these oyster beds; it is from the Morbihan and the Belon river that the best French oysters come. Eat them on the stone terrace of the restaurant overlooking the rocky entrance to the Aven River, or at that centre of painting Gauguin made famous, Pont Aven. But for huîtres grillées you must go to the north coast, to Lézardrieux. Here, in a little hotel unpretentiously named the Hotel de Commerce the Brenners once offered food the equal of any fish restaurant in France. Now they have a new restaurant, the Relais Brenner, built beside the bridge over the Pontrieux River with a magnificent view down the rock-strewn estuary. Here the spécialité de la maison is still Philippe Brenner's huîtres grillées.

One other delicacy—and a great delicacy this: langoustine. It is caught from Douarnenez south, and in little ports like

Loc Tudy you can buy them by the kilo on the quay. And somewhere close by you will find a shop with the word Crêpes. Inside, the owner, operating on an iron contraption as primitive as an old spit, will cook you pancakes, wafer thin, with the loving care of an artist, or pile them hot in paper for you to take away. There is cider to drink or Muscadet or the white wine of Anjou that does not travel.

Only at Roscoff, a little port behind Ile de Batz, where Mary Queen of Scots landed at the age of six on her way to marry France's future king, have I seen the coastal country really rich. Here, in June, the fields are green with the globes of artichoke. Here, in towns that lie at the head of long estuaries, the Breton countryside rubs shoulders with the fisherfolk; vegetables and fish, Breton smocks and Breton lace, and the women still in their traditional costumes—black, sometimes trimmed with velvet, with elaborately embroidered aprons and lace caps or bonnets that reach their most fantastic in *la coiffe bigoudène* of St. Pol de Léon, a piled-up cylinder of lace more than a foot high. Each locality favours a different dress, and the embroidery and lace are equally distinctive. The dialects differ, too, for these people have local pride and life still centres around the family.

Life in Brittany is hard. It is a good life so long as you don't give your soul to the Devil and your body to the deep. Fishermen and seamen, they start young. At L'Aberwrac'h there is a maritime school where the sons of fishermen are educated to the life that is their heritage. At Bénodet two top-sail schooners, the *Etoile* and the *Belle Poule*, sail daily in company, lovely as swans, training boys for the French Navy based on Brest.

The English landed 20,000 men on Belle-Ile and then exchanged it for Nova Scotia; Hawke demolished a whole fleet at Quiberon Bay—battle after battle between two maritime people who were cousins, and all the time the smuggling trade flourishing across the Channel. And in the last war, St. Nazaire saw the first amphibious operation into France, the Senans flocking to England in their boats, almost to a man, the tunny-men fishing more dangerously than ever before with agents on board and explosives for the Resistance. 'Toujours le bloody navy,' cried one young fisherman to me in Concarneau, mistaking my cap—a mocking salutation tinged with the admiration of one nautical race for another.

The sea—the Bretons live and breathe it; it is their father and mother, their devil, their other god . . . it gives them life, toil, hardship, independence; it gives them death. And though the land may change with time and the march of industry, the sea does not—nor will the Breton as long as he holds to his heritage.

IV

THE WESTERN ISLES

Lewis, Harris, North Uist, Benbecula, South Uist, Barra—
these islands lie like a visor of ice-worn gneiss across the
witch-head face of Scotland; lonely, remote, swept by the
winds of Atlantic depressions. Known collectively as the
'Long Island', they are as water-logged as the Labrador, a
mass of lakes and deep loch indentations strewn with rock
islets. From the top of Barra Head drips a chain of out-
islands with names that sing the Gaelic tongue—Sandray,
Pabbay, Mingulay, Berneray. Other out-islands lie to the
north and west, the Flannan Isles, Rona, Sula Sgeir, the
Monachs, and colossal and alone, fifty miles out into the
westerly winds, St. Kilda with its lofty sea-bird cluttered
crags.

It took me three journeys into the north of Canada to become suddenly fascinated by the thought of these islands
only two and a half flying hours from my own home. I wanted
to discover why in the Eskimo north of Canada the only white
people seemed to be Scots from these Western Isles, why
the Hudson's Bay Company sent their recruiting manager
over every other year.

> From the lone shieling of the misty islands
> Mountains divide us and the waste of seas—
> Yet still the blood is strong, the heart is Highland,
> And we in dreams behold the Hebrides!

It was cloudy when we took off from Inverness's lonely
airport with a glimpse of Loch Ness and the peat moors
of the true Highlands rolling out below us. My last mainland
glimpse was one of high deer forests falling in rocky spines
to the sea by Little Loch Broom. We were over the Minch
then and in less than twenty minutes we were slipping down
through a thin layer of cloud to a treeless land that was all
rock and heath bog, the line between land and sea made so
tenuous by the myriad lochs that I was reminded of the

231

north of Norway, rather than Canada, and felt instinctively that I was coming into a Viking land.

The sun came out, a pale, watery sun that caught the top of a weed-girt island and turned the lawn of its sheep-cropped grass to a brilliant emerald green. A glimpse of a lighthouse, and then the sea, white lines of surf beating on a silver strand of sand. We came in to land, and as I got out of the plane it began to rain, a gentle, soft rain with the drive of wind behind it. I was in the Western Isles and the people around me were talking in voices soft as the rain, the Scots accent overlaid with the lilt of the Gaelic.

Button-holed on the quay an hour later by an Ancient Mariner with bright, beady Nordic eyes, set in rheumy sockets, I was informed that he could remember the time when Stornoway's natural harbour was full of ships. 'All sail, man—nothing but sail. Square-rigged ships, you know. And drifters. Not these trawler things with their diesels, but sail, man, all sail.' His grip on my arm was tight as he recalled what it had been like when the quays were so tight-packed with boats you could walk right across the harbour without sight of water. 'Aye, like a bridge it was, man.' Then the trawlers had come, and fishing the Minches and the Sound of Sleat without restriction had ruined the breeding grounds so that the great herring shoals were gone and the few craft that lay along the quay wall were lucky if they brought in a dozen cran for a night's fishing. The whales had gone the same way, fished out, though I heard of an old man who could remember being called from his bed as a boy by the cry: 'Wake up, man. Hurry up. Stornoway is taken by whales.' Now the old whaling factory at Bunaveneadar in the south-west of Harris, started by Norwegians over sixty years ago, lies stripped of its machinery and buildings, a desolate concrete pad with only the tall brick chimney standing.

From the moment I landed in Stornoway I was conscious of the north—something in the nature of the sky, in the proximity of the sea, a feel in the atmosphere. It is a bleak, grey little town huddled tight round quay and loch, a lonely outpost on the edge of nowhere, the Atlantic and the Polar seas for ever beating at its door. Opposite my hotel a plaque set into the brown stone wall of a church read:

SIR ALEXANDER MACKENZIE
The Explorer
who was the first white man to follow the Mackenzie
River to the Arctic Ocean and the first to cross the
continent of North America north of Mexico was born
in the year 1763 in a house which stood on this site

This was the man who went out to Canada as a youth, trading
west as far as the Rockies with the old North West Company.

As I travelled through the islands, that plaque was often in
my mind, so many islanders had followed in the young Mackenzie's footsteps, peopling Canada with names like Mac-
eod, Macdonald, Morrison, MacIver, Nicolson and Mac-
Innes. The stream had become a flood when the notorious
evictions of Sutherland and Breadalbane had sent crofters in
their hundreds to pioneer Selkirk's Red River Settlement in
the early 1800s. Other migrations followed each period of
economic disaster, the most recent the result of the great
depression of the thirties and the collapse of Lord Leverhulme's ambitious plans, when more than a thousand Lewis-
men abandoned their homes within a few years and three
Canadian Pacific liners were regularly engaged, making direct
sailings from Stornoway to Montreal.

Canada and the Outer Isles—the link is instinctive, the
Atlantic route a natural one to a people who live with the perpetual beat of it in their ears, the great winds of it soughing
round their crofts. Almost a sixth of the *Stornoway Gazette*'s
2,000 circulation goes overseas, mainly to North America,
providing the last tenuous link with home to people who have
never quite forgotten the islands from which their forebears
came.

In a cloudburst of torrential rain I left Stornoway by the
northern road bound for the west coast. The sun came out, but
the great peat moors that form the central body of Lewis remained sombre and gloomy despite the heather bursting into
flower—a pattern of browns and purples shading into black
where the spade had trenched for winter fuel, and everywhere
great stacks of peat the colour of rotted manure beside the
single-track road. No trees relieved the dull monotony of the
landscape. Yet trees once grew there, for the blackened

stumps and roots of forest growth have been uncovered by
the peat-diggers, preserved and carbonised by the centuries.
They say the Vikings burned the woods when they invaded the
land from Norway, and the prophetic words of a Highland
seer two hundred years ago have almost come true, for the
black trenches that now score the roadside all the dozen miles
from Stornoway to Barvas show that the men of these two
towns will soon be digging peat side-by-side.

Coming down into Barvas the road parallels the best salmon
river in the Outer Hebrides. 'Aye, and when they're running
man, ye cin almost walk across the Barvas River, they're so
thick.' The sea again and a far glimpse of the Flannan Isles
low on the horizon beyond Loch Carloway, and then we were
climbing to one of those strange towers that stand witness to
the centuries that man has fought nature and his enemies in
the islands. There are Pictish *brochs* to be found all over the
Long Island, heaps of rubble in the middle of small lochans
with the remains of causeways full of twists and gaps to fool
the enemy, but most of them have been cannibalised to build
other and later dwellings. Only at Carloway, where the *broch*
is on the shoulder of a hill, can you see the structure as it was,
a great dry-stone tower with sloping apertureless walls rising
possibly to a point where it could be roofed with a single rock
slab. The only entrance, barely three feet high, leads into an
open enclosure, where the animals were herded. The walls
are double, tied with slabs of stone that go up in tiers like
an inner staircase. Here in the cavity of the wall, locked
securely against the outside world, the Pictish laird lay mured
up with his followers, a wild beast in his lair.

The wall structure of the 'black house', the traditional island home, may well have been based on these old Pictish
brochs. At any rate, the islanders were building homes with
cavity walls centuries before the technique was common practice in England. Black houses dot the islands' landscape in
all stages of use and disintegration. Some are still lived in,
others have become byres, many have only their walls standing, either fallen into disuse or used as sheep enclosures or
fanks.

They are very literally black houses, for the peat fire
smouldering in the centre was never allowed to go out and the

nly exit for the smoke was a solitary hole in the roof. As
a Celtic Brittany and in old buildings in Scottish cities, the
eds were a cavity in the wall. But when I wanted to photo-
raph the interior of one of these houses, I was told there
as not a person in the island who would permit it, the
ccupants of black houses having developed an inferiority
omplex about their homes.

This is a pity, for these compact, neat thatched homesteads
hat fit so snugly into their background are infinitely more
uited to the island life than the wretched little jerrybuilt
ouses that now clutter the landscape, architectural excres-
ences that are too often cracked and damp and draughty.
urely they could have adapted the near-perfect construction
f these little houses that stand so solid against the Atlantic
ales. The walls are a little above the height of a man, a yard
nd more thick. They are, in fact, two walls in one, the cavity
etween being filled with moss and heather, insulating the
terior against winter cold and summer heat. The roof is
hatch, low and curved like a bee-hive, snugged down tight
nto the thick walls and held in place against the winds by
many strands of rope weighted with rocks. Yet in one short
eneration the islanders have abandoned the tradition of cen-
uries, as though their ancestors had all been fools and had
nown nothing about the climate and the materials that lay
o hand.

Groups of these black houses stood beside the Callanish
ack as we drove to the Standing Stones. Bowered in roses,
hey were pretty as a picture in the bright sun, each with its
eat stack and the golden heaps of winter corn feed bound
nd netted against the wind. We left the car and walked
ush grass between lines of up-ended slabs. Framed in the
igh stones around the altar mound were the brown, bare
ountains of Harris, a humped-up range that prisoned its own
rivate rainstorm. Wrens darted, small as mice. The sun was
arm and there were meadow flowers. A place of peace and
range enchantment.

The stones themselves did not compare with Stonehenge;
hey were smaller and they had not been transported great
istances. But they were unique, the only megalithic forma-
on to be laid in the form of a cross. I thought of the great

stone circles a thousand miles to the south, in Brittany. Th
setting was so much the same—the sea, the grass, the nake
rock. Only the storm-blurred mountains of Harris reminde
me that I was in another, harsher world, where ancient ma
had been forced underground in search of shelter, buildir
beehive houses and burrowing like a rabbit. Had he, like th
Bretons, worshipped these stones? And why the cross forma
tion? They had been placed there before the Norse men cam
before St. Columba established his church on dry Iona, befor
Christ was born.

But why worry? Enough that I stood there where my ow
ancient forebears had stood, the view the same, the sea, th
rocks, the mountains all unchanged, and the great wide bov
of the sky filled with the scud of cloud galleons sailing fa
before the wind. No Scot can stand in such a place and n
be touched by some ancient call. It had a magic. So muc
so that I had an irresistible urge to walk westward into th
wind and the slanting sun, down to the purpling islands at m
feet where rocks like damaged bone pierced the thin gree
skin of sheep-grazed grass.

I was there, in those islands, the following day. It wa
Sunday and I crossed the bridge that now joins Great Berner
to Lewis in the company of a crofter, walking with him th
two and a half miles to his church at Breaclete in the island
centre. A bitter north wind blew in our faces, yet it was on
early September. Winter and summer he walked the fiv
miles to church and back twice each Sunday. The service l
said would last 'aboot an hoor and a half if the meenister fee
in a good mood.' If not it would likely be two hours.

He belonged to the 'Wee Frees', and as I left him at th
door of his church, refusing his kindly invitation to join hir
I was thinking how the St. Kildans had had the life knocke
out of them by the insensate demands of this drear religion.
reached such a pitch in that island under Macdonald's de
potic hold that none dared smile or speak above a whisper c
a Sunday, and no chore could be done, not even water draw
the blinds pulled down over the windows, the whole com
munity filled with a deathly hush.

The blinds are still drawn in many crofts on Lewis. N

oats put out. No buses run. The children are kept indoors.
The whole world stops dead for the Sabbath. There is a story
old that has in it the germ of truth. A minister, threatening
his flock with damnation and the fires of hell, storms at them:
And from the bottomless pit ye'll look up to the Laird and
ye'll cry—Laird, we didna ken. And the Guid Laird will look
down upon ye, and *in his infineet mer-rcy*, he'll say—Weel, ye
ken noo.'

Perhaps it is significant that I heard this story in Benbecula. Benbecula and South Uist are Roman Catholic. In these
islands there are even wayside shrines to the Virgin Mary.
Football on Sunday afternoons, buses parked outside village
halls for cinema shows in the evening, a relaxed, much happier
atmosphere. North Uist is the meeting place of these two
diametrically opposed faiths, for at the time of the Reforma-
tion the Papist priests were driven out of the islands and
nothing was brought in to replace the Catholic Church. By
the time John Knox's Calvinism had penetrated to the
Western Isles there had already been an invasion of Catholic
missionaries from Ireland. This in the seventeenth century.
The sea gaps between the islands proved sufficient barrier.
Calvinism failed to advance southward.

Women dressed all in black passed me as I walked north
to Bernera's highest point. The kirk's solitary bell tinkled its
call and was lost in a biting rain squall. I walked to Tobson,
a lobster fishing village on the west side, accompanied by a
friendly sheepdog, and from a little beach looked out across
the limpid sea loch to a litter of weed-grown islands. A thousand pounds' worth of lobsters had recently been landed there
in one day, proving what Leverhulme had always said, that
there was wealth in the sea round the Hebrides for those who
dared to go out after it.

Across country to the north I moved into a world of little
hills. Great ice-worn slabs of rock burst their cropped grass
covering. Shepherd's cairns pointed the way. I might have
been in the Barren Lands of the Canadian North, the slowly
turning radar screens of the RAF tracking station on Gallan
Head some lonely outpost of the DEW Line. But the small
dark scabious and orchids at my feet, the sudden outcrops of

heather, indicated the warming influence of the Gulf Stream
and the small mirror-bright lochans were full of iris and water
lily.

The sun came out. The sea turned instantly to a miraculous
blue. And away to the west the mountains of Uig were sleepy
giants in a purplish haze. Uig where the MacIvers had begun
trading to Greenock a century and a half ago and had then
moved to Liverpool to become the great Cunard Company.
A dry-stone wall, so solid it might have been built by the
Picts for their defence, and then the land sloped in lush
meadows to a sandy shore full of the wrack of countless gales.
I had reached the sea again, a bay encumbered with rock
and a long-fingered promontory ending in great stacs. The
remains of a black house had been used as a sheep dip and the
lazy-beds of that lone crofter's cultivation were all grown
over. As though to emphasise that this was a valley of the
dead, a scattering of gravestones stood in a walled enclosure
—it was almost as lonely a resting place as the Eskimo
cemetery I had found on a hill-top at Baker Lake far to the
west of Hudson's Bay.

The affinities with Northern Canada are almost endless in
these islands. The railway age passed them by, but the skeletal
remains of cars and trucks lie scattered across the landscape
and a man who has never seen a steam engine thinks nothing
of making his first trip out in a plane. Almost every village
has the raw cold look of a pioneer settlement. The roads,
single track, with passing points every few hundred yards,
have the same desperate loneliness as they wind into grim
and hostile territory, following the drunken lean of the gale-
slanted telegraph poles.

Go south into Harris, and where the mountain of Beinn a
Mhuil squeezes you close against the shores of the great loch
that gave the Seaforths their name, you enter a stretch of
road as lost and remote-seeming as any in the world. From
the settlement of Aline Lodge you look past the huge sugar
loaf of Seaforth Island to a glimpse of Skye sprawled across
the steep-sided entrance to the loch. Ahead stands Clisham
2,622 ft high, its shaggy head wrapped in clouds, its brown
flanks dripping rain. The burns everywhere run brown with
peat as you wind to the pass head round mountain shoulders

so soaked in water that even heather in bloom has a brown dead look.

And then suddenly you are over the pass and the land drops away to the sea in one bright sweep. It is lighter here and before you have reached West Loch Tarbert the rain will probably have ceased. At Tarbert, Harris is almost cut in two. This is the second town of the islands, a natural port, and there is something almost sunny about the place, the dour Norse lands beyond the mountains left behind.

From Tarbert south you are in a water-logged land of lochans until the road turns west and hits the coast below lush Taransay Island. Here all is green fertility, a *machair* of sand dune and grass where the crofts have pasture and there is the richer look of proper cultivation in place of a scraping among rock and peat bog for the means of existence. And at Leverburgh you meet up again with the sad relics of Lord Leverhulme's ambitions.

This millionaire chairman of a margarine empire once owned all Lewis and Harris. His bright dream was integrated farming of both land and sea. On the land he wanted economically large farms running dairy herds to supply the islanders with milk. Even now, so long after his death, fresh milk still has to be brought in from the mainland by boat, a sad commentary on the capabilities of the small croft as an agricultural unit. On the sea, he planned to organise the fishing, provide refrigeration storage and canning facilities, a port that would attract trawlers from all the coasts of Scotland. The hub of this dream was the little settlement of Obbe, which he had renamed Leverburgh. It was central. It had a fine deepwater approach. It was sheltered. The great quay he built is now slowly crumbling to decay. The harbour lights and entrance beacons rust unlit. No boats now, only sea birds, use those sheltered waters, and the houses he constructed for his workpeople are occupied by pensioned islanders, retired teachers, postmen and the like.

Some say his schemes foundered on the stupidity of local opposition. Others that it was political sabotage in Edinburgh.

A new generation of islanders now bitterly regrets that lost opportunity. He had wealth, vision and the urge to transform the island economy. Now all they have to show for his frus-

trated period as Laird of the Isles is a disused quay and a
pseudo-baronial castle turned technical college overlooking
Stornoway harbour.

South from Harris the island road is barred by a broad
stretch of sea encumbered by countless islands, rocks and
reefs. You take the steamer from Rodil and in just over an
hour you are at Lochmaddy. I first crossed the new causeway
between North Uist and Benbecula shortly after it was
opened, a five-mile embankment interspersed with bridges
through which the North Ford tide ebbs and flows, the road
a 'velvet cushion' of sea sand sprayed with tar, very similar
to the 'black tops' of North America. The South Ford was
bridged during the war and now you can drive a car from
Lochmaddy down through North Uist, across the flat *machair*
country of Benbecula, some sixty miles to Lochboisdale at
the bottom end of South Uist. But driving shows you little
of the real character of these three islands, for the road keeps
mainly to the *machair* lands of the western coast, where the
beaches are flat and uninteresting, the land given over to
cultivation.

It is the eastern coast that is fantastic, so deeply indented
by the two fords and the deep sea lochs of Eynort, Skiport,
Sheilavaig, Laip, Uskavagh, Eport and Maddy, so pock
marked with countless islands that the coastline must be well
over a thousand miles. Loch Maddy alone, though only half
a dozen miles deep, has a coastline length of no less than three
hundred miles. It is only by boat that you can get the full
flavour of these southern islands. Deep-water channels and
weed-grown shallows—you can take risks here, for the rocks
are so cushioned with weed that there is little risk of damage
Of all the lochs, Skiport, dominated by the mountain bulk
of Hecla, is perhaps the most beautiful. I saw it in the warmth
of a perfect afternoon, still water mirroring the islands, the
shores and islets ablaze with the purple of heather in full
bloom, the lawn-like grass a brilliant green, Hecla cloud
capped, bulking huge, all shades of brown. There were seal
and shags, the quick erratic flight of snipe, and at the loch
head a narrow lead of water sounded to the slap of salmon
leaping.

The wind rose as we headed the boat north, charting our

way through an island maze, where each stretch of water seemed a dead end until suddenly the narrow channel opened up. And to the east the Island of Skye lay sprawled along the horizon. In the late afternoon light we felt our way among the low tide rocks awash to an old quay so overgrown with sea-weed that it was almost indistinguishable from the surrounding rocks. This was Scarilode, and it was from this same quay that Bonnie Prince Charlie embarked for Skye with a price of £30,000 on his head.

This last Stuart bid for the English throne had begun in the islands, for it was in the bay on Eriskay, now known as Cailleag a' Phrionnsa that he first set foot on his native soil, chased there by British men o' war. The date was 3rd August, 1745. Ten months later he was back again, a hunted man, tramping South Uist in disguise, his clansmen having been cut to pieces at Culloden after getting as far south as Derby and so frightening the Hanoverian king that he signed his abdication papers. There is another Prince's Cove on the south-east side of Hecla. He spent a night there searching for a boat and there is a story of £2 million in French gold buried in a cave there, all the money that should have gone to pay his troops. The islanders, who never gave him away despite the price on his head, still preserve the birthplace of Flora Macdonald on the west side of the island, the Clanranald girl who saved his life by taking him out to Skye disguised as her maidservant. But the most haunting memory of Prince Charlie now belongs to that weed-grown pier. And in the last of the evening light we came back to our anchorage at Carnan by the South Ford, the rock islands black against the setting sun, the loch waters a steel highway, burnished and translucent. Every sound we made was sharp and defined in the absolute stillness.

No journey through the Western Isles can be complete without a glimpse of at least one of the outlying island crags, their towering cliffs and satellite stacs white with the packed mass of sea birds that flock there to breed. Sula Sgeir and St. Kilda are two of the largest breeding haunts in the world of the gannet, the big solan-goose whose hunting dives into the sea for fish are as exhilarating to watch as the stoop of a falcon. Rona is the home of Leach's fork-tailed petrel.

Like the stormy petrel it breeds in burrows. Fulmars—oil-squirters like the petrels—abound on all the islands; puffins, too, with their parrot beaks and quaint manners. Great black-backed gulls, kittiwakes, guillemots, shags, razorbills . . . the out-islands are as crowded as Manhattan, every ledge of the skyscraper cliffs and stacs an overcrowded bird slum without sewage-disposal, the noise as shattering as the smell.

I would like to have gone to Rona; not only for the night flighting of the petrel, but because St. Ronan's cell is still largely intact after all these centuries. But Rona is difficult to reach and when I arrived in Stornoway the yearly expedition to neighbouring Sula Sgeir—the Romans' Ultima Thule—had already gone and the boat returned after landing ten men. They go there for the guga, the young of the solan-goose. Split and salted, the inch-thick layer of flesh spread like a great oval pancake, they are regarded as a delicacy by the people of the Ness district of Lewis, the true Norsemen. It is an acquired taste, for the flesh is tainted with oil and has a fishy flavour, which is hardly surprising considering the quantities of herring the bird consumes.

St. Kilda, the most remote of the out-islands, is really a group. Hirta, together with the sheep-cropped crag of Soay and the dragon spine of Dun, forms the central block. The names are Norse. Boreray, with its two attendant stacs, Lli and an Armin, is a little removed to the north-east, and to the south-east lies the isolated, bird-white rock of Levenish. Beginning with Martin Martin's *Late Journey to St. Kilda* in 1698, a whole library of books has been written about these seven lonely piles of rock that had once, some 30 million years ago, been the outriders of that great volcanic belt which covered all the north-west with its basalt lava. The stories handed down from book to book are endless—of a matriarchal community ruled by an Amazon Queen; of a bird-raiding party marooned eight months on Boreray because a smallpox epidemic had so decimated the population that there were not enough men to man the boat; of two men who set fire to the whole community in the kirk and were banished to the stacs to die in solitude for their crime; of the dour Macdonald who killed all laughter on the island; of the eight-day sickness that carried off children almost at birth; of the St. Kilda mail buoyed by a sheep's stomach and borne by the Gulf Stream to the mainland coast; of the final evacuation in 1930. But it was the birds and the way the islanders lived off them that formed the main attraction. Nowhere in the world were men so nimble on rock, climbing barefoot down the highest cliffs in Britain, dangling a thousand feet above the ever-pounding swell, held by a frail hand-made rope woven of hairs from horses' tails. These ropes, or even the horse-hair to make puffin snares, were a girl's dowry, and she would watch whilst her boy passed the ordeal by rock, climbing to the steep-tilted point of the Lover's Stone, 850 ft above the sea, and there, clinging by the toes of one foot whilst he bent and held the other in his hand, he would convince her of his ability to support a family.

Visitors were attracted by these colourful stories, and in the late 1800s naturalists, like Harvie-Brown and Buckley and the brothers Kearton with their specially-constructed camera, gave a scientific slant to the outside world's interest. The Soay sheep were a unique species, directly descended from Viking stock. There were species of field mice and over-sized wrens that existed nowhere but on St. Kilda. Ornithologists joined with tourists to make regular steamer excursions a part of the summer season. The end was inevitable. Demoralised by too close a contact with the mainland, and by the switch from barter to a money economy, the islanders sold their unique heritage for the blandishments of civilisation and in 1930 opted for evacuation.

For almost ten years they continued to return for the summer tourist season, a community of souvenir-sellers. Then the war came. The houses, pillaged by sheltering trawlermen, fell into ruins and the island was left to the sheep and the birds. Finally a guided weapons range was established on South Uist and this required a tracking station out in the Atlantic. St. Kilda was the answer and in 1957 the RAF moved in and built a road. The Army then took over, paying token rent to a new Laird, the Scottish Nature Conservancy.

As I stood beside the plane waiting to take off for this island group the wind tugged at my clothing. We were supposed to be making a mail-drop to the isolated Army unit, but the wind was already blowing 25 knots, the cloud base down

to 1,000 ft and conditions worsening. The pilot shook his head.
'Not very promising, but we may as well go and have a look.'
We took off in a hurry and ten minutes later we flew into
thick cloud at just over 3,000 ft. Seated in the co-pilot's seat
I had time to consider the navigational problem. The aircraft
was a piece of Nevil Shute's world, a development of the
machine he had designed in the early thirties. The radio
crackled—with speed at St. Kilda now 40 knots plus, the
ceiling less than 1,000 ft. We cleared the overcast at 6,000,
flying in bright sunlight, the pilot doing his navigation on his
knee the way the early fliers did and hoping for sight of an
orographical cloud, an umbrella-shaped protuberance in the
cloud layer that would mark the position of Hirta's highest
point, Conachair. There was no such cloud formation, and
five miles beyond Conachair's estimated position we dropped
into the opaque void of the cloud layer and started on our
long descent, a slow spiral with visibility nil and the knowledge that if the pilot's dead reckoning were wrong, then instead of coming out over the sea, the void ahead would suddenly darken as we crashed into the 1,400 ft heights of the
island group.

Our nerves were taut as the altimeter hand unwound—four
thousand, three, two, one—eight hundred, six hundred, five
—and then a sudden darkening below, a corrugated surface,
the long lines of breaking waves. We skimmed the sea, banking with one wing-tip almost touching the water. A rain
squall then, and we came out of it with rock ahead, the sheer
thousand foot cliffs of Boreray. Hirta came up, dead ahead.
A glimpse of Village Bay, the line of the old houses grey and
roofless, the slopes above, dotted with the small stone circles
of old cleits, disappearing into cloud. The bay was full of
white-caps, the wind gusting straight into it from the south-
east. We flew over the gap that separates Dun from the main
bulk of Hirta and banked to a view of sheer cliffs, sea birds
wheeling, specks of white, the swell foaming at their base, the
tops veiled in cloud so that the great basalt wall seemed to
reach up into infinity, to the heavens themselves. It was a
magnificent, appalling sight. Another turn, the T that marked
the dropping zone white against a lawn of green grass, and
the plane dropping like a stone in a down-draught.

The pilot shook his head. 'No good. Too risky.' He circled Village Bay again; a glimpse of the gannet-white top of the bare rock islet of Levenish and we were headed for home. We flew back across the Monach Islands, so low it was like riding in a double-decker bus, for these islands are a complete contrast to St. Kilda, flat and green like a lawn, pitted with sand bunkers like a well-kept golf course. The sea was breaking white on the reefs and the only buildings were the lighthouse and three empty crofts.

Next day we tried again, the morning bright and clear, the wind south-west, a bare 15 knots. This time we saw St. Kilda from 5,000 ft, a smiling pattern of greens and browns seen through dark layers of cloud that looked themselves like islands. Three Spanish trawlers were sheltering in Village Bay. We went into a dive, swept low over Dun and turned to follow the cliff line, all the base laced with the foam of the breaking swell, sea birds wheeling, a drift of snowflakes. Soay loomed gigantic. We swept through the steep-cliffed gap between it and Hirta, banked sharply into Glen Bay and took the wet grass slope of the Glen in a low level climb, banked again at the top of it and roared down the narrow spine that runs out to Dun. One man was already holding the fuselage door open against the slip-stream. The despatcher knelt in the roaring draught. 'Drop—drop—drop.' The aircraft bucked as the down-draughts caught us, the pilot fighting the controls.

Five packages cleared. We repeated the performance. This time the pilot made an error of fifty yards and a bad down-draught slammed us towards jagged outcrops. One package still to go. A third run, the ridge so close I could see the expression on the faces of men on the ground waiting to retrieve the drop. And as we set course for home, the pilot yelled to me, 'Well, that was easy. Second easiest drop I've ever had.' I wondered what it would have been like if he'd tried the previous day. Once he had come low over the back of the island in a south-easterly gale and, caught by the vacuum of the vertical cliff face on the western side, had plummeted 1,000 ft before finding air sufficient to cushion his fall.

There are many islands in the world even more difficult to reach than St. Kilda, but none I think so near to a great centre of civilisation. Seeing it from the air is one thing, to set foot on it quite another. It took me three visits to the Western Isles, spread over a period of two years, before I was able to land in Village Bay and walk Hirta from one end to the other. At close quarters the island has an extraordinary atmosphere, the misted luminosity of the air magnifying the steepness of the slope surrounding the bay, the crags of Dun, black and savage, the clouds above pressing suffocatingly down. It is almost incredible that people lived out their lives in this solitary isolation century after century, yet there, behind the boulder-strewn beach, is the evidence, the roofless walls of the village they evacuated and the stone-heap remains of much older dwellings; and on the heights above the dry-stone mounds of innumerable cleits. But though the sense of isolation was overwhelming at close quarters, it is still that first sight of Hirta's black cliffs seen from a tiny plane in thick weather that remains most vividly in my mind. There, in a flash, I caught the mood, the feel of an island fortress standing in the path of the great depressions that sweep continually up out of the Atlantic towards Iceland and the Arctic seas. It so fascinated me that I wrote a novel about it—*Atlantic Fury*.

V

TREASURE IN THE MARITIMES

The Canadian boom of the early fifties, which gave me the background for *Campbell's Kingdom*, was like the unlocking of a vast treasure chest. It was based on oil and uranium and the key to it was American finance and American know-how. Hand-in-hand went the strategic requirements of the cold war. Money and men poured west into the oil-rich prairies, north into the trackless forests of the Laurentian Shield, and beyond into the Polar wastes. It was a colossal opening up of territory that had only just been properly mapped from the air. In the next ten years I saw a great deal of Canada—into the Labrador for the building of the iron ore railway and the background for *The Land God Gave to Cain*, up into the white spruce country of northern British Columbia, following the old gold rush route of the Caribou Trail, into the Barren Lands of the far north for a film company, to the furthest trading stations of the Hudson's Bay Company serving remote Eskimo people who still live off the dwindling caribou herds on the edge of the Arctic Sea. By the early 1960s I knew almost the whole of Canada, except the Mackenzie River and the Maritimes.

The Maritimes are the oldest part of this huge country, the relatively small Atlantic Provinces of the eastern seaboard that we and the French originally settled and developed. In the boom of the fifties they had become a backwater, almost forgotten in the drive for new development, their maritime tradition threatened by the slump in shipping and the St. Lawrence Seaway, their European markets for coal and agriculture casualties of the war. These provinces became what we would term distressed areas, and though I could see little evidence of any real distress when I visited them in September 1963, the sense that they were out of the mainstream of development in modern Canada was very strong, and I had the impression that, as in the remoter parts of

Scotland, the feeling that the rest of the country owed them a living was carefully nurtured.

The contrast is especially marked if your approach to the Maritimes is by way of Montreal. There the Americanisation of Canada is typified by the skyscraper development of the Place Ville Marie, all glass and aluminium. But a bare three hours by plane and you are in the tree-ed backwaters of New Brunswick's capital, Fredericton, where old colonial-style houses glimmer white in a riot of hydrangeas and where the tempo of life has hardly changed in a hundred years. The contrast for me was even more marked, for within less than twenty-four hours I was in a canoe shooting the rapids of the St. Croix River, back in time nearly 300 years to the mode of travel of the French *voyageurs*. Plunging down rapids, back-paddling into pools of quiet water to cast for salmon, trout and bass; the sun beat down, the air sang with the sound of water rushing over rock, and the forest wall on either side blazed with the violent reds of the Canadian autumn. Like the *voyageurs*, we camped the night on the bank, cooking our fish over a fir-wood fire, and as dusk fell and the moon rose, we drifted gently on the stream watching for game. There are deer in the forests and some moose; black bear, too.

As a fisherman's paradise New Brunswick is probably only surpassed by the unfished areas of the Canadian North, the Miramichi alone yielding over 50,000 salmon a year, all caught by rod and line with each fisherman limited by law to four fish a day. The fishing—and the hunting, too—is mainly done by the local inhabitants. New Brunswick is, of course, beginning to cater for American sportsmen, erecting lush log cabins with names like Loon Bay Lodge, but the hunting as well as the fishing is controlled so that there will never be the wholesale slaughter of animals that the Federal Government has permitted, and even encouraged, in the north. In fact, it is not the visitors who contravene the game laws; it is the New Brunswickers themselves. The day I arrived back in Fredericton they were auctioning firearms that had been confiscated by forest wardens—and the farmers who purchased them looked as though they would use them for exactly the same purpose. The farms in New Brunswick, hemmed in be-

veen highway and forest, are generally poor. I heard the
ord 'slum farmers' used to describe them and was told that
) per cent of all farmers came into this category. A little
rming, a little lumbering, fishing, hunting—a lot of effort,
would seem, to achieve something approaching self-suffi-
ency; a way of life rather than efficient living.

The sad thing is that, if the people of New Brunswick had
it as much effort into farming their forests as they have into
tching fish or shooting game, the province would indeed
e rich. God gave them one of the finest tree growing soils
the world and as a forester myself I was appalled at what
ey had done with their heritage. The near-empty roads run
r hundreds of miles through close-packed forest that has
en laid waste for pulp as though a fire had run through it.
here is not a full grown tree to be seen anywhere. Step off
e road or ashore from a canoe and there are seedlings com-
g up with a profusion that I have seen only in the tropics.
atural regeneration seems a reasonable method of silvi-
lture in such circumstances, but since the law says no tree
all be cut with a bole diameter of less than 9 inches, trees
e invariably felled as soon as they achieve this size. The
st of this haphazard extraction in man hours must be
ormous, since roads and even forest tracks are few and far
tween. Companies owning vast tracts are obliged to re-
ck the areas they cut over, but they still do so largely by
tural regeneration. Significantly, almost the only individual
anting up in the efficient British manner was a St. John oil
dustrialist. He will get the high-yielding species he wants
d the low cost of extraction. For the rest, New Brunswick,
hich seen from the roads or from the air appears as one
st forest interspersed with water, is a variegated mixture of
l sorts of species—Norway spruce, white and black spruce,
lsam fir, western hemlock, western red cedar, white cedar,
l mixed with hardwoods of maple, ash, hornbeam, oak,
ech, poplar, hazel and the white and yellow birches. This
riety enhances the autumn colouring. The flaming reds and
lds against the dark evergreen back-cloth are beautiful bend description.

It was the trees that attracted the Vikings to this part of
orth America more than a thousand years ago. Straumey,

wintering home of the only recorded expedition, may well ha
been Deer Island off the mouth of the St. John river. T'
description in the Icelandic sagas fits and is supported by t
legends of the Passamaquoddy Indians. I did not see De
Island myself when I crossed to Nova Scotia, for though t'
sun was shining when I left the Lord Beaverbrook Hotel,
was thick fog fifty miles down the St. John where the lo
jammed river runs into the Bay of Fundy. The tides he
range fifty feet, the highest rise and fall in the world exce
for Ungava in the north of Labrador, and there are bold pla
to build a series of tidal barrages across the Bay's upp
reaches. The theoretical electrical output from only one
these projects, Minas Basin, is estimated at 150 billi
kilowatt hours per year. But even the pilot project would ta
ten years to complete and there is as yet no prospect of
being started. Nevertheless, the tides and the enormous pote
tial are there, and one day, like the St. Lawrence Seaway th
was argued over for so long, it will be developed. The Feder
Government, or perhaps I should say Canada itself with
fantastic natural resources, has a way of attracting capital
itself when it needs it most.

Moving from the fog and forests of the New Brunswi
shore to Nova Scotia was like moving into a different worl
the island smiling in the sunshine, the grass as emerald gree
as it is in the Outer Hebrides, the farms along the Annapo
valley rich with three and a half centuries of husbandr
Whoever sold the idea that the Maritimes are a depressed ar
of Canada must have looked at these old eastern provinc
through the materialistic spectacles of an industrialist. Wag
are lower, the standard of living measured by gadgetry le
but in Nova Scotia and Prince Edward Island at least t'
people are well fed, well housed—more important, they a
happy. You can see it in their faces, in the way they li
and work. Like the old country of Scotland, the pace in No
Scotia is slower, the atmosphere somewhat parochial. But
is a pleasant atmosphere nevertheless, and the country is ve
beautiful, being much fuller of contrasts than the rest
Canada.

Nova Scotia, and Cape Breton in particular, are as full
quick changes of scene as they are of race. The mixture

ace is the legacy of history, for this was where modern
anada had its beginning. It was five centuries after the
iking long ships lay in Passamaquoddy Bay before Cabot
ade his landfall somewhere on these coasts. The French
ollowed—Jacques Cartier, the discoverer of new lands, then
hamplain with his settlers. They established themselves at
ort Royal on Nova Scotia's north shore in 1605. After that
vents moved swiftly—wars with the Indians, wars between
ie British and the French, Wolfe's capture of Louisburg, the
viction of the Acadians. But though the rule of Britain was
nally established, the French still number 88,000 out of
ova Scotia's population of three-quarters of a million. In-
eed in one area of Cape Breton I was told that five survivors
f the deportation had grown in two centuries to a community
f fifteen thousand and all the west coast with its countless
illages is known as the French Shore. So populated is it, so
uilt up, so absolutely French in language and outlook that
is regarded by English-speaking people as the longest main
reet in North America. In minuscule this is the problem that
edevils all eastern Canada. Memories are long and militant
oung separatists in Montreal resort to violence.

In Nova Scotia, however, the English predominate—over
quarter of a million, stemming partly from Loyalist stock
oming north in the late eighteenth century after the American
evolution—the War of Independence is still called a revolu-
on in the Maritimes! With them they brought their Negro
aves and east of Halifax you can see the somewhat run-
own settlements of their descendants. Another eviction, every
it as brutal as that suffered by the Acadians (but in this case
flicted by Highland landowners on their own tenants),
rought Scots crofters, and the potato famine brought the
rish. The Scots and the Irish between them total another
uarter of a million, and practically every other European race
represented.

The South Shore and the East Shore are deeply indented
nd studded with islands so that from the coast road there is
ie impression of an endless series of Scottish lochs. This is
ie centre of the inshore fishing—lobster, cod, halibut, hake,
addock, and pollock. It is the coast for salt-water sport fish-
ig, and offshore the tunny run up to 1,000 lbs., the sword-

fish even bigger. Here each homestead with its few acres
tilled land and woodland is duplicated by a fish and gear she
that is like a little grey shingled doll's house perched on stil
above the water. Much publicised Peggy's Cove catches th
mood of the coast at its wildest; the bald rocks scoured l
centuries of ice reminded me of the inner leads of th
Swedish coast that I had sailed two years before. And look
ing at the paintings of the artist John de Garthe in his hon
in Peggy's Cove I got the smell of the Grand Banks fisher
Around Lunenburg, where the Dutch have settled, deep se
fishing boats—draggers and long-liners—were being built
massive timbers to withstand the ice. I talked with Capta
Angus Walters, aged 81, who beat all comers, including th
Americans, in his famous *Bluenose*, the fastest Grand Ban
schooner ever built. And at Smith & Rhuland's yard in Lune
burg, where she was built, and which also built the fil
version of the *Bounty*, I walked the decks of *Bluenose II*,
replica designed to promote a well-known beer.

Not far from Lunenberg, there is an island called Oa
Island that is as steeped in mystery as any island in th
world. There I talked to Bob Restall and his English wif
Bloodshed, mystery, the pot of gold at the rainbow's end-
this is the stuff of youthful dreams. But for most of us suc
dreams vanish in adolescence, crowded out by the competiti
drive of the modern educational system. What is one to thi
then of a grown man, not young and with children to brir
up, who had spent the last four years of his life searching f
buried treasure? Was it greed or innocence? Was he one
those who never grow up or was this the physical expressio
of a much more complex character at odds with the mu
danity of ordinary life? Or was he like the explorer, the i
ventor even, seeking some concrete end to the goal he h
set himself? The search had already cost him $85,000—h
own savings and others' as well; four years of his life, years
hardship and toil, with nothing to show for them. Yet st
he was going on, his confidence unshaken.

Oak Island is to my mind one of the two great treasu
stories of the world. The other is Cocos Island. They a
fundamentally opposites. In the case of the Cocos Islar
treasure everybody knows what is supposed to be buried the

—all the wealth of the great cathedral built by the Conquis-
adors on Lima's Plaza de Armas, including two life-size
tatues in solid gold. It was consigned to Spain in the Bristol
rigantine, *Mary Dier* (after which my own boat is named).
The captain was a man named Mary Thompson and once
ut in the Pacific he is supposed to have dropped the Jesuit
riests who accompanied the treasure overboard and sailed
or Cocos Island, which is a wet hell of a place bedevilled
y landslides. What is not known is the exact location of the
reasure and an element of mystery surrounds Keating, the
Newfoundland fisherman (or was he Nova Scotian?) who
nounted the first three expeditions little more than a century
go.

Where the Oak Island treasure differs is that there has
ever been any doubt about its location. Anybody with a few
lollars to spare could hire Bill's boat and go across to the
sland and watch Restall at work and stare down into the
Money Pit as it is called. Six hundred tourists had been that
ear. But what is at the bottom of the Pit nobody knows. The
opular theory is that Captain Kidd buried his ill-gotten
ains there—an obvious choice, since pirates and treasure go
ogether. More sophisticated theorists talk of Inca gold, even
French state papers. Whatever it is, the fascination of Oak
sland's Money Pit is that with all the modern techniques
t their disposal, the treasure seekers—and there have been
lmost a dozen individuals or groups who between them have
pent something like $1½ million—have all failed to get to the
ottom of it. The secret is locked—locked in by water.

'A theory about the treasure? I have none. The only thing
know about Oak Island is that it's a great mystery.' We were
n the lounge of the Isle Royal in Sydney, Nova Scotia, and
alking to me was M. R. Chappell, son of the man who first
robed the Money Pit with a drill some seventy years ago.
Chappell was sixtyish, tall with a long pale face and glasses.
That night he had abandoned a bridge party at his home to
ome and talk to me about Oak Island—for five minutes he
aid on the phone. He talked for an hour. He was a successful
uilding contractor who had acquired, not only the treasure
rove licence originally taken out by Judge Blair in 1895, but
lso physical ownership of the relevant part of the island.

He has, in fact, taken all necessary steps to safeguard his
interests should anybody find treasure. And though my impression was that he had never himself invested money in the
search, he has certainly provided at various times machinery
workmen and also advice, and he admits to being entirely
fascinated by the mystery.

The story of the discovery of the Money Pit is this: Three
men, whose names are given as Anthony Vaughan, Jack
Smith and Dan McInnes, were shooting over Oak Island
There were at that time three oaks standing on the high
ground back of the cove now called Smith's Cove. One of
the party lay down to rest under one of these oaks and looking up he saw that a branch had been sawn off short. Since
this shooting trip is supposed to have occurred in 1795 there
could have been very few people living in the district. A sawn-
off branch was, therefore, something unusual, sufficient at any
rate to excite the hunter's curiosity. He climbed the tree and
found the limb deeply scored as though by a chain that had
borne a heavy weight. Looking down, he noticed that directly
below there was a shallow depression in the ground.

The three of them rowed back to the mainland, and after
procuring implements and stores, returned to the island and
began to dig. About ten feet down they uncovered a platform
of oak timbers. Below this it was earth again, until at the
20-ft level they struck another platform, and again another
at 30 ft. At this point they ran out of provisions and, failing
to enlist help, owing to the evil reputation of the place, they
gave up. Six years later they managed to interest some
Boston people, a company was formed and work renewed
The pattern continued to repeat itself—every ten feet a staging of oak timbers. They came very near to success as later
drilling showed, but the people who had originally dug that
pit and put in the oak platforms did not intend that their
secret should yield to pick and shovel. At 95 ft the shaft
flooded and all attempts to pump it free of water failed.

The reason for the failure is not known. At 111 ft—this
was the depth given me by Chappell—the makers of the pit
drove a sloping tunnel out to Smith's Cove. Just back of the
cove there is now a shaft intersecting this tunnel at the 80 ft
level. The tunnel was packed with stones and small boulders

o that water could pass through it without destroying it. And o finish off this whole neat piece of engineering a dam was onstructed in Smith's Cove so that even at low water prings the water supply would never fail. The extraordinary hing is that this simple device has baffled every searcher, including Restall. He thought he could seal the water tunnel by orcing cement in under pressure the way you deal with orous rock around a dam, but he was only partially successful nd when I saw him he was laboriously pulling pipe because he couplings were worn and he could no longer keep his ump working.

The trouble with Oak Island is that so many people have rodded around in that one spot that virtually nothing of the riginal construction remains. When I saw it the Money Pit ooked like the shaft head of a primitive coal mine. The sun as shining and the mosquitoes were biting ferociously. I had notored into the tiny settlement of Marriott's Cove, which is bout 40 miles west of Halifax, had turned down where a ign pointed to 'Bill's Boat for Oak Island', had waited in he little shed where two coopers were making fish barrels ntil Bill had finished his lunch, and had finally embarked n his open launch, heading out to the dark, thickly tree-ed sland. We landed in Smith's Cove at a rickety wooden jetty. Below us as we tied up I could see the piled-up rocks of the de dam. At low water the top of it is awash. A red-painted aunch with a rusty-looking outboard stood with its bows mongst the trees, surrounded by the debris of this and previ-us expeditions. Back of the shore was the remains of a shaft ttle more than a yard square. The supporting timbers were otting and in the centre was the top of the iron casing hrough which Restall had forced cement into the water nnel 80 ft below. A path led up to the top of the island, and fter walking little more than two hundred yards, we came uddenly upon a wired enclosure that dropped away to a rimitive-looking mine working where great baulks of sawn mber bolted together formed the head of the shaft. There was big diesel generator and floodlights, a pump and iron iping. And on the edge of the clearing stood a small hut bout the size of a caravan.

I have said that Restall's confidence was unshaken, but he

was more positive than that. 'The treasure's there all right. know what it is and I know how to get to it.' More than tha he would not say. 'I have to protect my interest and that o the other shareholders.' Fair enough, but when a man has bee working without success for four years it's difficult to asses such absolute confidence. Was he kidding himself, hiding hi failure from his wife and his eldest son who was helping him They showed me a stone that was supposed to have come from the water tunnel. It had a date scratched on it—1704. I didn't look very convincing and I wondered whether it wa not just a convenient way of passing on to tourists and th more gullible members of the press the laboratory findings o test samples of wood and coconut fibre taken from the Pit.

Restall talked about a false treasure, insisted that the rea treasure was off to one side; as soon as the pump was going again and he was back to the 130-ft level, he'd get bot treasures. 'The sooner the better,' his wife said. 'I'm getting tired of this place.' And she excused herself, to go off an help her youngest with his schooling, which was by correspond ence course. She had been on the island for three years, he only home through the hot, mosquito-ridden summers and th bitter frozen winters that tiny hut.

I went up then to another clearing where Bill showed m some stones of what looked like cut granite. They had fain markings on them and some people believe them to be th work of an Inca priest. But as Chappell said, so much i hearsay and conjecture. Even after his father started using a oil drill on the Pit in 1895 incidents became exaggerated an distorted in the telling. For instance, there is a story that o one occasion a driller brought up three links of gold chai and made off with it. What, in fact, happened was that th tool-pusher took some sort of a sample from the drill bi put it in his pocket and told the others it would be examine and he'd give the results when they returned to the Pit. In th event, he never came back. He had to go and see to his ow mine and was blown up the following day in an explosion.

There was never any gold chain. But Chappell's father di bring up something—a few oak chips and a piece of parch ment about the size of a finger-nail. It is this minute piece o parchment that gave rise to the idea that the treasure migh rove to be no more than French state papers. Moreover, on this occasion the drill did not go down straight. Somewhere along the line of probe the bit struck an obstruction and veered off in an unknown direction. It was not quite clear to me how they knew this, but I suspect that it was based on the knowledge that the bed-rock lies at 190 ft. Probably the depth of the bit at the time it brought up a core sample of oak chips and parchment was greater than this. As a result subsequent expeditions have drilled all round the Money Pit and you can still see their drill holes. That these holes have not caved in is due to the fact that the ground is all heavy clay right down to the bed-rock. It was this clay that enabled the buriers of the 'treasure' to go straight down with pick and shovel without the need of shoring.

Chappell first became interested in the 1920s. But though he will talk for hours on the subject, he is neither a crank nor a dreamer. He is a hard-headed, practical business man who has become fascinated by a mystery. 'If I have had one theory, I have had hundreds. I go to bed thinking about it and wake up thinking about it.' He certainly wouldn't stake his life savings as Restall had done. But then Restall was entirely different. According to Chappell, he had travelled in many countries with the only Globe of Death in the world, and his wife, an ex-dancer, rode pillion. Restall's concession ran out at the end of that year. 'Let him bring up some oak chips or a piece of parchment and I'd certainly let him go on.'

He did, in fact, renew the concession and it resulted in tragedy. Two years after I talked with him in 1963, Restall was killed. He was overcome by gas at the bottom of the Money Pit, and his eldest son and two other men, who tried to get him out, also lost their lives.

Did Restall really believe he had discovered the final resting place of the Cocos Island treasure? Though the dates do not appear to tie up, Keating provides a tenuous connection. The *Mary Dier* was finally captured by a Peruvian warship. Captain Mary Thompson's life was spared on the understanding that he would show them where the treasure was buried. Instead, he took them to the Galapagos and there escaped. Nothing very much is known of him after that and there is uncertainty about where he died—some accounts say England, some Nova Scotia. All that is known for certain is that in 1841 a fisherman named Keating had in his possession a map purporting to give the treasure's location and in June of that year he and a Captain Boag reached Cocos Island in the brig *Edgcombe*. On Keating's return he apparently had sufficient resources to commission the building of a 120-ton clipper schooner, the *Red Gauntlet*. This vessel never returned to Nova Scotia. She is supposed to have foundered off Cape Horn on the return journey. But a Judge Prowse tells how Keating, who was supposed to have deserted at Panama, was able to buy one of the finest business premises in St. John's, Newfoundland, and how on his return he astonished his wife by throwing a heap of gold and jewels on her bed. Keating made one more expedition to Cocos Island in 1846. He died in 1882 leaving a number of maps of the treasure's location, all of them inaccurate.

When I mentioned this treasure to Chappell he immediately said, 'Yes, Restall has a theory about that, too.' He wouldn't say that the Cocos Island treasure and the Oak Island treasure were one and the same, but that was the inference. There is one major snag to this idea, the date of the Oak Island burial. Carbon 14 tests on the oak chips and parchment, on the coconut fibre, even acorns found in the Money Pit, have proved inconclusive, since this type of test can only be a rough guide to antiquities several thousand years old, the margin of error being some 300 years. And I certainly do not accept the stone with 1704 scratched on it. But if the date of the original discovery of the Pit is really 1795 then that rules out any connection with the Cocos Island treasure for that was not put on board the *Mary Dier* until more than twenty years later. If, on the other hand, this date is entirely spurious, then Restall's theory—if it was his theory—could easily hold water. Keating's behaviour during the course of the *Red Gauntlet* expedition has in it the germ of all sorts of possibilities.

One final thing Chappell told me as we parted. He is convinced that once the influx of water has been satisfactorily controlled searchers will find a huge chamber, perhaps as much as 50 ft high, immediately above the bed-rock. His reasoning here is based partly on his father's drilling—at one point the drill indicated a void—and partly on the original construction of the Money Pit. If the buriers, having sunk their shaft through the clay to a depth of more than 100 ft, had then excavated a large chamber, they would not then have dared back-fill with the whole 100 ft column of loose earth resting on the chamber's roof beams. Not only would the beams have collapsed, but the subsidence of that amount of earth would have revealed their excavation to the first hunter or fisherman who climbed to the top of Oak Island. In other words, they would have had to do exactly what they did, insert staging at intervals.

Thus the method of construction becomes understandable. But if one accepts this as a reasonable theory it still remains for Restall's successors to discover who built that chamber and why—and whether the two vastly different island treasure stories, so tenuously linked by Keating, are in fact connected. There is, of course, much more to the two stories than I have been able to give here. Books have been written about both, and even the short talk I had with Malcolm Campbell before he died, about his expedition to Cocos Island in 1925, would fill pages. Attempt after attempt, expedition after expedition —the one attracting miners, the other sailors. And all, so far, to no avail. An enormous waste of human effort—or is it? Are these seekers after the pot of gold at the rainbow's end not real treasure seekers after all, but simply men in love with the excitement of living?

I only wish I could have met the one man in this part of Canada for whom the adventure of life was entirely unselfish. But I had to be content with a visit to the beautiful little museum at Baddeck on the Bras d'Or, for Alexander Graham Bell died in 1922. A Scot, educated at Edinburgh University, he was threatened with tuberculosis and emigrated to Canada in 1870. He moved to Boston the following year, became an American citizen and ran a school for deaf mutes. His involvement with the problems of the deaf was the spark that stimulated his inventive genius and the use of a magnetic aid led to the telephone. But though it is the telephone with which his name is mainly associated, many things we now take for granted came within the scope of this man's brilliant brain. He never stopped, one thing leading to another right up to the time he died.

Cape Breton Island is now connected to Nova Scotia by a causeway across the narrow Canso Straits. Here you move into a world of forest and water, the whole island like a hollow tooth, its golden centre of beauty the huge inland sea of Bras d'Or Lake. It was on the north shore of the Bras d'Or that Alexander Graham Bell finally built his home. He chose it because it reminded him of Scotland. All through my journey in the Maritimes people kept saying to me, 'Doesn't this remind you of Scotland?' And each time I had to reply, 'No—it's different.' The tang in the air, the colder light, the sense of illimitable space and a vastness reaching up towards the Pole. But here at Baddeck, looking across the Bras d'Or, it really is like Scotland. Here the first public flight was made, the first hydrofoils used, the first tricycle undercarriage, echo-sounders, sea-water distillation. It is all there in that fascinating little museum, the life of a man whose ever-inventive, ever-searching, restless mind could never stop. The museum, very modern, very suited to the man, fits most perfectly into its background of fir and birch and water.

North from Baddeck the Cabot Trail sweeps round the coastal perimeter of the Cape Breton Highlands. The forests, the fine highway, the neat, ordered camping sites with plug-ins for electricity in the caravan parks—the Canadians, like the Americans, have a built-in urge to tame the wild and make it neat and ordered as a suburban housing estate. It remains, however, the most beautiful stretch of country in the Maritimes. In contrast, Prince Edward Island, known as the Garden Province, or more generally, as P.E.I., is flat as an aerodrome with a soil as red and rich as Devon and a vested interest in the potato. In summer the shallow waters of the Gulf of St. Lawrence on which it seems to float give it the highest sea temperature north of Florida—70°. In winter the pack ice jammed against the beautiful sand beaches of its northern shore pile up in a cold bleak wall 20 ft high. P.E.I. is the smallest of Canada's ten provinces, and Charlottetown, founded in 1764, is the smallest and oldest of the provincial capitals. Here, in the little Georgian Provincial Building, Canada was born, and to mark the centenary of the first meeting of the Fathers of the Confederation a big new Memorial Building, which I had seen nearing completion and which included theatre, library, museum and art gallery, was opened in 1964 by the Queen.

Affection for the Crown—and for the 'Old Country' itself —is common to all the Maritimes. This loyalty is almost an anachronism in the Americanised rest of Canada, but here it is solidly based, stemming as much from geographical position as from race. These eastern provinces face the Atlantic. They are essentially maritime islands, looking to the old world for trade; it is, after all, often cheaper to ship goods the two and a half thousand miles across the ocean into the great natural harbour of Halifax than to bring them by road or rail the near-thousand miles from Montreal, Toronto or New York. I could not suppress whilst I was there an instinctive feeling that race and ocean and way of life all combine to form an inescapable link between the old world and this small section of the new.

Beaverbrook had this same feeling—in fact, throughout his long, turbulent, energetic life his most cherished aim was to bridge the gap that had opened up between his homeland and the land of his adoption. His father, William Aitken, was minister of Newcastle, a small New Brunswick town. It was here that Beaverbrook spent the formative years of his life on which his career in Britain, his beliefs and hopes, were founded. He never wavered in his conviction that if only the British people would spend time and energy in cultivating those eastern provinces of Canada the gap would be bridged, the link firmly re-established through trade. I never met him, but just before he died I had a letter from him thanking me for writing about some of the things in which he had always believed. One day perhaps the unflagging faith of this man from the dark timber lands of Eastern Canada will prove to have been justified.

VI

ADDU ATOLL

Gan. It was a name to me, no more—a name that had stuck in my mind all through the writing of *Atlantic Fury*, ever since an official of the Air Ministry had suggested it as a possible background for a novel. I did not realise then that it was the key to one of the least-known and most fascinating island groups in the world; one, moreover, that because of its strategic position could become as important to us in the future as Malta was in the past. I knew Gan was an RAF staging post and that it was in the Maldives, but that was all. I barely knew where the Maldives were, and it wasn't until I took the Air Ministry up on their suggestion that I realised there was a political problem—no writer had ever been allowed to visit the island, no journalist had even been permitted to stage through for fear he aggravated the situation by writing about it.

The Maldives are a group of 19 coral atolls stretching south from Ceylon like a great barrier reef 500 miles into the Indian Ocean. The most southerly and remote are Suvadiva and Addu Atoll. Gan lies like a huge aircraft carrier stranded on the coral reefs of Addu Atoll, one of a dozen or so small islands fringing a deep water lagoon just below the equator. Governed from Malé, 300 miles to the north, their meagre exports of dried fish, copra, coir rope and cowrie shells subject to crippling taxes, the peoples of these two atolls had formed a breakaway state—the United Suvadivan Republic. My request to visit the islands came at a bad time. The RAF had been accused by the Malé Government of fostering rebellion. Long conferences at the Air Ministry finally resulted in the RAF agreeing to give me facilities for visiting the islands provided that the political situation did not form an integral part of any novel that might result.

Now it was late afternoon, January 29, 1963, and I was in a Transport Command Comet. The Gurkha major sitting next to me was describing how, as a young paymaster during the war, he had been given a million pounds in cash and ordered to get it through Cairo. The sun sank in tropical splendour, a furnace glow of red with the anvil shapes of cunim standing like stacs along the western horizon. England had been in the grip of the worst cold in living memory when we had taken off the previous night. We had had breakfast at El Adem in the Libyan desert, lunch at Aden, and now we were high over the Indian Ocean.

Night closed in as we crossed the equator and then the whispering descent, the stars blotted out by cloud, rain streaming in torrents off the wings. Suddenly we were below the cloud. The plane banked and in the darkness a fleeting glimpse of red lights shining like rubies. Our landing lights were switched on, shone on a void of driving rain, and then sheets of spray as we hit the runway, and the wet earth smell of the land seeping into the fuselage. We came to rest, and with the opening of the fuselage door the hot humid jungle scent of quick growth and quick decay hit us in the face, and with it came another smell, fainter, more astringent— the smell of the sea all around us.

Gan is the last stage on the long air route from the UK to Singapore. This island was once, like all the other islands of Addu Atoll, covered in a tropical growth of palm trees, pawpaws, yams, bananas, and the big branching kanda tree from which the inhabitants make their boats. But a few years back the people of Gan agreed to transfer to the neighbouring islands of Fedu and Maradu. Gan was bulldozed flat, all the jungle growth, all the Adduan houses of coral cement and palm tree fronds pushed into the sea. Now it is a flat bare expanse, a great concrete runway flanked by all the paraphernalia of any aerodrome anywhere in the world.

Five hundred British servicemen live here in complete isolation, a year at a stretch; no wives, no families, confined to Gan and barred from visiting any of the other islands of this atoll group. But life there has its compensations. Addu Atoll is as near to an island paradise as you will find anywhere in the seven seas. The water temperature is a permanent 82°F, the reefs swarm with fish, the shade temperature varies between 70° and 90° F and though the rainfall is 100 inches a year it tends to fall in short, concentrated bursts; the rest of the time the sun shines and the waters of the lagoon sparkle with the trade wind breeze.

But it is the Adduans themselves who are largely responsible for the happy atmosphere of the place. There are over 7,000 of them on Addu Atoll—a small, dark, sensitive people full of laughter. Many of the women have the fragile beauty of the Ceylonese, big-eyed and fine-boned. The men are tough and wiry despite their diminutive stature. They are predominantly Sinhalese stock infiltrated by Arab and African. Several hundred of them work on the base, and the first morning I was there I watched them coming in from their islands. A line of palm fringed the beach and beyond the palms the coloured sails of their dhonis glided silently on the first zephyr of the day's breeze as they sailed close inshore towards the landing place.

These long, narrow, squaresail-rigged craft with their curved-up prow are not unlike the Viking ships of the Inner Lead. The larger ones—the bondo-dhonis—are ten-oared and will hold 30 to 40 men. The kuda-dhoni is six-oared. Both are for use mainly inside the reefs and the *hunganu hif-meeha*, the helmsman, steers with his foot on the helm, holding on to the stern post, the *atteli*. In the sunbright morning air these crowded boats had a timeless quality. In them this isolated people had moved across their lagoon for centuries past. The sense of continuity was very strong. So also was the sense of peace, of absolute tranquillity. And then the quiet was rent by the screams of jets and the first plane of the day taxied out to the runway-end behind me. It took off with a shattering roar, climbing steeply and banking as it set course for Singapore 2,000 miles away.

The sudden impact of the twentieth century upon an isolated seafaring people was for me the chief fascination of Addu Atoll. I can write about it now for the political situation has been resolved. The Adduan People's Republic is no more. We have shipped the rebel president off to the Seychelles and the Adduans are back under the Maldivian Government, nominally at any rate.

It wasn't the jets that produced a new mood of defiance to the established government. The desire for independence had

ong been there. What sparked it off was the construction of
he base in 1957. The Adduans provided the labour force and
he money they earned enabled them to purchase rice, flour,
sugar, cigarettes, even radios. Whereas before they had existed
argely on what they harvested from the sea or grew in their
gardens, a diet so restricted that their physical stature was
stunted, they were suddenly able to obtain all the things for
which their pitiful exports of dried fish and shells had been
insufficient. Then the Malé Government stepped in and demanded its cut.

This was too much for Afif Didi, the small, dapper, ambitious Adduan leader. In 1959, confident that the RAF, however unwillingly, would be forced to support him, he joined
his people with the neighbouring atoll of Suvadiva and set up
his own government. The result was disastrous for Suvadiva.
The Malé Government mounted a punitive expedition. They
had two launches armed with machine-guns. The people of the
atolls had no arms. Suvadiva was brought to heel and Addu
Atoll isolated, the big trading vessels—the vedis—all laid up
and unable to put to sea.

'Pir-racy,' Afif Didi told me, speaking in a high, waspish
voice. 'Because Malé men make pir-racy on the high seas.'
We were in his high palm-raftered office in the Adduan
Trading Corporation's building close by the Gan jetty. He
did not refer to the Malé Government. As self-styled president
of the Adduan People's Republic he did not recognise Malé.
They say we make rebellion. But it is not rebellion to form
a government where before there is no government.'

He ruled through a People's Council of 52 representatives.
I still have an envelope with a crest on the back showing a
dhoni under sail and a lone palm tree, three stars and a
crescent above, and inscribed below: *People's Council of
Addu Atoll*. He was slightly built, not exactly effeminate, but
a man more at home in an office than on the waters of the
lagoon. He had a thinnish, clean-shaven face, large dark
brown eyes, black hair. He was a born politician, an oppor-
tunist and tactically clever. For instance, he could have taken
much more violent and vengeful action when the Malé Government sent representatives to Gan to negotiate a settlement
with the RAF. Feeling was running very high amongst the

Adduans following the attack on Suvadiva. The four delegates
were housed for the night in quarters close to the dhoni park.
It would not have been very difficult to arrange for their
throats to be slit. Maldivians are not squeamish about such
things. The machete is in constant use and as recently as 1953
the lopping off of a hand was re-introduced by the Sultan for
offences against the Malé Government.

His approach, however, was much more subtle. In the dead
of the tropic night he had practically the whole male population of Addu afloat in their dhonis. The boats congregated
opposite the delegates' quarters, dark shadows under the stars,
and for an hour and more the delegates were subjected to the
full-throated roar of nearly 2,000 men chanting: 'Malé men
go home. Go home, Malé men.' They went the next day, in a
great hurry.

By a demonstration, rather than vicious action, Afif Did
ensured that the Malé Government was made aware of the
strength of his support in Addu Atoll. Locally, of course, he
had gone out of his way to make himself indispensable to the
RAF, particularly at a time when Gan was being cleared and
the aerodrome constructed. But he was fishing in waters too
big for him. Economically he was not a free agent and this was
his weakness.

Nevertheless, he had plans that might have helped both the
Adduans and himself. In 1960 he had formed the Adduan
Trading Corporation with a capital of £6,000 in £1 shares.
The maximum holding for a village was 100 shares, for an
individual 10. When I saw him the capital had been increased to £40,000, so presumably every village and a lot of
individuals had expressed their confidence in him by subscrib-
ing for the maximum. The Corporation was a monopoly with
shops in each village through which was channelled the pay of
all the men working on the base. He had also founded a bank
—the People's Bank of Addu Atoll. This enabled him to
borrow money from the Adduans to finance his government.
He told me he paid interest quarterly, but he failed to explain
how he earned the money to pay that interest. With the vedi
laid up there was no means of trading unless it was done
clandestinely with the ships calling at Gan; the market for

cowrie shells was Ceylon and Singapore and the dried fish lay rotting in store.

'Addu can produce about seventy-five tons of dried fish a year,' he told me. 'But it is better and more profitable if we are able to can it.' He was very anxious to get one of the big British food firms interested in setting up a cannery. 'Addu has plenty of fish.' This was true. Any day you could go out to the reefs and see the lateen-sailed battelis hauling in bonito and tunny fish, using long bamboo rods and bent nails that gleamed in the water like small fry. 'And there is good swimming also.' He was thinking of the deep water lagoon and cruise ships. During the war Addu Atoll had been known as Port T, a centre for convoys and re-fuelling. The *Queen Mary* had put in there on a trooping voyage to the Far East.

Was all this a pipe dream? I am not certain. Afif Didi was a very astute man with a smart business sense. But he is gone now, and even whilst his Adduan flag—a very colourful one of blue, green and red in horizontal bars with white stars and a crescent—flew over the islands, the price the people had to pay for independence was a very high one. They were completely cut off from their own kind, isolated and at the mercy of benevolent strangers, their vedis lying rotting on the beaches like the dried fish in the store.

Those vedis were one of the most pathetic sights I have ever seen. 'Mothballed' was the way somebody described them to me and the description was exact. They had mothballed them against the heat of the sun in the only way they could, in great thatched houses of palm tree fronds.

I saw them first from a helicopter. We had flown up the western shores of the lagoon, skimming the tree-green islands of Fedu, Maradu, Abuhera, past the tall radio masts on the southern tip of Hittadu. There was a mosque I remember with white flags flying in the trade wind breeze like Monday's washing on a housing estate, flags for the dead; and some children flying a kite, bright eyes gazing up at us and the flash of white teeth in small dark faces. The island streets were clean and white and straight, the houses neat rectangles half buried with their gardens amongst the trees. And along the beaches palm-thatched boathouses for the dhonis that were surplus to requirement now that most of the men went to work each day on Gan. And then we were winging our way up the white sword slash of Hittadu's main street. Hittadu is the largest of the islands and the seat of government. We hovered for a moment over the red tiled roof of the council building, circled a mosque built of coral cement, blinding in the sunglare, and then we turned east, sidling towards the reef shallows where the water was a brilliant green darkening to purple as the depth increased.

The pale sand line of a man-made channel cut through the dark of the reef-weed growth to a shore lagoon shot with colours of bright chemical green. There were several dhoni moored here and also the little sailing boat that Afif Didi had imported. And along the shore great thatched buildings like Malayan longhouses.

These were the vedis, their dark hulks crouched below the thatch, their bowsprits pointing towards the sea. In some cases the bowsprits themselves had been wrapped in palm fronds to protect them from the sun. I counted more than a dozen still resting on the palm bole rollers on which the Adduans had hauled them up out of the water. Their masts lay beside them, the wood sun-tired and cracked. The air shimmered in the morning heat and I could not believe that they would ever put to sea again.

We turned east, flying low over the reefs that are the northern bastion of the great lagoon. Big manta rays winged with slow beat through the green water at the edge of the Kudu Kanda Channel. The currents are fierce here and there were whirlpools. We flushed a large flock of grey terns by Bushy Island, the birds diving for small fry which were in their turn being chased by larger fish. A batteli, with a curved white sail like a dhow, was fishing by one of the buoys in the Man Kanda Channel. And then we were coming in to Midu, the second largest island. Again the pale cut of a man-made channel through the reef and back from the shore the long straight line of the village street gleaming white between banks of tropical growth. A crowd of people here mostly women and girls, all smiling and waving as the 'chopper' pilot danced the helicopter in till the blades whipped

he waters of the lagoon in their faces. And behind this
hrilled and colourful crowd the mothballed bulk of more vedis
nder their thatch. Gan was ten miles away across the big
lgoon. Most of the men were working there and the vedis lay
weltering in the burning sun, immobile hulks, abandoned now
nd no longer a part of the people's lives.

Later, when I visited the islands, I was able to examine
hem more closely. I was accompanied by Musafta, one of the
reatest of the Adduan *malimi*, or navigators. He had been
nany times to Ceylon, also to the Nicobar Islands. And
nce, coming from Suvadiva, he had been blown past Addu
Atoll far to the south and in a great storm had lost both masts
nd with his vedi almost sinking under him had been picked
p by a steamer and taken with his crew to Australia. He
vas taller than the average Adduan, a slender, wiry man with
. gentle smile and prominent ears. Like the Polynesians, he
lavigated by using a gourd half filled with water to give him
n artificial horizon.

We left the main jetty at Gan immediately after breakfast
n a bondo-dhoni, ten men rowing. It was an old boat, the
vood hard and silvered by the sun. But though rough and
vorn now, it was still beautifully made, all hand work that any
•oatyard would have been proud of. The Adduans rowed till
hey were clear of the reef, then they raised the mast, slot-
ing it into a tabernacle and securing it with a forestay. The
quaresail was hoisted by a rope passed over a metal sheave.

For those who know something about boat design the rig
•f these craft is interesting. The squaresail boom has two
;uys, one at each end, and these are knotted together and
•assed round a wooden protrusion in the stern. By adjusting
hese guys the wind can be spilled if the dhoni heels so much
hat water comes in over the gunnel. There are also two
heet ropes, one for the bows and one aft, and there is a long
•ole, an atteli, which slots into one of two cringles on the luff.
Chis holds the luff taut and has the effect of converting the
quaresail into something approaching a fore-and-aft-rig
vhen going to windward. These cringles are on both sides
•f the squaresail so that either edge can become the luff
ls they go about. The oars, home-made like everything else,

are blades of wood shaved thin, slotted into a pole and boun
with coir rope. They are secured to wooden thole pins o
the gunnels by twisted rushes.

The phrase 'ten men rowing' is typical of the pidgin Englis
used in the islands. There appears to be no plural. If yo
are referring to more than one it requires the prefix of
numeral. Verbs do not seem to be conjugated, hence the per
sistent use of -ing. Man having or not having. . . . This sor
of bastard phraseology has crept into RAF signals: 'Ref you
etc engineer looking but not having necessary spare parts.'

The dhoni is an extraordinarily fast boat. Going to wind
ward with five men rowing on one side to give the effect o
power-assisted sailing the boat seems capable of about 5 knot
some five points off the wind. With the wind aft of the beam
the speed rises to nearer 8 knots.

The sun blazed down and the spray sparkled as it hit ou
faces. The trade wind breeze was on the starboard beam, th
dhoni heeled hard over and the only sound the hiss of th
water as it slid past, lipping the top of the port gunnel and
occasionally sloshing into the boat. I asked Musafta whethe
in his voyages he had ever seen the 'white water'. Yes, he had
seen the white water—not once, but twice. Both times he had
been very frightened.

The white water is a phenomenon more often seen in th
Red Sea or off the coast of India. The best description of it i
given in the West Coast of India Pilot under the heading
'Luminosity of the Sea'. It is described by the master of th
Ariosto in one of the most exact and descriptive passages
have ever read by an untrained writer:

At 7.30 p.m., on the 17th February 1912, in latitude 23°
37′N, longitude 67° 20′E, the weather at the time being very
fine, with a clear and cloudless sky, full of stars, sea smooth
wind moderate, breeze from NW, the ship steaming 9½ knots
and perfectly steady, steamed into the most curious and
weird atmospheric phenomenon it has been my lot to see in al
my 40 years' experience of sea life. As we approached it,
had the appearance of breakers on a low beach, but when w
got into it, it looked, at first, like flashes of light (not bright
coming from all directions in quick time. After some minute
of this the flashes assumed a lengthened shape, following

quickly one after the other from the north, and these continued for some minutes, steadily veering to east and south and to SW into NW. All the time this was going on, the surface of the sea appeared to be violently agitated, at times very high seas, as if they would completely engulf the ship, the imagined waves always going in the same direction as the waves of light, and at the time the waves of light were from opposite directions. At the same time the sea appeared like a boiling pot, giving one a most curious feeling—the ship being perfectly still, and expecting her to lurch and roll every instant. It turned me dizzy watching the moving flashes of light, so that I had to close my eyes from time to time. . . . I have seen the 'white water' many times in the Arabian sea, but this did not appear like that in any way; it gave one the idea of the cinematograph without the brightness, the flashes being so quick in their movements.

Unfortunately Musafta's knowledge of English was not sufficient for him to describe the white water to me as he had seen it nor could he tell me anything about it. But in my conversation with Afif Didi I discovered that the white water was part of the mythology of the islands. Before the Adduans were converted to the Moslem faith they believed in a whole range of djinns or devils, one of which was Ran-a-Maari.

This meeting took place in Afif's house on Hittadu. I had arrived on the daily launch at the Hittadu transmitter jetty at the south end of the island where the 'president's' secretary had met me with a bicycle. We had ridden together through the afternoon heat along a tree-ed track where new Kadjan houses were being erected—as in Western countries an improved standard of living had resulted in a demand for separate homes from young married couples. It was stiflingly hot, the trade wind breeze killed by the dense tree growth. The palm-thatched vedis stood black and huge against the sun glare of the lagoon. Afif, dressed in immaculate white, was waiting for me in the shaded gloom of a room that was part office, part bedroom. There was a very expensive-looking chromium plated radio and the top of his desk was glass —covered with chart 2067 (the large-scale chart of Addu Atoll) spread out below the glass. I was presented with two very fine helmet-like shells polished with coconut oil so that

the strange orange colouring of the hard surface gleamed a
though it were lacquered. He apologised for not offering an
refreshment. It was Ramadan.

'The first man the Adduans recognise,' Afif Didi told me
'is Adam. The second is Noah and the third is Suleiman
Suleiman made a copper ball in which to imprison Ran-a
Maari, but when he thrust the djinn into the ball, he foun
it was too small. The ball would accommodate no more than
the djinn's body and when it was closed his legs stuck out of it
Suleiman threw the copper ball into the sea and it sank
Smilingly he added, 'The djinn's legs still thrash about as h
tries to release himself from his prison and it is this thrash
ing of Ran-a-Maari's legs that is supposed to be the cause o
the white water.'

It was after this meeting with Afif Didi that Musafta too
me to see the vedis and standing in the shadow of one of th
laid-up trading craft the tragedy of what had happened wa
mirrored on his face—a mixture of pride and frustration. H
had his small son with him and he stood leaning against th
dried-up bows with his arm round the boy's shoulders starin
out across the lagoon to the Kudu Kanda Channel. There wa
no mistaking the look of longing in his eyes. Whether he wa
the owner of the boat, the *odi vari meehi*, or merely the helms
man—*hunguna hifa meeha*—I do not know. Probably it wa
family owned. But it was certainly the boat in which he ha
made his last voyages, for he showed me round it with th
air of a man introducing a stranger to his mistress; there wa
pride and affection in the way he caressed the sun-drie
wood.

It was not a large boat, though by comparison with th
dhonis it seemed so. It was about 60 ft long by some 15 f
wide, a thick-bodied tubby craft with a blunt-nosed clippe
bow and the square stern of a dhow. There was some rough
carving and the remains of gilding, but for the most part th
paint had long since flaked off her topsides revealing th
weather-worn wood. Her planks were dry to the touch, th
caulking withered in the seams.

Other vedis I saw varied in size up to 90 ft long. They ar
built in the islands, all of them two-masted, with the foremas
carrying a squaresail and raffee for downwind sailing on th

monsoon. They are without engine and, being entirely dependent on the wind in an area where the sea is littered with coral reefs and the currents strong, the safety of both boat and crew is very much in the hands of the navigator—and Allah also!

I did not, of course, see one of these boats under construction. But I did see a small dhoni almost finished. There are no plans for the construction of the island craft; it is all done by eye. The lines were perfect. The morticed joints would have done credit to the best work of a British yard. She was copper fastened. Normally honest, the Adduans will do anything to obtain copper, or any other non-corrosive metal. This and the sail cloth are the only things they cannot produce in the islands. The planking was tightly caulked with white cotton between the seams, the bare wood polished with coconut oil to a warm gloss finish.

It was Musafta who first introduced me to the interior of an Adduan house. It was strongly built of coral cement with the drinking well in front and the washing well behind. A small shy girl presented me with the inevitable glass of *dhora,* which is palm juice. She looked about twelve and was already married. Ages, however, are deceptive in the islands owing to their small stature. A boy of eighteen is comparable in physique to our eleven-year-old. Palm juice comes in several guises. It is collected from the stem of the *faan* or coconut palm which is cut and tied down in a certain manner with an empty coconut shell hung from the end to catch the juice. Trees treated in this way have pegs slotted into the bole at intervals for ease of climbing. Drunk immediately from the tree, the juice is cool and refreshing, slightly sweet with a flavour of lime. Allowed to ferment, it produces an alcoholic liquor rather like saké. This is the toddy of the sailor's vernacular. Boiled, it becames *hakuru,* a kind of syrup rather like cod-liver oil, and if heated a little longer it turns solid. It is then called *hukara* or *gandu-hakuru* and can be eaten much like halwa.

This house had a palm-thatched roof. Dwellings on Fedu built to house the inhabitants of Gan are tin-roofed. But most of the houses on Addu Atoll are kadjan built. Kadjan is the same as the Arabian barasti, a screen of plaited palm fronds.

The kadjan house is typical of a seafaring community. A wooden frame is first constructed, all the timbers being tied with coir rope. Kadjan thatch is about two inches thick and this is capable of withstanding the heaviest rain. The walls are of kadjan screens, most of them a natural brown colour, but they also come in mat form and are then dyed either green or red. The main bed, which can also be used as a stretcher for carrying the sick in dhonis, is slung by ropes from the roof beams so that it swings to and fro.

I went into several houses on Maradu when I visited the island with the RAF hygiene squad. These hygiene squads are responsible for pest control and work the islands one by one in rotation. In the centre of each island is a small swamp, a sort of catchment area that gives the island a water table. These are regularly sprayed and so are the wells. The result is that since the RAF came malaria and elephantiasis, two of the great scourges of the islands, have been almost entirely stamped out. Moreover, a more varied diet, with the necessary protein and the full range of vitamins, has already had an effect on the stature of the young Adduans.

The interior of a kadjan house on Maradu was composed of one main room with a single great bed slung from the rafters. There was a big, elaborate Victorian dresser panelled with mirrors and filled with cheap English china. There were tables and chairs and a little kadjan porch or verandah. The cookhouse at the back was separate and there was a little prayer house for the women. The well in the front was circular and constructed of coral cement. There was a coral cement wall in front and the rest of the big garden area, which included palms and bread-fruit trees, bananas, paw-paws and the ubiquitous alah plant, which is a yam and gives a root not unlike sweet potatoes, was surrounded by a kadjan fence. The floor of the house was of coral sand, as also were the paths around it. The street outside, too, was of coral chippings, spotlessly clean for it is swept by the inhabitants once a week on the orders of the local headman.

A family's wealth seems to be carried by the women and the children. Most of the babies had a sort of harness-cum-necklace of black strings with gold or silver coins shining bright against the black velvet softness of the skin. And at the waist, where the sarong is tied, a rope of silver wound perhaps six or eight times round the body. The women wore beautiful necklaces of silver and gold coins. Some had bangles, even anklets.

The social system goes back undisturbed many centuries, which is perhaps why it seems to work so smoothly. Even in marital relations there is a sense of freedom. A woman can be divorced for five shillings by the headman after he has heard the case. And it works both ways, for at the RAF hospital for Adduans there was a woman dresser called Rosina who had been married twice and divorced twice. She was then eighteen and earning more than most men.

There is an uninhabited island just to the east of Gan called Wilingili that is used as a penal settlement. The coconut plantations are government-owned and during the term of their sentence the convicts collect and process the coconuts. Flogging is confined to religious offences. The men who are marooned on Wilingili without benefit of boat are mostly there for robbery or failing to pay their taxes or for resisting authority in some way or another. They can also be sent there for rape or adultery. Both are rare, for a woman convicted of adultery must be banished to a distance of at least 48 miles from her home. To avoid the impossible, Adduan law requires that four men, each with two eyes, must testify that they actually witnessed the act. Four male witnesses to either rape or adultery is unusual to say the least and this gets over the difficulty.

Children attend school for four hours a day and learn reading, writing and arithmetic in addition to the religious and moral teachings that are to be expected in Moslem schools. Their main preoccupation out of school hours is kite-flying. The design of the kite is not unlike one of those extraordinary flat fish caught in the Arabian Sea. Often they have a face painted on them and there is an extra string attached so that the kite can be tilted to catch the up-draughts. When high above the trees it can then be made to dance and bow and nod. The tail is of twisted palm fronds. Kite-flying is probably a child's first instruction in the use of wind for sailing. Also, it probably stems from the religious enthusiasm for flying white flags on the mosques, some of them swallow-tailed, rather like a commodore's pennant.

The number of mosques on the islands is considerable, most of them built of coral cement with palm thatching. The coral cement, incidentally, is a small industry in itself. Men who are specialists in this trade dig and bag coral sand from certain off-lying islands so newly-formed that the sand is clear of vegetation. It is transported in dhonis to the island where it is to be used and is then laid in pits and covered with palm fronds weighed down by coral boulders. This generates heat and with the addition of water it is then slaked to produce the equivalent of lime.

The religious leader is the khatib, and each village has two khatibs. Most of the inhabitants are Moslem and one of the things that makes the Adduans different from the rest of the Maldives is that they were early converts to the Faith, whereas the northern atoll groups were at one time Buddhists. Previously all the atolls were pagan, the people worshipping a whole series of djinns, most of which were connected with the sea, the sky, the weather and the four quadrants of the compass.

There is little doubt that the conversion of the Adduans to the Moslem faith was due to its being a staging post for the age-old traffic between the Hadhramaut in south-east Arabia and Java and Sumatra. This is readily understandable when you examine the charts. The Maldives are a dangerous reef barrier for men sailing the monsoon round the south of India and Ceylon. There is hardly an island that is more than six feet above high water and in the whole 470-mile chain of atolls there are only three major channels—the Equatorial, the One-and-a-Half Degree and the Eight Degree Channel. Many dhow captains would undoubtedly have headed south outside the main groups, despite the less reliable winds on the equator, particularly on the outward voyage where they would have the benefit of a 5-knot east-going current through the Equatorial Channel between Suvadiva and Addu Atoll.

The mythology of the Maldivian conversion to the Moslem faith was given to me by Afif Didi. It is the same sort of story that haunts the mythology of so many nations—the equivalent of St. George and the Dragon or the rescuing of Andromeda. The interest in this particular version is that it is definite confirmation that the Maldive channels were used since early times by the dhow traffic between the Hadhramaut and Java.

'A navigator from the Arabian coast came to Malé in a dhow.' Afif Didi was speaking slowly, his eyes half closed as though he were trying to recall a story he had heard long ago. 'There on the quay he saw a woman crying and when he asked her why she was crying, he discovered that her daughter was to be sacrificed to Gospi—the God of the Sea.' Afif Didi opened his eyes and stared at me. 'They were barbaric peoples and this was a monthly sacrifice.'

The navigator had then offered to take the girl's place. After some dispute with the Malé leaders he was finally left alone on the reef. He was to stay there all night, and in the small hours a light came towards him from out of the sea. He was reading the Koran and he continued to read. Presumably there was a moon. Just before the light reached the reef it disappeared.

When the burial party arrived at dawn there was the Arab navigator alive and still reading the Koran. The Malé leaders then offered him a reward, but he told them he wanted nothing, except that they should believe in Allah, and not in such a primitive god.

'They would not agree to do this thing,' Afif Didi went on. 'But when, after he had stayed a month, the Arab again spent the whole night out on the reef in place of the sacrifice, and when again the light came out of the sea and vanished, then the headman and all the other leaders were converted.'

'What was this Gospi?' I asked.

Afif Didi shrugged. 'Perhaps it is all in their imagination?' But then he added quickly that strange things did come out of the sea, including sea cows which I think he called koel. No, it was nothing like a giant squid. There are no giant squids in the Maldives, only octopus. 'Perhaps the girls died of fright?' He smiled, but a little uncertainly.

What is the origin of this story then? If you go out on to the reefs at night alone, wading out through the shallows to the outer edge where the perpetual Indian Ocean swell sucks and gurgles at the reef face—the sea all black and the stars like diamonds overhead—then, after a time, the imagination takes command. Is that a whale venting, or just the surge and suck of the swell? And that streak of phosphorescence—a shark or something bigger? And then a sound along the reef, a sound like a cork popping—are there really no giant squids? A star shoots, falling in a white firework blaze across the sky, and at your feet something wavers in the water and you hope it isn't a moray eel.

And what was it Corporal Marshall heard? He was out fishing for shark on the south side of Gan at night and a voice called 'Oi' from out on the reef three hundred yards away. It was some time around 0300 hours in the morning and there was nobody about; no dhoni, not even a batteli. Several times this same sound, like a human voice, called out to him, and the Corporal was certainly not an over-imaginative man.

Even the reefs themselves are a mystery. There was some story that the Navy, either during or immediately after the war, had planned a submarine cable from Addu Atoll to Ceylon. But when they started to take soundings, they found that the reef went down absolutely sheer and that the sea close in against the reef face was deeper than anywhere else in the Indian Ocean. Whether this is true I do not know. The Admiralty Chart shows only one line of soundings in the vicinity of Addu Atoll. These vary between 1011 and 654 fathoms and at its closest point to Addu Atoll, within two miles of the north-easternmost island of Midu, the depth is 838 fathoms. A little further south and about the same distance off there is 477 fathoms, and about one mile off the island of Wilingili there is a reading of 376 fathoms. Even this is well over 2,000 ft.

The origins of atolls have puzzled scientists for a long time. Most theories depend on what Daly called glacial control. Coral does not thrive in depths greater than about 30 fathoms and exposure above water for more than an hour or two is fatal. Daly's theory, which was little more than an extension of Darwin's, was that during the last Ice Age the sea level fell by anything up to 200 ft. The exposed coral reefs were eroded by the action of waves into a platform and as the sea rose again with the passing of the Ice Age the coral reef built up on the outside of the formation. This theory was based on the knowledge that coral, which needs oxygen, grows best on the seaward side of reefs, so that growth is always an outward movement.

Darwin's theory was that during the Ice Age, when the sea level was low, coral grew round the shores of exposed volcanic peaks. Thus the atoll ring was already there and as the sea level rose so the coral growth followed it upwards until finally it covered the entire peak.

None of these theories would account for a sheer depth of 2,000 ft off the reefs, certainly not for a depth of anything approaching 2,000 fathoms. We may know much more about this mystery when the scientists have had an opportunity to examine the results of the International Indian Ocean Survey carried out in 1964. In the meantime, I must admit I am inclined to support a theory postulated by Hans Hass.

Hass was diving from his marine research vessel *Larifa* along the reef faces of Addu Atoll in January 1959. In his book *Expedition into the Unknown* he states that whilst exploring the inner structure of atoll reefs he found undoubted evidence of central subsidence. The inner, or lagoon structure of these reefs, being composed of heavily branched corals, was loose and shifting and so brittle that it collapsed under pressure.

There is no doubt that great pressure exists in an atoll lagoon, particularly after heavy rains. And in an atoll as big as Addu, with only four channels through the surrounding reef line, the build-up of pressure due to tides alone must be considerable. In one flight by helicopter, the pilot took me up to 4,000 ft over the north-east corner of Addu. Below us were the two northern channels—Kudu and Kanda and Man Kanda—and the sluice of water through them showed that the sea level inside the lagoon was much higher than it was outside.

From the helicopter I had an armchair view of Addu Atoll, lying in a great heart-shaped fringe of reefs and islands round the wind-dappled waters of the lagoon. The shallows, which are very extensive in the region of Hittadu, were magnificent in their vivid colouring. The whole atoll was like a great green platter floating in the sea—the sea-green of the lagoon bordered by the almost continuous darker green of island vegetation. To the south I could just see the concrete dagger line of the Gan runway; to the north the first low islands of Suvadiva showed vague through the haze like a fungus growth on the sea's surface. To the north-east the island of Fua Mulaku was so small and isolated that I felt sure the coral must be resting on a volcanic peak. Thin lines of cirrus flaked the sky, a dirty white with the atmosphere so hazed with humidity that they had the appearance of islands floating in a void.

The sea below me was very clear and from that height I should have been able to see down into it for a considerable depth. I could see the reef spreading out under water from the surface face, but only for a very short distance, and then suddenly the grey line of it vanished and there was nothing but the dark purple-blue that denoted really deep water.

It is a strange feeling to be sitting there in the sky, high above such an extraordinary land formation, and particularly so when the pilot cuts the engine leaving the rotor feathering free and you drop like Icarus out of the sun towards swell-beaten shallows shot with colours from pure white to the most livid green.

Hass makes the point that the bigger an atoll becomes, the greater is the volume of water enclosed within the circumference of the reef, and that the weight of this water plus the age of the reef determines the depth of water within the lagoon. Thus he says that with a ring diameter of about one sea mile, the depth of the lagoon would be 5 to 10 fathoms; a diameter of four sea miles gives a depth of up to 20 fathoms; a diameter of twelve sea miles up to 35 fathoms and a diameter of thirty sea miles up to 50 fathoms. This is certainly borne out by the Admiralty chart. The heart-shaped lagoon of Addu Atoll is nearly ten miles across and the greatest depth is 36 fathoms, the average being around 20 fathoms.

But Addu Atoll is not typical of the Maldives. None of the other eighteen groups are so perfectly enclosed; nor are the lagoons so clear of coral obstructions. Several flights in the nose gunner's position of a Shackleton on patrol gave me a unique opportunity to view these atolls from the air. From Suvadiva north they are mostly very complex. I had the Admiralty charts with me and it was extraordinary how the shape of these complex formations, seen from about 1,000 feet, matched exactly the hydrographical survey information so finely printed on the charts; despite the multiplicity of coral outcrops and islands, I never had any doubt about our position. From that height it was as though the chart itself had suddenly come to life, unfolding in the sea below me, island upon island, reef upon reef, no longer minute printed outlines on paper, but imbued with colour and reality despite the haze—a constant living pattern of marine growth developing into the green of vegetation.

These flights were made in the afternoon. The sun was high and the heat beneath the unshaded perspex canopy intense. The sweat rolled off me to be replaced with paper cupfuls of iced lime juice which one of the crew brought round at intervals. The exposed skin of my hands and face burned, my eyelids drooped with the glare and my head was bursting with the pumping of my blood. It would have been impossible to stay awake if it had not been for the fact that, through my earphones, I was in contact with the nine members of the crew, and that my mind was kept alert by the fascination of what my eyes were seeing.

Here below me was the whole marine development of atoll life. I could see it from the very beginning of time, for I was looking at coral reefs and islands, even atolls, in every stage of development.

The main atoll groups all have the same general formation, an outline fringe of islands enclosing a great area of water. But unlike Addu Atoll, the groups to the north have their island fringe shot through with channels to the sea. As a result the water of the lagoon within the fringe is not open water as is the case with Addu, but is studded with above-water reefs, miniature atolls, drifts of white coral sand, even isolated niggerheads of coral standing like rotten nails above the glass mirror of the lagoon. And where the sea swept in and out of the reef channels, or broke on the outer fringe of islands, I could follow the whole above-water development, from the birth of an island to the point where it became habitable. In the foetus state of birth it was no more than white water breaking on a strip or plate of coral, and in the centre the green of the shallows fading to white where a deposit of coral was forming; then the actual break of water against a narrow strip of coral sand just showing a line of brilliant white above the surface of the sea; and then again an exposed strip of white sand with a thin line of green along its back. The build-up of coral sand is then quite fast, and so is the growth of vegetation. The strips of green become denser, instead of minute plants they are bushes. Then the first palm trees. And as the island develops, so the vegetation becomes more varied, the green of growth darker as trees and shrubs take hold, the shade more dense.

Except at Malé I saw no concentrations of population to equal the Adduan villages. Nor were there indications of quite the same high social development and sense of culture. It was all much more primitive, the occupied islands more scattered. It appeared that whether an island was inhabited or not depended on access through the coral reef, for many of the small islands I looked down on were completely surrounded by shallows impassable to any boat.

Malé itself was a much smaller island than I had expected. On the occasion of our visit we were dropping mail for the political resident and for the frigate on which he was then living. For political reasons we had to avoid over-flying the town, but in our various runs we flew several times along the Malé waterfront. Some sort of breakwater had been constructed and the sheltered water within its long protective arm was massed with boats, including the mock-up of a gunboat. The harbour was backed by a mass of buildings, some of them quite large, palaces or government buildings, and all blinding white in the sunlight. The effect was of an Arab town, something like Mukalla, the gateway to the Hadhramaut in Arabia, nearly two thousand miles away to the north-east.

It was during these flights that I was able to see how the atoll develops. In explaining his theory Hans Hass says, 'As soon as a reef reaches the surface of the sea and begins to spread out in all directions, a barren area forms in the middle, something like a bald patch on a man's crown. . . . In this way a reef of not more than perhaps 1,000 ft in diameter will become a miniature atoll whose centre grows progressively barer as subsidences set in.'

There is no doubt that subsidence does occur in the centre of atolls, and since the coral is very largely of the types acropora and echinopora, both branching corals, the tendency must be for these to collapse as they die in the centre. The weight of this detritus, increasing over thousands, possibly millions of years, must inevitably compress the centre, thus developing an inner basin within the outgrowing coral reef circle.

Such a multiplicity of islands and reefs inevitably produces variegated marine life, some of which, because of isolation, is highly specialised. In particular, there is a variety of crayfish peculiar to the Maldives—it looks not unlike a large marine scorpion—and the flesh from the barrel of the body is exquisite eating. Fish of the most fantastic markings and colours swarm along the reef faces, making underwater swimming peculiarly fascinating as one searches for variations upon known species. Earplugs, however, are advisable, for coral sand hangs suspended like dust in the sunlit water and the effect of this in the ear passage is bad, producing a fungus growth that softens and destroys the tissue. Any cut or graze is also attacked by the coral sand, either in the sea or on land, and if not treated within the hour the injury has to be scrubbed to bare unaffected flesh, and even then the process of healing is slow.

The moray eel in the reef shallows, the stonefish in the sand—both are deadly. The stonefish, the most poisonous of all seafish, buries itself in the sand like a stone till only the spines show. Infection from the prick of one of these spines produces a pain so excruciating that the pain itself can kill. One of the medical officers told me that eight men were needed to hold down one small Adduan during the eight to ten hours his body writhed in agony. If the pain of the most intense toothache is measured as 4, he said, then the sting of the stonefish is 10 plus.

Apart from the crayfish and the cowrie shells, the Adduans are mainly interested in the bonito, barracuda and tunny. These are much larger, of course, outside the reefs, and it is in the open sea that the lateen-sailed battelis mainly operate.

There are sail-fish and black marlin inside the lagoon, also manta rays and tarpon. Outside there are sharks, both sand shark and the hammerhead, and sea cows, a mammal related to the seal and walrus, rather like a hippopotamus in appearance. The whale is an irregular visitor, but there are dolphins and for some reason these are regarded with superstitious aversion.

As might be expected, with so much marine life and such dense tropical growth, there are great numbers of birds. Some, like the tern, plovers, and shearwaters, are well-known to us. Even the whimbrel is a winter visitor. However, most of them originate from India and Ceylon. There is a crab plover and both the paler and the darker Maldivian little herons. The terns are particularly common, but the white tern breeds on Addu Atoll only, due to the fact that this is the one atoll not occupied by the house-crow which feeds on the tern's eggs.

The fauna, of course, is much more limited than either fish or bird life. Like the birds, they stem mostly from the Indian peninsula. Rabbits of a domestic type have been loosed on some islands and these have reverted to the wild. There is the murk shrew, the common rat and the eastern house mouse. The toads are everywhere, dinning their way through the twilight hours. And as the sun sinks in a furnace blaze of red and the sky darkens to purple, the Maldivian flying fox comes in with the slow beat of a rook to its roosting point in the branches of large evergreens like the kanda tree. These big fruit bats will cross the lagoon from island to island, and even cross the sea to reach another atoll.

But it is not its marine life or its birds, or even its people, that makes Addu unique. It is the physical structure of the atoll, its climate and its geographical position. Here is a remote island group right in the centre of the Indian Ocean. It is half-way between Africa and South East Asia, less than 3,000 miles from Australia. Its strategic position has already been recognised in one great war, though in the brief space of twenty years little remains of the naval shore establishments that made Port T—only the concrete supports of a light railway that linked the islands of Gan, Fedu and Maradu and the disintegrating rusting hulks of some landing craft already

uried in new tropical growth. But it is still a bunkering point
or the Navy with an old tanker, the *Wave Victor*, perman-
ntly moored there and kept constantly supplied with fuel oil.

Since 1887 the Maldives as a whole have been under British
rotection. By a strange coincidence the complete independ-
nce of the Sultan's government at Malé was established on
uly 26, 1965, the very day that *The Strode Venturer*, the
ovel I had by then written about Addu Atoll, was published
n England. Under the agreement, which made the Maldives
ndependent, the lease of the island of Gan in Addu Atoll
vas confirmed and the British were granted certain other
ights. Now, if Aden were to go and ultimately Singapore, and
ur presence East of Suez had to be maintained, the strategic
otential of Addu Atoll would be greatly increased, for its
2-square-mile lagoon is almost all deep water and it is pro-
ected by a sea wall of reefs and islands with only four
pproach channels. What effect this would have on the
Adduans themselves it is difficult to say. So far they have
aken the abrupt incursion of the twentieth century into their
sland solitude in their stride. This has been mainly due to
he RAF's policy of isolating the Gan base from the rest of
he islands, the Adduans who work there leaving it each
vening for their own homes. The happy nature of this people
nd their cultural life has thus been kept inviolate. This would
ardly be possible if the base were enlarged. Their future thus
angs in the balance, the geographical position of their atoll
lacing them at the mercy of the world's political pressures.
But at least their remoteness insulates them from the prob-
em facing so many islands I have visited—the drift of the
oung to the mainland centres of civilisation with its conse-
quent disruption of family life.

Hammond Innes

The Conquistadors £1·95

Hammond Innes's brilliantly told, lavishly illustrated history
of the Spanish conquest of the New World. 'Mr. Innes's
lucid and fast-moving prose is enhanced by the traveller's
feel for the land and the sailor's experience of the vagaries
of the sea. With its high quality and superb photographs
The Conquistadors deserves a wide audience.'

Times Literary Supplement

Hammond Innes has also written two travel books, tracing
his own journeys to remote parts of the globe to collect the
raw material for his novels.

Sea and Islands 45p

In his ocean-going yacht, the *Mary Deare*, Hammond Innes
and his wife Dorothy explored the coasts of Europe from
Scandinavia to Turkey, as well as the Indian Ocean and the
Western Isles. 'Here is a book which makes you feel that a
lifetime passed without cruising in your own boat from one
to another of the Greek islands is a lifetime wasted.'

Maurice Wiggin, The Bookman

Harvest of Journeys 45p

The story of Hammond Innes's many journeys overland—
with a survey team in the Rockies, with the Hudson's Bay
eskimos, with Arabs in the Hadhramaut on the explosive
Yemen border—to the very outposts of civilization. 'It has
all the punch of a Hammond Innes novel plus the qualities
of the great travel books.'   *Books and Bookmen*

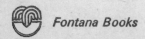

Fontana Books

Alistair MacLean

His first book, *HMS Ulysses*, published in 1955, was out-standingly successful. It led the way to a string of best-selling novels which have established Alistair MacLean as the most popular thriller writer of our time.

Bear Island *35p*

Caravan to Vaccarès *35p*

Puppet on a Chain *35p*

Force 10 from Navarone *35p*

The Guns of Navarone *35p*

Where Eagles Dare *35p*

South by Java Head *35p*

Ice Station Zebra *35p*

Fear is the Key *35p*

The Satan Bug *35p*

The Golden Rendezvous *35p*

When Eight Bells Toll *35p*

HMS Ulysses *35p*

The Last Frontier *35p*

The Dark Crusader *35p*

Night Without End *35p*

 *Fontana Books*

Fontana Books

Fontana is best known as one of the leading paperback publishers of popular fiction and non-fiction. It also includes an outstanding, and expanding section of books on history, natural history, religion and social sciences.

Most of the fiction authors need no introduction. They include Agatha Christie, Hammond Innes, Alistair MacLean, Catherine Gaskin, Victoria Holt and Lucy Walker. Desmond Bagley and Maureen Peters are among the relative newcomers.

The non-fiction list features a superb collection of animal books by such favourites as Gerald Durrell and Joy Adamson.

All Fontana books are available at your bookshop or newsagent; or can be ordered direct. Just fill in the form below and list the titles you want.

FONTANA BOOKS, Cash Sales Department, P.O. Box 4, Godalming, Surrey. Please send purchase price plus 5p postage per book by cheque, postal or money order. No currency.

NAME (Block letters) _____

ADDRESS _____

_____

_____

While every effort is made to keep prices low, it is sometimes necessary to increase prices at short notice. Fontana Books reserve the right to show new retail prices on covers which may differ from those previously advertised in the text or elsewhere.